Catherine Sinclair

Holiday house

A book for the young

Catherine Sinclair

Holiday house

A book for the young

ISBN/EAN: 9783337290993

Printed in Europe, USA, Canada, Australia, Japan

Cover: Foto ©Andreas Hilbeck / pixelio.de

More available books at **www.hansebooks.com**

HOLIDAY HOUSE;

A

BOOK FOR THE YOUNG.

BY

CATHERINE SINCLAIR,

AUTHOR OF

"*Modern Accomplishments;*" "*Mysterious Marriage;*" "*Jane Bouverie;*"
"*Beatrice;*" "*Modern Flirtations;*" "*London Homes;*" etc.

"Young heads are giddy, and young hearts are warm,
And make mistakes for manhood to reform."
COWPER.

WARD, LOCK AND CO.
LONDON: WARWICK HOUSE, SALISBURY SQUARE, E.C.
NEW YORK: 10, BOND STREET.

PREFACE.

> "Of all the paper I have blotted, I have written nothing without the intention of some good. Whether I have succeeded or not, is for others to judge."
>
> Sir William Temple.

The minds of young people are now manufactured like webs of linen, all alike, and nothing left to nature. From the hour when children can speak, till they come to years of discretion or of indiscretion, they are carefully prompted what to say, and what to think, and how to look, and how to feel; while in most school-rooms Nature has been turned out of doors with obloquy, and Art has entirely supplanted her.

When a quarrel takes place, both parties are generally in some degree to blame; therefore if Art and Nature could yet be made to go hand in hand towards the formation of character and principles, a graceful and beautiful superstructure might be reared, on the solid foundation of Christian faith and sound morality; so that while many natural weeds would be eradicated, and many wild flowers pruned and carefully trained, some lovely blossoms that spring spontaneously in the uncul

tivated soil, might still be cherished into strength
and beauty, far excelling what can be planted or
reared by art.

Every infant is probably born with a character
as peculiar to himself as the features in his countenance, if his faults and good qualities were permitted to expand according to their original tendency; but education, which formerly did too little
in teaching the "young idea how to shoot," seems
now in danger of overshooting the mark altogether,
by not allowing the young ideas to exist at all. In
this age of wonderful mechanical inventions, the
very mind of youth seems in danger of becoming
a machine; and while every effort is used to stuff
the memory, like a cricket-ball, with well-known
facts and ready-made opinions, no room is left for
the vigour of natural feeling, the glow of natural
genius, and the ardour of natural enthusiasm. It
was a remark of Sir Walter Scott's many years
ago, to the author herself, that in the rising generation there would be no poets, wits, or rators,
because all play of the imagination is now carefully discouraged, and books written for young
persons are generally a mere dry record of facts,
unenlivened by any appeal to the heart, or any excitement to the fancy. The catalogue of a child's

library would contain Conversations on Natural Philosophy,—on Chemistry,—on Botany,—on Arts and Sciences,—Chronological Records of History, and travels as dry as a road-book, but nothing on the habits or ways of thinking, natural and suitable to the taste of children; therefore, while such works are delightful to the parents and teachers who select them, the younger community are fed with strong meat instead of milk, and the reading which might be a relaxation from study becomes a study in itself.

In these pages the author has endeavoured to paint that species of noisy, frolicsome, mischievous children, now almost extinct, wishing to preserve a sort of fabulous remembrance of days long past, when young people were like wild horses on the prairies, rather than like well-broken hacks on the road; and when amidst many faults and eccentricities, there was still some individuality of character and feeling allowed to remain. In short, as Lord Byron described "the last man," the object of this volume is to describe "the last boy." It may be useful, she thinks, to shew, that amidst much requiring to be judiciously curbed and corrected, there may be the germs of high and generous feeling, and of steady, right principle, which should be the chief objects of culture and encouragement. Plodding industry is in the present day at a very high premium in education; but it requires the leaven of mental energy and genius to make it work well; while it has been remarked by one whose experience in education is deep and practical that "those boys whose names appear most frequently in the black book of transgression, would sometimes deserve to be also most commonly recorded, if a book were kept for warm affections and generous actions."

The most formidable person to meet in society at present, is the mother of a promising boy, about nine or ten years old; because there is no possible escape from a volume of anecdotes, and a complete system of education on the newest principles. The young gentleman has probably asked leave to bring his books to the breakfast-room, —can scarcely be torn away from his studies at the dinner-hour,—discards all toys,—abhors a holiday,—propounds questions of marvellous depth in politics or mineralogy,— and seems, in short, more fitted to enjoy the learned meeting at Oxford than the exhilarating exercise of the cricket-ground; but, if the axiom be true, that "a little learning is a dangerous thing," it has also been proved by frequent, and sometimes by very melancholy experience, that, for minds not yet expanded to maturity, a great deal of learning is more dangerous still, and that in those school-rooms where there has been a society for the suppression of amusement, the mental energies have suffered as well as the health.

A prejudice has naturally arisen against giving works of fiction to children, because their chief interest too often rests on the detection and punishment of such mean vices as lying and stealing, which are so frequently and elaborately described that the way to commit those crimes is made obvious; while a clever boy thinks he could easily avoid the oversights by which another has been discovered, and that if he does not yield to similar temptations, he is a model of virtue and good conduct.

In writing for any class of readers, and especially in occupying the leisure moments of such peculiarly fortunate young persons as have leisure moments at all, the author feels conscious of a deep responsibility, for it is at their early age that the seed can best be sown which shall bear fruit unto eternal life; therefore it is hoped this volume may be found to inculcate a pleasing and permanent consciousness, that religion is the best resource in happier hours, and the only refuge in hours of affliction.

Those who wish to be remembered for ever in the world,—and it is a very common object of ambition,—will find no monument more permanent, than the affectionate remembrance of any children they have treated with kindness; for we may often observe in the reminiscences of old age, a tender recollection surviving all others, of friends in early days who enlivened the hours of childhood by presents of playthings and comfits. But above all, we never forget those who good-humouredly complied with the constantly-recurring petition of all young people in every generation, and in every house,—" Will you tell me a story?"

In answer to such a request, often and importunately repeated, the author has from year to year delighted in seeing herself surrounded by a circle of joyous eager faces, listening with awe to the terrors of Mrs Crabtree, or smiling at the frolics of Harry and Laura. The stories, originally, were so short, that some friends, aware of their popularity, and conscious of their harmless tendency, took the trouble of copying them in manuscript for their own young friends; but the tales have since grown and expanded during frequent verbal repetitions, till, with various fanciful additions and new characters, they have enlarged into their present form, or rather so far beyond it, that several chapters are omitted, to keep the volume within moderate compass.

Paley remarks, that "any amusement which is innocent, is better than none ; as the writing of a book, the building of a house, the laying out of a garden, the digging of a fish-pond, even the raising of a cucumber," and it is hoped, that, while the author herself has found much interesting occupation in recording those often repeated stories, the time of herself and her young readers may be employed with some degree of profit, or she will certainly regret that it was not better occupied in the rearing of cucumbers.

It may add something to the interest, and yet more to the usefulness of those scenes and circumstances relative to the return from abroad and premature death of Frank Graham, to mention, that they are not fictitious ; and the author is mournfully touched by the consciousness that some tears of juvenile sympathy have fallen from eyes that never saw him, for the early fate of a brother deeply loved and deeply lamented. With every endearing and admirable quality of head and heart, few ever held out a brighter promise of excellence, than he who, being restored as is here described for a few weeks to his family, dying, resigned himself without a murmur, to the will of God, and has long slumbered in a premature grave, his name being thus commemorated on a tombstone in the churchyard of Hackney :

In Memory

OF

LIEUTENANT JAMES SINCLAIR,

AGED 20,

WHO WAS ARRESTED BY THE HAND OF DEATH

ON HIS WAY HOME,

AFTER AN ABSENCE OF SOME YEARS, DURING WHICH HE LOST HIS

HEALTH ON SERVICE AGAINST THE BURMESE,

20TH JUNE 1826.

"It is the Lord, let Him do what seemeth Him good."
"For I know that my Redeemer liveth."

HOLIDAY HOUSE.

CHAPTER I.

CHIT CHAT.

*A school-boy, a dog, and a walnut tree,
The more you strike 'em, the better they be.*

LAURA and Harry Graham could scarcely feel sure that they ever had a mama, because she died while they were yet very young indeed; but Frank, who was some years older, recollected perfectly well what pretty playthings she used to give him, and missed his kind, good mama so extremely, that he one day asked if he might "go to a shop and buy a new mama?" Frank often afterwards thought of the time also, when he kneeled beside her bed to say his prayers, or when he sat upon her knee to hear funny stories about good boys and bad boys—all very interesting, and all told on purpose to shew how much happier obedient children are, than those who waste their time in idleness and folly. Boys and girls all think they know the road to happiness without any mistake, and choose that which looks gayest and pleasantest at first, though older people, who have travelled that road already, can tell them that a very difficult path is the only one which ends agreeably; and those who begin to walk in it when they are young will really find that " Wisdom's ways are ways of pleasantness, and all her paths are peace." It was truly remarked by Solomon, that " even a child is known by his doings, whether his work be pure, and whether it be right." Therefore, though Frank was yet but a little boy, his friends, who observed how carefully he attended to his mama's instructions, how frequently he studied his Bible, and how diligently he learned his lessons, all prophesied that this merry, lively child, with laughing eyes and dimpled cheeks, would yet grow up to be a good and useful man; especially when it became evident that, by the blessing of God, he had been early turned away from the broad road that leadeth to destruction, in which every living person would naturally walk, and led into the narrow path that leadeth to eternal life.

When his mama, Lady Graham, after a long and painful illness, was at last taken away to the better world, for which she had been many years preparing her only sorrow and anxiety seemed to be that she left behind her three such very dear children, who were now to be entirely under the care of their papa, Sir Edward Graham; and it was with many prayers and tears that she tried to make her mind more easy about their future education, and future happiness.

Sir Edward felt such extreme grief on the death of Lady Graham, that instead of being able to remain at home with his young family, and to interest his mind as he would wish to have done, by attending to them, he was ordered by Dr Bell to set off immediately for Paris, Rome, and Naples, where it was hoped he might leave his distresses behind him while he travelled, or, at all events, forget them.

Luckily the children had a very good, kind uncle, Major David Graham, and their grandmama, Lady Harriet Graham, who were both exceedingly happy to take charge of them, observing that no house could be cheerful without a few little people being there, and that now they would have constant amusement in trying to make Frank, Harry, and Laura, as happy as possible, and even still happier.

"That is the thing I am almost afraid of!" said Sir Edward, smiling. "Uncles and grandmamas are only too kind, and my small family will be quite spoiled with indulgence."

"Not if you leave that old vixen, Mrs Crabtree, as governor of the nursery," answered Major Graham, laughing. "She ought to have been the drummer of a regiment, she is so fond of beating! I believe there never was such a tyrant since the time when nurserymaids were invented. Poor Harry would pass his life in a dark closet, like Baron Trenck, if Mrs Crabtree had her own way!"

"She means it all well. I am certain that Mrs Crabtree is devotedly fond of my children, and would go through fire and water to serve them; but she is a little severe, perhaps. Her idea is, that if you never forgive a first fault, you will never hear of a second, which is probably true enough. At all events, her harshness will be the best remedy for your extreme indulgence; therefore let me beg that you and my mother will seldom interfere with her 'method,' especially in respect to Harry and Laura. As for Frank, if all boys were like him, we might make a bonfire of birch-rods and canes. He is too old for nursery discipline now, and must be flogged at school, if deserving of it at all, till he goes to sea next year, with my friend Gordon, who has promised to rate him as a volunteer of the first class, on board the Thunderbolt."

In spite of Mrs Crabtree's admirable "system" with children, Harry and Laura became, from this time, two of the most heedless, frolicsome beings in the world, and had to be whipped almost every morning; for in those days it had not been discovered that whipping is all a mistake, and that children can be made good without it; though some old-fashioned people still say—and such, too, who take the God of truth for their guide—the old plan succeeded best, and that those who "spare the rod will spoil the child." When Lady Harriet and Major Graham spoke kindly to Harry and Laura about any thing wrong that had been done, they both felt more sad and sorry, than after the severest punishments of Mrs Crabtree, who frequently observed, that " if those children were shut up in a dark room alone, with nothing to do, they would still find some way of being mischievous, and of deserving to be punished."

" Harry!" said Major Graham, one day, " you remind me of a monkey which belonged to the colonel of our regiment. He was famous for contriving to play all sorts of pranks when no one supposed them to be possible, and I recollect once having a valuable French clock, which the malicious creature seemed particularly determined to break. Many a time I caught him in the fact, and saved my beautiful clock, but one day being suddenly summoned out of the room, I hastily fastened his chain to a table, so that he could not possibly, even at the full extent of his paw, so much as touch the glass case. I observed him impatiently watching my departure, and felt a misgiving that he expected to get the better of me; so, after shutting the door, I took a peep through the key-hole, and what do you think Jack had done, Harry? for, next to Mr Monkey himself, you are certainly the cleverest contriver of mischief I know."

"What did he do?" asked Harry, eagerly; "did he throw a stone at the clock?"

"No! but his leg was several inches longer than his arm, so having turned his tail towards his object, he stretched out his hind-paw, and before I could rush back, my splendid alabaster clock had been upset and broken to shivers."

Laura soon became quite as mischievous as Harry, which is very surprising, as she was a whole year older, and had been twice as often scolded by Mrs Crabtree. Neither of these children intended any harm, for they were only heedless, lively romps, who would not for twenty worlds have told a lie, or done a shabby thing, or taken what did not belong to them. They were not greedy either, and would not on any account have resembled Peter Grey, who was quite an old boy, at the same school with Frank, and who spent all his own pocket-money and borrowed a great deal of other people's, to squander at the pastry-cook's, saying, he wished it were possible to eat three dinners, and two breakfasts, and five suppers every day.

Harry was not a cruel boy either; he never lashed his pony, beat his dog, pinched his sister, or killed any butterflies, though he often chased them for fun; and one day he even defended a wasp at the risk of being stung, when Mrs Crabtree intended to kill it.

" Nasty, useless vermin !" said she, angrily. " What business have they in the world! coming into other people's houses, with nothing to do ! They sting and torment every body ! Bees are very different, for they are useful, making honey."

" And wasps make jelly !" said Harry, resolutely, while he opened the window, and shook the happy wasp out of his pocket-handkerchief.

Mrs Crabtree allowed no pet of any description in her territories, and ordered the children to be happy without any such nonsense. When Laura's canary-bird escaped one unlucky day out of its cage, Mrs Crabtree was strongly suspected by Major Graham of having secretly opened the door, as she had long declared war upon bullfinches, white mice, parrots, kittens, dogs, bantams, and gold fish, observing that animals only made a noise and soiled the house, therefore every beast should remain in its own home, " birds in the air, fish in the sea, and beasts in the desert." She seemed always watching, in hopes Harry and Laura might do something that they ought to be punished for: and Mrs Crabtree certainly had more ears than other people, or slept with one eye open, as, whatever might be done, night or day, she overheard the lowest whisper of mischief, and appeared able to see what was going on in the dark.

When Harry was a very little boy, he sometimes put himself in the corner, after doing anything wrong, apparently quite sensible that he deserved to be punished, and once after being terribly scolded by Mrs Crabtree, he drew in his stool beside her chair, with a funny, penitent face, twirling his thumbs over and over each other, and saying, " Now, Mrs Crabtree! look what a good boy I am going to be!"

" You a good boy!" replied she, contemptuously: " No! no! the world will be turned into a cream-cheese first!"

Lady Harriet gave Harry and Laura a closet of their own, in which she allowed them to keep their toys, and nobody could help laughing to see that, amidst the whole collection, there was seldom one unbroken. Frank wrote out a list once of what he found in this crowded little storeroom, and amused himself often with reading it over afterwards. There were three dolls without faces, a horse with no legs, a drum with a hole in the top, a cart without wheels, a churn with no bottom, a kite without a tail, a skipping-rope with no handles, and a cup and ball that had lost the string. Lady Harriet called this closet the hospital for decayed toys, and she often employed herself as their doctor, mending legs and arms for soldiers, horses, and dolls, though her skill seldom succeeded long; because playthings must have been made of cast-iron to last a week with Harry. One cold winter morning, when Laura entered the nursery, she found a large fire blazing, and all her wax dolls sitting in a row staring at the flames. Harry intended no mischief on this occasion, but great was his vexation when Laura burst into tears, and shewed him that their faces were running in a hot stream down upon their beautiful silk frocks, which were completely ruined, and not a doll had its nose remaining. Another time, Harry pricked a hole in his own beautiful large gas-ball, wishing to see how the gas could possibly escape, after which, in a moment, it shrivelled up into a useless empty bladder; and when his kite was flying up to the clouds, Harry often wished that he could be tied to the tail himself, so as to fly also through the air like a bird, and see every thing.

Mrs Crabtree always wore a prodigious bunch of jingling keys in her pocket, that rung whenever she moved, as if she carried a dinner-bell in her pocket, and Frank said it was like a rattlesnake, giving warning of her approach, which was of great use, as everybody had time to put on a look of good behaviour before she arrived. Even Betty, the under nurserymaid, felt in terror of Mrs Crabtree's entrance, and was obliged to work harder than any six housemaids united. Frank told her one day that he thought brooms might soon be invented, which would go by steam and brush carpets of themselves; but, in the mean time, not a grain of dust could lurk in any corner of the nursery without being dislodged. Betty would have required ten hands, and twenty pair of feet, to do all the work that was expected; but the grate looked like jet, the windows would not have soiled a cambric handkerchief, and the carpet was switched with so many tea-leaves, that Frank thought Mrs Crabtree often took several additional cups of tea in order to leave a plentiful supply of leaves for sweeping the floor next morning.

If Laura and Harry left any breakfast, Mrs Crabtree kept it carefully till dinner time, when they were obliged to finish the whole before tasting meat; and if they refused it at dinner, the remains were kept for supper. Mrs Crabtree always informed them that she did it " for their good," though Harry never could see any good that it did to either of them ; and when she mentioned how many poor children would be glad to eat what they despised, he often wished the hungry beggars had some of his own hot dinner, which he would gladly have spared to them ; for Harry was really so generous, that he would have lived upon air, if he might be of use to anybody. Time passed on, and Lady Harriet engaged a master for some hours a-day to teach the children lessons, while even Mrs Crabtree found no other fault to Harry and Laura, except that in respect to good behaviour their memories were like a sieve, which let out everything they were desired to keep in mind. They seemed always to hope, somehow or other, that when Mrs Crabtree once turned her back, she would never shew her face again ; so their promises of better conduct were all " wind without rain," very loud, and plenty of them, but no good effect to be seen afterwards.

Among her many other torments, Mrs Crabtree rolled up Laura's hair every night on all sides o. her head, in large stiff curl-papers, till they were as round and hard as walnuts, after which she tied on a night-cap, as tightly as possible above all, saying this would curl the hair still better. Laura could not lay any part of her head on the pillow, without suffering so much pain, that, night after night, she sat up in bed, after Mrs Crabtree had bustled out of the room, and quietly took the cruel papers out, though she was punished so severely for doing so, that she obeyed orders at last, and lay wide awake half the night with torture; and it was but small comfort to Laura afterwards, that Lady Harriet's visitors frequently admired the forest of long, glossy ringlets that adorned her head, and complimented Mrs Crabtree on the trouble it must cost her to keep that charming hair in order. Often did Laura wish that it were ornamenting any wig-block, rather than her own head; and one day Lady Harriet laughed heartily, when some strangers admired her little grandaughter's ringlets, and Laura asked, very anxiously, if they would like to cut off a few of the longest, and keep them for her sake.

"Your hair does curl like a cork-screw," said Frank, laughing. "If I want to draw a cork out of a beer bottle any day, I shall borrow one of those ringlets, Laura!"

"You may laugh, Frank; for it is fun to you, and death to me," answered poor Laura, gravely shaking her curls at him. "I wish we were all bald, like uncle David! During the night I cannot lie still, on account of those tiresome curls, and all day I dare not stir for fear of spoiling them; so they are never out of my head."

"Nor off your head! How pleasant it must be to have Mrs Crabtree combing and scolding, and scolding and combing, for hours every day! Poor Laura! we must get Dr Bell to say that they shall be taken off on pain of death, and then, perhaps, grandmama would order some Irish reapers to cut them down with a sickle."

"Frank! what a lucky boy you are, to be at school, and not in the nursery! I wish next year would come immediately, for then I shall have a governess, after which goodbye to Mrs Crabtree, and the wearisome curl-papers."

"I don't like school!" said Harry. "It is perfect nonsense to plague me with lessons now. All big people can read and write, so, of course I shall somehow be able to do like others. There is no hurry about it!"

Never was there a more amiable, pious, excellent boy than Frank, who read his Bible so attentively, and said his prayers so regularly every morning and evening, that he soon learned both to know his duty and to do it. Though he laughed heartily at the scrapes which Harry and Laura so constantly fell into he often also helped them out of their difficulties, being very different from most elderly boys, who find an odd kind of pleasure in teasing younger children—pulling their hair—pinching their arms—twitching away their dinners—and twenty more plans for tormenting, which Frank never attempted to enjoy, but he often gave Harry and Laura a great deal of kind, sober, good advice, which they listened to very attentively while they were in any new distress, but generally forgot again as soon as their spirits rose. Frank came home only upon Saturdays and Sundays, because he attended during most of the week at Mr Hannay's academy, where he gradually became so clever that the masters all praised his extraordinary attention, and covered him with medals, while Major Graham often filled his pockets with a reward of money, after which he ran towards the nearest shop to spend his little fortune in buying a present for somebody. Frank scarcely ever wanted any thing for himself, but he always wished to contrive some kind, generous plan for other people; and Major Graham used to say, " if that boy had only sixpence in the world, he would lay it all out on penny tarts to distribute among half-a-dozen of his friends." He even saved his pocket-money once, during three whole months, to purchase a gown for Mrs Crabtree, who looked almost good-humoured during the space of five minutes, when Frank presented it to her, saying, in his joyous, merry voice, "Mrs Crabtree! I wish you health to wear it, strength to tear it, and money to buy another!"

Certainly there never was such a gown before! It had been chosen by Frank and Harry together, who thought nothing could be more perfect. The colour was so bright an apple-green, that it would have put anybody's teeth on edge to look at it, and the whole was dotted over with large, round spots of every colour, as if a box of wafers had been showered upon the surface. Laura wished Mrs Crabtree might receive a present every day, as it put her in such good humour, and nearly three weeks passed without a single scold being heard in the nursery; so Frank observed that he thought Mrs Crabtree would soon be quite out of practice.

"Laura!" said Major Graham, looking very sly one morning, "have you heard all the new rules that Mrs Crabtree has made?"

"No!" replied she, in great alarm; "what are they?"

"In the first place, you are positively not to tear and destroy above three frocks a-day; secondly, you and Harry must never get into a passion, unless you are angry; thirdly, when either of you take medicine, you are not to make wry faces, except when the taste is bad; fourthly, you must never speak ill of Mrs Crabtree herself, till she is out of the room; fifthly, you are not to jump out of the windows, as long as you can get out at the door"——— ———

"Yes!" interrupted Laura, laughing, "and sixthly, when uncle David is joking, we are not to be frightened by anything he says!"

"Seventhly, when next you spill grandmama's bottle of ink, Harry must drink up every drop."

"Very well! he may swallow a sheet of blotting paper afterwards, to put away the taste."

"I wish every body who writes a book, was obliged to swallow it," said Harry. "It is such a waste of time reading, when we might be amusing ourselves. Frank sat mooning over a book for two hours yesterday when we wanted him to play. I am sure some day his head will burst with knowledge."

"That can never happen to you, Master Harry," answered Major Graham; "you have a head, and so has a pin; but there is not much furniture in either of them."

CHAPTER II.

THE GRAND FEAST.

*She gave them some tea without any bread,
She whipp'd them all soundly, and sent them to bed.*
Nursery Rhymes.

LADY HARRIET GRAHAM was an extremely thin, delicate, old lady, with a very pale face and a sweet, gentle voice, which the children delighted to hear, for it always spoke kindly to them, and sounded like music, after the loud, rough tones of Mrs Crabtree. She wore her own grey hair, which had become almost as white as the widow's cap which covered her head. The rest of her dress was generally black velvet, and she usually sat in a comfortable arm-chair by the fireside, watching her grandchildren at play, with a large work-bag by her side, and a prodigious Bible open on the table before her. Lady Harriet often said that it made her young again to see the joyous gambols of Harry and Laura; and when unable any longer to bear their noise, she sometimes kept them quiet, by telling them the most delightful stories about what had happened to herself when she was young.

Once upon a time, however, Lady Harriet suddenly became so very ill, that Dr Bell said she must spend a few days in the country, for change of air, and accordingly she determined on passing a quiet week at Holiday House with her relations, Lord and Lady Rockville. Meanwhile, Harry and Laura were to be left under the sole care of Mrs Crabtree, so it might have been expected that they would both feel more frightened for her, now that she was reigning monarch of the house, than ever. Harry would obey those he loved, if they only held up a little finger; but all the terrors of Mrs Crabtree, and her cat-o'-nine-tails, were generally forgotten soon after she left the room; therefore he thought little at first about the many threats she held out, if he behaved ill, but he listened most seriously when his dear, sick grandmama told him, in a faint, weak voice, on the day of her departure from home, how very well he ought to behave in her absence, as no one remained but the maids to keep him in order, and that she hoped Mrs Crabtree would write her a letter full of good news about his excellent conduct.

Harry felt as if he would gladly sit still without stirring till his grandmama came back, if that could only please her; and there never was any one more determined to be a good boy than he, at the moment when Lady Harriet's carriage came round to the door. Laura, Frank, and Harry, helped to carry all the pillows, boxes, books, and baskets, which were necessary for the journey, of which there seemed to be about fifty; then they arranged the cushions as comfortably as possible, and watched very sorrowfully when their grandmama, after kindly embracing them both, was carefully supported by Major Graham and her own maid Harrison, into the chariot. Uncle David gave each of the children a pretty picture-book before taking leave, and said, as he was stepping into the carriage, " Now, children! I have only one piece of serious, important advice to give you all, so attend to me! Never crack nuts with your teeth."

When the carriage had driven off, Mrs Crabtree became so busy scolding Betty, and storming at Jack the foot-boy, for not cleaning her shoes well enough, that she left Harry and Laura standing in the passage, not knowing exactly what they ought to do first, and Frank, seeing them looking rather melancholy and bewildered at the loss of their grandmama, stopped a moment as he passed on the way to school, and said in a very kind, affectionate voice,

" Now, Harry and Laura, listen, both of you—

here is a grand opportunity to shew everybody that we can be trusted to ourselves, without getting into any scrapes, so that if grandmamma is ever ill again and obliged to go away, she need not feel so sad and anxious as she did to-day. I mean to become nine times more attentive to my lessons than usual this morning, to shew how trustworthy we are, and if you are wise, pray march straight up to the nursery yourselves. I have arranged a gown and cap of Mrs Crabtree's on the large arm-chair, to look as like herself as possible, that you may be reminded how soon she will come back, and you must not behave like the mice when the cat is out. Goodbye! Say the alphabet backwards, and count your fingers for half-an-hour; but when Mrs Crabtree appears again, pray do not jump out of the window for joy."

Harry and Laura were proceeding directly towards the nursery, as Frank had recommended, when unluckily they observed in passing the drawing-room door, that it was wide open; so Harry peeped in, and they began idly wandering round the tables and cabinets. Not ten minutes elapsed before they both commenced racing about as if they were mad, perfectly screaming with joy, and laughing so loudly at their own funny tricks, that an old gentleman who lived next door very nearly sent in a message to ask what the joke was.

Presently Harry and Laura ran up and down stairs till the housemaid was quite fatigued with running after them. They jumped upon the fine damask sofas in the drawing-room, stirred the fire till it was in a blaze, and rushed out on the balcony, upsetting one or two geraniums and a myrtle. They spilt Lady Harriet's perfumes over their handkerchiefs,—they looked into all the beautiful books of pictures,—they tumbled many of the pretty Dresden china figures on the floor,—they wound up the little French clock till it was broken —they made the musical work-box play its tunes and set the Chinese mandarins a-nodding, till they very nearly nodded their heads off. In short, so much mischief has seldom been done in so short a time, till at last Harry, perfectly worn out with laughing and running, threw himself into a large arm-chair, and Laura, with her ringlets tumbling in frightful confusion over her face, and the beads of her coral necklace rolling on the floor, tossed herself into a sofa beside him.

"Oh! what fun!" cried Harry, in an ecstacy of delight. "I wish Frank had been here, and crowds of little boys and girls, to play with us all day! It would be a good joke, Laura, to write and ask all our little cousins and companions to drink tea here to-morrow evening! Their mamas could never guess we had not leave from grandmama to invite everybody, so I daresay we might gather quite a large party! oh! how enchanting!"

Laura laughed heartily when she heard this proposal of Harry's, and without hesitating a moment about it, she joyously placed herself before Lady Harriet's writing-table, and scribbled a multitude of little notes, in large text, to more than twenty young friends, all of whom had at other times been asked by Lady Harriet to spend the evening with her.

Laura felt very much puzzled to know what was usually said in a card of invitation; but after many consultations, she and Harry thought at last that it was very nicely expressed, for they wrote these words upon a large sheet of paper to each of their friends :—

"Master Harry Graham and Miss Laura wish you to have the honour of drinking tea with us to-morrow at six o'clock.

(Signed)   "HARRY and LAURA."

Laura afterwards singed a hole in her muslin frock, while lighting one of the Vesta matches to seal these numerous notes; and Harry dropped some burning sealing-wax on his hand, in the hurry of assisting her; but he thought that little accident no matter, and ran away to see if the cards could be sent off immediately.

Now, there lived in the house a very old footman, called Andrew, who remembered Harry and Laura since they were quite little babies; and he often looked exceedingly sad and sorry when they suffered punishment from Mrs Crabtree. He was ready to do any thing in the world when it pleased the children, and would have carried a message to the moon, if they had only shewn him the way. Many odd jobs and private messages he had already been employed in by Harry, who now called Andrew up stairs, entreating him to carry out all those absurd notes as fast as possible, and to deliver them immediately, as they were of the greatest consequence. Upon hearing this, old Andrew lost not a moment, but threw on his hat, and instantly started off, looking like the twopenny postman, he carried such a prodigious parcel of invitations, while Harry and Laura stood at the drawing-room window, almost screaming with joy when they saw him set out, and when they observed that, to oblige them, he actually ran along the street at a sort of trot, which was as fast as he could possibly go. Presently, however, he certainly did stop for a single minute, and Laura saw that it was in order to take a peep into one of the notes, that he might ascertain what they were all about; but as he never carried any letters without doing so, she thought that quite natural, and was only very glad when he had finished, and rapidly pursued his way again.

Next morning, Mrs Crabtree and Betty became very much surprised to observe what a number of smart livery-servants knocked at the street door, and gave in cards, but their astonishment became still greater, when old Andrew brought up a whole parcel of them to Harry and Laura, who immediately broke the seals, and read the contents in a corner together.

"What are you about there, Master Graham?" cried Mrs Crabtree, angrily. "How dare anybody venture to touch your grandmama's letters?"

"They are not for grandmama!—they are all for us! every one of them!" answered Harry, dancing about the room with joy, and waving the notes over his head. "Look at this direction! For Master and Miss Graham! put on your spectacles, and read it yourself, Mrs Crabtree! What delightful fun! the house will be as full as an egg?"

Mrs Crabtree seemed completely puzzled what to think of all this, and looked so much as if she did not know exactly what to be angry at, and so ready to be in a passion if possible, that Harry burst out a-laughing, while he said, "Only think, Mrs Crabtree! here is everybody coming to tea with us!—all my cousins, besides Peter Grey, John Stewart, Charles Forrester, Anna Perceval,

Diana Wentworth, John Fordyce, Edmund Ashford, Frank Abercromby, Ned Russell, and Tom ———"

"The boy is distracted!" exclaimed Betty, staring with astonishment. "What does all this mean, Master Harry?"

"And who gave you leave to invite company into your grandmama's house?" cried Mrs Crabtree, snatching up all the notes, and angrily thrusting them into the fire. "I never heard of such doings in all my life before, Master Harry! but as sure as eggs are eggs, you shall repent of this, for not one morsel of cake or anything else shall you have to give any of the party; no! not so much as a crust of bread, or a thimbleful of tea!"

Harry and Laura had never thought of such a catastrophe as this before; they always saw a great table covered with everything that could be named for tea, whenever their little friends came to visit them; and whether it rose out of the floor, or was brought by Aladdin's lamp, they never considered it possible that the table would not be provided as usual on such occasions; so this terrible speech of Mrs Crabtree's frightened them out of their wits. What was to be done! They both knew by experience that she always did what she threatened, or something a great deal worse, so they began by bursting into tears, and begging Mrs Crab-free for this once to excuse them, and to give some cakes and tea to their little visitors; but they might as well have spoken to one of the Chinese mandarins, for she only shook her head with a positive look, declaring over and over and over again that nothing should appear upon the table except what was always brought up for their own supper—two biscuits and two cups of milk.

"Therefore say no more about it!" added she, sternly. "I am your best friend, Master Harry, trying to teach you and Miss Laura your duty; so save your breath to cool your porridge."

Poor Harry and Laura looked perfectly ill with fright and vexation when they thought of what was to happen next, while Mrs Crabtree sat down to her knitting, grumbling to herself, and dropping her stitches every minute, with rage and irritation. Old Andrew felt exceedingly sorry after he heard what distress and difficulty Harry was in; and when the hour for the party approached, he very good-naturedly spread out a large table in the dining-room, where he put down as many cups, saucers, plates, and spoons, as Laura chose to direct; but in spite of all his trouble, though it looked very grand, there was nothing whatever to eat or drink except the two dry biscuits, and the two miserable cups of milk, which seemed to become smaller every time that Harry looked at them

Presently the clock struck six, and Harry listened to the hour very much as a prisoner would do in the condemned cell in Newgate, feeling that the dreaded time was at last arrived. Soon afterwards several handsome carriages drove up to the door, filled with little Masters and Misses, who hurried joyfully into the house, talking and laughing all the way up stairs, while poor Harry and Laura almost wished the floor would open and swallow them up; so they shrunk into a distant corner of the room, quite ashamed to shew their faces.

The young ladies were all dressed in their best frocks, with pink sashes, and pink shoes; while the little boys appeared in their holiday clothes, with their hair newly brushed, and their faces washed. The whole party had dined at two o'clock, so they were as hungry as hawks, looking eagerly round, whenever they entered, to see what was on the tea-table, and evidently surprised that nothing had yet been put down. Laura and Harry soon afterwards heard their visitors whispering to each other about Norwich buns, rice-cakes, spunge biscuits, and macaroons; while Peter Grey was loud in praise of a party at George Lorraine's the night before, where an immense plum-cake had been sugared over like a snow-storm, and covered with crowds of beautiful amusing mottoes; not to mention a quantity of noisy crackers, that exploded like pistols; besides which, a glass of hot jelly had been handed to each little guest before he was sent home.

Every time the door opened, all eyes were anxiously turned round, expecting a grand feast to be brought in; but quite the contrary—it was only Andrew shewing up more hungry visitors; while Harry felt so unspeakably wretched, that, if some kind fairy could only have turned him into a Norwich bun at the moment, he would gladly have consented to be cut in pieces, that his ravenous guests might be satisfied.

Charles Forrester was a particularly good-natured boy, so Harry at last took courage and beckoned him into a remote corner of the room, where he confessed, in whispers, the real state of affairs about tea, and how sadly distressed he and Laura felt, because they had nothing whatever to give among so many visitors, seeing that Mrs Crabtree kept her determination of affording them no provisions.

"What is to be done?" said Charles, very anxiously, as he felt extremely sorry for his little friends. "If mama had been at home, she would gladly have sent whatever you liked for tea, but unluckily she is dining out! I saw a loaf of bread lying on a table at home this evening, which she would make you quite welcome to! Shall I run home, as fast as possible, to fetch it? That would, at any rate, be better than nothing!"

Poor Charles Forrester was very lame; therefore, while he talked of running, he could hardly walk; but Lady Forrester's house stood so near that he soon reached home, when, snatching up the loaf, he hurried back towards the street with his prize, quite delighted to see how large and substantial it looked. Scarcely had he reached the door, however, before the housekeeper ran hastily out, saying,

"Stop, Master Charles! stop! sure you are not running away with the loaf for my tea; and the parrot must have her supper too. What do you want with that there bread?"

"Never mind, Mrs Comfit!" answered Charles, hastening on faster than ever, while he grasped the precious loaf more firmly in his hand, and limped along at a prodigious rate: "Polly is getting too fat, so she will be the better of fasting for one day."

Mrs Comfit, being enormously fat herself, became very angry at this remark, so she seemed quite desperate to recover the loaf, and hurried forward to overtake Charles; but the old housekeeper was so heavy and breathless, while the young gentleman was so lame, that it seemed an even chance which won the race. Harry stood at his own door, impatiently hoping to receive the prize, and eagerly stretched out his arms to encourage his friend, while it was impossible to say which of the runners might arrive first. Harry had sometimes heard of a race between two old women tied up in sacks, and he thought they could scarcely move with more difficulty; but at the very moment when Charles had reached the door, he stumbled over a stone, and fell on the ground. Mrs Comfit then instantly rushed up, and, seizing the loaf, she carried it off in triumph, leaving the two little friends ready to cry with vexation, and quite at a loss what plan to attempt next.

Meantime, a sad riot had arisen in the dining-room, where the boys called loudly for their tea; and the young ladies drew their chairs all round the table, to wait till it was ready. Still nothing appeared; so everybody wondered more and more how long they were to wait for all the nice cakes and sweetmeats which must, of course, be coming; for the longer they were delayed, the more was expected.

The last at a feast, and the first at a fray, was generally Peter Grey, who now lost patience, and seized one of the two biscuits, which he was in the middle of greedily devouring, when Laura returned with Harry to the dining-room, and observed what he had done.

"Peter Grey!" said she, holding up her head,

and trying to look very dignified, " you are an exceedingly naughty boy, to help yourself! As a punishment for being so rude, you shall have nothing more to eat all this evening."

"If I do not help myself, nobody else seems likely to give me any supper! I appear to be the only person who is to taste any thing to-night," answered Peter, laughing, while the impudent boy took a cup of milk, and drank it off, saying, "Here's to your very good health, Miss Laura, and an excellent appetite to everybody!"

Upon hearing this absurd speech, all the other boys began laughing, and made signs, as if they were eating their fingers off with hunger. Then Peter called Lady Harriet's house "Famine Castle," and pretended he would swallow the knives, like an Indian juggler.

"We must learn to live upon air, and here are some spoons to eat it with," said John Fordyce. "Harry! shall I help you to a mouthful of moonshine?"

"Peter! would you like a roasted fly?" asked Frank Abercromby, catching one on the window. "I daresay it is excellent for hungry people,—or a slice of buttered wall?"

"Or a stewed spider?" asked Peter. "Shall we all be cannibals, and eat one another?"

"What is the use of all those forks, when there

is nothing to stick upon them?" asked George Maxwell, throwing them about on the floor. " No buns!—no fruit!—no cakes!—no nothing!"

" What are we to do with those tea-cups, when there is no tea?" cried Frank Abercromby, pulling the table-cloth, till the whole affair fell prostrate on the floor. After this, these riotous boys tossed the plates in the air, and caught them, becoming, at last, so outrageous, that poor old Andrew called them a "meal mob!" Never was there so much broken china seen in a dining-room before! It all lay scattered on the floor, in countless fragments, looking as if there had been a bull in a china shop, when suddenly Mrs Crabtree herself opened the door and walked in, with an aspect of rage enough to petrify a milestone. Now old Andrew had long been trying all in his power to render the boys quiet and contented. He had made them a speech,—he had chased the ring-leaders all round the room,—and he had thrown his stick at Peter, who seemed the most riotous,—but all in vain; they became worse and worse, laughing into fits, and calling Andrew " the police officer and the bailiff." It was a very different story, however, when Mrs Crabtree appeared, so flaming with fury, she might have blown up a powder-mill.

Nobody could help being afraid of her. Even

Peter himself stood stock still, and seemed withering away to nothing, when she looked at him; and when she began to scold in her most furious manner, not a boy ventured to look off the ground. A large pair of tawse then became visible in her hand, so every heart sunk with fright, and the riotous visitors began to get behind each other, and to huddle out of sight as much as possible, whispering, and pushing, and fighting, in a desperate scuffle to escape.

"What is all this!" cried she, at the full pitch of her voice; "has bedlam broke loose? who smashed these cups? I'll break his head for him, let me tell you that! Master Peter! you should be hissed out of the world for your misconduct; but I shall certainly whip you round the room like a whipping-top."

At this moment, Peter observed that the dining-room window, which was only about six feet from the ground, had been left wide open; so instantly seizing the opportunity, he threw himself out with a single bound, and ran laughing away. All the other boys immediately followed his example, and disappeared by the same road; after which, Mrs Crabtree leaned far out of the window, and scolded loudly, as long as they remained in sight, till her face became red, and her voice perfectly hoarse.

Meantime, the little misses sat soberly down before the empty table, and talked in whispers to each other, waiting till their maids came to take them home, after which they all hurried away as fast as possible, hardly waiting to say "Goodbye," and intending to ask for some supper at home.

During that night, long after Harry and Laura had been scolded, whipped, and put to bed, they were each heard in different rooms, sobbing and crying, as if their very hearts would break, while Mrs Crabtree grumbled and scolded to herself, saying she must do her duty, and make them good children, though she were to flay them alive first.

When Lady Harriet returned home some days afterwards, she heard an account of Harry and Laura's misconduct from Mrs Crabtree, and the whole story was such a terrible case against them, that their poor grandmama became perfectly astonished and shocked, while even uncle David was preparing to be very angry; but before the culprits appeared, Frank most kindly stepped forward, and begged that they might be pardoned for this once, adding all in his power to excuse Harry and Laura, by describing how very penitent they had become, and how very severely they had already been punished.

Frank then mentioned all that Harry had told him about the starving party, which he related with so much humour and drollery, that Lady Harriet could not help laughing; so then he saw that a victory had been gained, and ran to the nursery for the two little prisoners.

Uncle David shook his walking-stick at them, and made a terrible face, when they entered; but Harry jumped upon his knee with joy at seeing him again, while Laura forgot all her distress, and rushed up to Lady Harriet, who folded her in her arms, and kissed her most affectionately.

Not a word was said that day about the tea-party, but next morning Major Graham asked Harry, very gravely, " if he had read in the newspaper the melancholy accounts about several of his little companions, who were ill and confined to bed from having eat too much at a certain tea-party on Saturday last. Poor Peter Grey has been given over; and Charles Forrester, it is feared, may not be able to eat another loaf of bread for a fortnight!"

" Oh! uncle David! it makes me ill whenever I think of that party!" said Harry, colouring perfectly scarlet; " that was the most miserable evening of my life!"

" I must say it was not quite fair in Mrs Crabtree to starve all the strange little boys and girls, who came as visitors to my house, without knowing who had invited them," observed Lady Harriet. " Probably those unlucky children will never forget, as long as they live, that scanty supper in our dining-room."

And it turned out exactly as Lady Harriet had predicted; for though they were all asked to tea, in proper form, the very next Saturday, when Major Graham showered torrents of sugar-plums on the table, while the children scrambled to pick them up, and the sideboard almost broke down afterwards under the weight of buns, cakes, cheesecakes, biscuits, fruit, and preserves, which were heaped upon each other — yet, for years afterwards, Peter Grey, whenever he ate a particularly enormous dinner, always observed, that he must make up for having once been starved at Harry Graham's; and whenever any one of those little boys or girls again happened to meet Harry or Laura, they were sure to laugh and say, " When are you going to give us another

"GRAND FEAST.'

CHAPTER III.

THE TERRIBLE FIRE.

*Fire rages with fury wherever it comes,
If only one spark should be dropped ;
Whole houses, or cities, sometimes it consumes,
Where its violence cannot be stopped.*

ONE night, about eight o'clock, Harry and Laura were playing in the nursery, building houses with bricks, and trying who could raise the highest tower without letting it fall, when suddenly they were startled to hear every bell in the house ringing violently, while the servants seemed running up and down stairs, as if they were distracted.

"What can be the matter?" cried Laura, turning round and listening, while Harry quietly took this opportunity to shake the walls of her castle till it fell.

"The very house is coming down about your ears, Laura!" said Harry, enjoying his little bit of mischief. "I should like to be Andrew, now, for five minutes, that I might answer those fifty bells, and see what has happened. Uncle David must be wanting coals, candles, tea, toast, and soda-water, all at once! What a bustle everybody is in! There! the bells are ringing again, worse than ever! Something wonderful is going on! What can it be?"

Presently Betty ran breathlessly into the room, saying that Mrs Crabtree ought to come down stairs immediately, as Lady Harriet had been suddenly taken very ill, and, till the Doctor arrived, nobody knew what to do; so she must give her advice and assistance.

Harry and Laura felt excessively shocked to hear this alarming news, and listened with grave attention, while Mrs Crabtree told them how amazingly well they ought to behave in her absence, when they were trusted alone in the nursery, with nobody to keep them in order, or to see what they were doing, especially now, as their grandmama had been taken ill, and would require to be kept quiet.

Harry sat in his chair, and might have been painted as the very picture of a good boy during nearly twenty minutes after Mrs Crabtree departed; and Laura placed herself opposite to him, trying to follow so excellent an example, while they scarcely spoke above a whisper, wondering what could be the matter with their grandmama, and wishing for once to see Mrs Crabtree again, that they might hear how she was. Any one who had observed Harry and Laura at that time, would have wondered to see two such quiet, excellent, respectable children, and wished that all little boys and girls were made upon the same pattern; but presently they began to think that probably Lady Harriet was not so very ill, as no more bells had rung during several minutes, and Harry ventured to look about for some better amusement than sitting still.

At this moment Laura unluckily perceived on the table near where they sat, a pair of Mrs Crabtree's best scissors, which she had been positively forbid to touch. The long troublesome ringlets were as usual hanging over her eyes in a most teasing manner, so she thought what a good opportunity this might be to shorten them a very little, not above an inch or two ; and without considering a moment longer, she slipped upon tiptoe, with a frightened look, round the table, and picked up the scissors in her hand, then hastening towards a looking-glass, she began snipping off the ends of her hair. Laura was much diverted to see it showering down upon the floor, so she cut and cut on, while the curls fell thicker and faster, till at last the whole floor was covered with them, and scarcely a hair left upon her head. Harry went into fits of laughing when he perceived what a ridiculous figure Laura had made of herself, and he turned her round and round to see the havoc she had made, saying,

"You should give all this hair to Mr Mills the upholsterer, to stuff grandmama's arm-chair with! At any rate, Laura, if Mrs Crabtree is ever so angry, she can hardly pull you by the hair of the head again! What a sound sleep you will have to-night, with no hard curl-papers to torment you!"

Harry had been told five hundred times never to touch the candles, and threatened with twenty different punishments if he ever ventured to do so; but now he amused himself with trying to snuff one till he snuffed it out. Then he lighted it again, and tried the experiment once more, but again the teasing candle went out, as if on purpose to plague him; so he felt quite provoked. Having lighted it once more, Harry prepared to carry the candlestick with him towards the inner nursery, though afraid to make the smallest noise, in case it might be taken from him. Before he had gone five steps, down dropped the extinguisher, then followed the snuffers with a great crash; but Laura seemed too busy cropping her ringlets, to notice what was going on. All the way along upon the floor, Harry let fall a perfect shower of hot wax, which spotted the nursery-carpet from the table where he had found the candle, into the next room, where he disappeared, and shut the door, that no one might interfere with what he liked to do.

After he had been absent some time, the door was hastily opened again, and Laura felt surprised to see Harry come back with his face as red as a stick of sealing-wax, and his large eyes staring wider than they had ever stared before, with a look of rueful consternation.

"What is the matter?" exclaimed Laura, in a terrified voice. "Has anything dreadful happened? Why do you look so frightened and so surprised?"

"Oh dear! oh dear! what shall I do?" cried Harry, who seemed scarcely to know how he spoke, or where he was. "I don't know what to do Laura!"

"What can be the matter? do tell me at once, Harry," said Laura, shaking with apprehension. "Speak as fast as you can!"

"Will you not tell Mrs Crabtree, nor grand-mama, nor anybody else?" cried Harry, bursting into tears. "I am so very, very sorry, and so frightened! Laura! do you know, I took a candle into the next room, merely to play with it."

"Well! go on, Harry! go on! What did you do with the candle?"

"I only put it on the bed for a single minute, to see how the flame would look there. Well! do

you know, it blazed away famously, and then all
the bedclothes began burning too ! Oh ! there is
such a terrible fire in the next room ! you never
saw anything like it ! what shall we do ? If old
Andrew were to come up, do you think he could
put it out ? I have shut the door, that Mrs Crabtree may not see the flames. Be sure, Laura, to
tell nobody but Andrew."

Laura became terrified at the way she saw poor
Harry in, but when she opened the door to find
out the real state of affairs, oh ! what a dreadful
sight was there ! all the beds were on fire, while
bright, red flames were blazing up to the roof of
the room with a fierce, roaring noise, which it was
perfectly frightful to hear. She screamed aloud
with terror at this alarming scene, while Harry
did all he could to quiet her, and even put his
hand over her mouth, that her cries might not be
heard. Laura now struggled to get loose, and
called louder and louder, till at last every maid
in the house came racing up stairs, three steps at
a time, to know what was the matter. Immediately upon seeing the flames, they all began screaming
too, in such a loud, discordant way, that it sounded as if a whole flight of crows had come into
the passages. Never was there such an uproar
heard in the house before ; for the walls echoed
with a general cry of " Fire ! fire ! fire !"

THE TERRIBLE FIRE.

Up flew Mrs Crabtree towards the nursery like a sky-rocket, scolding furiously, talking louder than all the others put together, and asking who had set the house on fire, while Harry and Laura scarcely knew whether to be most frightened for the raging flames or the raging Mrs Crabtree; but, in the mean time, they both shrunk into the smallest possible size, and hid themselves behind a door.

During all this confusion, old Andrew luckily remembered that in the morning there had been a great washing in the laundry, where large tubs full of water were standing, so he called to the few maids who had any of their senses remaining, desiring them to assist in carrying up some buckets, that they might be emptied on the burning beds, to extinguish the flames if possible. Everybody was now in a hurry, and all elbowing each other out of the way, while it was most extraordinary to see how old Andrew exerted himself, as if he had been a fireman all his life, while Mrs Marmalade, the fat cook, who could hardly carry herself up stairs in general, actively assisted to bring up the great, heavy tubs, and to pour them out like a cascade upon the burning curtains, till the nursery-floor looked like a duck-pond.

Meantime, Harry and Laura added to the confusion as much as they could, and were busier than anybody, stealing down the back stairs whenever Mrs Crabtree was not in sight, and filling their little jugs with water, which they brought up, as fast as possible, and dashed upon the flames, till at last, it is to be feared, they began to feel quite amused with the bustle, and to be almost sorry when the conflagration diminished. At one time, Laura very nearly set her frock on fire, as she ventured too near, but Harry pulled her back, and then courageously advanced to discharge a shower from his own little jug, remaining stationary to watch the effect, till his face was almost scorched.

At last the fire became less and less, till it went totally out, but not before the nursery furniture had been reduced to perfect ruins, besides which, Betty had her arm sadly burned in the confusion. Mrs Marmalade's cap was completely destroyed, and Mrs Crabtree's best gown had so large a hole burned in the skirt, that she never could wear it again.

After all was quiet, and the fire completely extinguished, Major Graham took Laura down stairs to Lady Harriet's dressing-room, that she might tell the whole particulars of how this alarming accident happened in the nursery; for nobody could guess what had caused so sudden and dreadful a fire, which seemed to have been as unexpected as a flash of lightning.

Lady Harriet had felt so terrified by the noise and confusion, that she was out of bed, sitting up in an arm-chair, supported by pillows, when Laura entered, at the sight of whom, with her well-cropped head, she uttered an exclamation of perfect amazement.

" Why! who on earth is that? Laura, my dear child! what has become of all your hair? Were your curls burned off in the fire? or did the fright make you grow bald? What is the meaning of all this?"

Laura turned perfectly crimson with shame and distress, for she now felt convinced of her own great misconduct about the scissors and curls; but she had been taught on all occasions to speak the truth, and would rather have died than told a lie, or even allowed any person to believe what was not true, therefore she answered in a low, frightened voice, while the tears came into her eyes, " My hair has not been burned off, grandmama! but—but—"

" Well, child! speak out!" said Lady Harriet, impatiently. " Did some hairdresser come to the house and rob you?"

" Or, are you like the ladies of Carthage, who

gave their long hair for bows and arrows?" asked Major Graham. "I never saw such a little fright in my life as you look now; but tell us all about it."

"I have been quite as naughty as Harry!" answered Laura, bursting into tears, and sobbing with grief; "I was cutting off my hair with Mrs Crabtree's scissors all the time that he was setting the nursery on fire!"

"Did any mortal ever hear of two such little torments!" exclaimed Major Graham, hardly able to help laughing. "I wonder if anybody else in the world has such mischievous children!"

"It is certainly very strange that you and Harry never can contrive to be three hours out of a scrape!" said Lady Harriet, gravely; "now Frank, on the contrary, never forgets what I bid him do. You might suppose he carried Mrs Crabtree in his pocket, to remind him constantly of his duty; but there are not two such boys in the world as Frank!"

"No," added Major Graham; "Harry set the house on fire, and Frank will set the Thames on fire!"

When Laura saw uncle David put on one of his funny looks, while he spoke in this way to Lady Harriet, she almost forgot her former fright, and became surprised to observe her grandmama busily preparing what she called a coach-wheel, which had been often given as a treat to Harry and herself when they were particularly good. This delightful wheel was manufactured by taking a whole round slice of the loaf, in the centre of which was placed a large teaspoonful of jelly, after which long spokes of marmalade, jam, and honey, were made to diverge most tastefully in every direction towards the crust; and Laura watched the progress of this business with great interest and anxiety, wondering if it could be hoped that her grandmama really meant to forgive all her misconduct during the day.

"That coach-wheel is, of course, meant for me!" said Major Graham, pretending to be very hungry, and looking slyly at Laura. "It cannot possibly be intended for our little hairdresser here!"

"Yes, it is!" answered Lady Harriet, smiling. "I have some thoughts of excusing Laura this time, because she always tells me the truth, without attempting to conceal any foolish thing she does. It will be very long before she has any hair to cut off again, so I hope she may be older and wiser by that time, especially considering that every looking-glass she sees for six months will make her feel ashamed of herself. She certainly deserves some reward for having prevented the house to-night from being burned to the ground."

"I am glad you think so, because here is a shilling that has been burning in my pocket for the last few minutes, as I wished to bestow it on Laura for having saved all our lives, and if she had behaved still better, I might perhaps have given her a gold watch!"

Laura was busily employed in eating her coach-wheel, and trying to fancy what the gold watch would have looked like which she might probably have got from uncle David, when suddenly the door burst open, and Mrs Crabtree hurried into the room, with a look of surprise and alarm, her face as red as a poppy, and her eyes fixed on the hole in her best gown, while she spoke so loud and angrily, that Laura almost trembled.

"If you please, my lady! where can Master Harry be? I cannot find him in any corner!— we have been searching all over the house, up stairs and down stairs, in vain. Not a garret or a closet but has been ransacked, and nobody can guess what has become of him!"

"Did you look up the chimney, Mrs Crabtree?" asked Major Graham, laughing to see how excited she looked.

"'Deed, Sir! it is, no joke," answered Mrs Crabtree, sulkily; "I am almost afraid Master Harry has been burned in the fire! The last time Betty saw him, he was throwing a jug of water into the flames, and no one has ever seen or heard of him since! There is a great many ashes and cinders lying about the room, and——"

"Do you think, in sober seriousness, Mrs Crabtree, that Harry would melt away like a wax-doll, without asking anybody to extinguish him?" said Major Graham, smiling. "No! no! little boys are not quite so easily disposed of. I shall find Harry in less than five minutes, if he is above ground."

But uncle David was quite mistaken in expecting to discover Harry so easily, for he searched and searched in vain. He looked into every possible or impossible place—the library, the kitchen, the garrets, the laundry, the drawing-room, all without success,—he peeped under the tables, behind the curtains, over the beds, beneath the pillows, and into Mrs Crabtree's bonnet-box,—he even opened the tea-chest, and looked out at the window, in case Harry had tumbled over; but nowhere could he be found.

"Not a mouse is stirring!" exclaimed Major Graham, beginning now to look exceedingly grave and anxious. "This is very strange! The house-door is locked, therefore, unless Harry made his escape through the key-hole, he must be here! It is most unaccountable what the little pickle can have done with himself!"

When Major Graham chose to exert his voice,

it was as loud as a trumpet, and could be heard half a mile off; so he now called out, like thunder, from the top of the stairs to the bottom, saying, " Hollo, Harry! Hollo! Come here, my boy! Nobody shall hurt you! Harry! where are you?"

Uncle David waited to listen, but all was still— no answer could be heard, and there was not a sound in the house, except poor Laura at the bottom of the stairs, sobbing with grief and terror about Harry having been lost, and Mrs Crabtree grumbling angrily to herself, on account of the large hole in her best gown.

By this time Lady Harriet nearly fainted with fatigue, for she was so very old, and had been ill all day; so she grew worse and worse, till everybody said she must go to bed, and try if it would be possible to fall asleep, assuring her that Harry must soon be found, as nothing particular could have happened to him, or some person would have seen it.

" Indeed, my lady! Master Harry is just like a bad shilling, that is sure to come back," said Mrs Crabtree, helping her to undress, while she continued to talk the whole time about the fire, shewing her own unfortunate gown, describing the trouble she had taken to save the house from being burned, and always ending every sentence with a wish that she could lay hands on Harry, to punish him as he deserved.

"The truth is, I just spoil and indulge the children too much, my lady!" added Mrs Crabtree, in a self-satisfied tone of voice. "I really blame myself often for being over-easy and kind."

"You have nothing to accuse yourself of in that respect," answered Lady Harriet, unable to help smiling.

"Your ladyship is very good to say so. Major Graham is so fond of our young people, that it is lucky they have some one to keep them in order. I shall make a duty, my lady, of being more strict than ever. Master Harry must be made an example of this time!" added Mrs Crabtree, angrily glancing at the hole in her gown. "I shall teach him to remember this day the longest hour he has to live!"

"Harry will not forget it any how," answered Lady Harriet, languidly. "Perhaps, Mrs Crabtree, we might as well not be severe with the poor boy on this occasion. As the old proverb says, 'There is no use in pouring water on a drowned mouse.' Harry has got a sad fright for his pains; and at all events you must find him first, before he can be punished. Where can the poor child be hid?"

"I would give sixpence to find out that, my lady!" answered Mrs Crabtree, helping Lady Harriet into bed, after which she closed the shutters, put out the candles, and left the room, angrily muttering, "Master Harry cares no more for me than the poker cares for the tongs; but I shall teach him another story soon."

Lady Harriet now feebly closed her eyes, being quite exhausted, and was beginning to feel the pleasant, confused sensation that people have before going to sleep, when some noise made her suddenly start quite awake. She sat up in bed to listen, but could not be sure whether it had been a great noise at a distance, or a little noise in the room; so after waiting two or three minutes, she sunk back upon the pillows, and tried to forget it. Again, however, she distinctly heard something rustling in the bed-curtains, and opened her eyes to see what could be the matter, but all was dark. Something seemed to be breathing very near her, however, and the curtains shook worse than before, till Lady Harriet became really alarmed.

"It must surely be a cat in the room!" thought she, hastily pulling the bell-rope, till it nearly came down. "That tiresome little animal will make such a noise, I shall not be able to sleep all night!"

The next minute Lady Harriet was startled to hear a loud sob close beside her; and when everybody rushed up stairs to ask what was the matter, they brought candles to search the room, and there was Harry! He lay doubled up in a corner, and crying as if his heart would break, yet still endeavouring not to be seen; for Harry always thought it a terrible disgrace to cry, and would have concealed himself anywhere, rather than be observed weeping. Laura burst into tears also, when she saw what red eyes and pale cheeks Harry had; but Mrs Crabtree lost no time in pulling him out of his place, being quite impatient to begin her scold, and to produce her tawse, though she received a sad disappointment on this occasion, as uncle David unexpectedly interfered to get him off.

"Come now! Mrs Crabtree," said he, good-naturedly; "put up the tawse for this time; you are rather too fond of the leather. Harry seems really sorry and frightened, so we must be merciful. The cataract of tears he is shedding now, would have extinguished the fire if it had come in time! Harry is like a culprit with the rope about his neck; but he shall not be executed. Let me be judge and jury in this case; and my sentence is a very dreadful one. Harry must sleep all to-night in the burned nursery, having no other covering than the burned blankets, with large holes in them, that he may never forget

CHAPTER IV

THE PRODIGIOUS CAKE.

> Yet theirs the joy
> That lifts their steps, that sparkles in their eyes,
> That talks or laughs, or runs, or shouts, or plays,
> And speaks in all their looks, and all their ways.
> CRABBE.

NEXT day after the fire, Laura could think of nothing but what she was to do with the shilling that uncle David had given her; and a thousand plans came into her head, while many wants entered her thoughts which never occurred before; so that if twenty shillings had been in her hand instead of one, they would all have gone twenty different ways.

Lady Harriet advised that it should be laid by till Laura had fully considered what she would like best; reminding her very truly, that money is lame in coming but flies in going away. "Many people can get a shilling, Laura," said her grandmama; "but the difficulty is to keep it; for you know the old proverb tells that A fool and his money are soon parted.'"

" Yes, Miss ! so give it to me, and I shall take care of your shilling !" added Mrs Crabtree, holding out her hand to Laura, who felt that if her money once disappeared into that capacious pocket, she would never see it again. " Children have no use for money! That shilling will only burn a hole in your purse, till it is spent on some foolish thing or other. You will be losing your thimble soon, or mislaying your gloves; for all these things seem to fly in every direction, as if they got legs and wings as soon as they belong to you ; so then that shilling may replace what is lost."

Mrs Crabtree looked as if she would eat it up; but Laura grasped her treasure still tighter in her hand, exclaiming,

" No ! no ! this is mine ! Uncle David never thought of my shilling being taken care of ! He meant me to do whatever I liked with it ! Uncle David says he cannot endure saving children, and that he wishes all money were turned into slates, when little girls keep it longer than a week."

" I like that !" said Harry, eagerly ; " it is so pleasant to spend money, when the shopkeeper bows to me over the counter so politely, and asks what I please to want."

" Older people than you like spending money, Master Harry, and spend whether they have it or no; but the greatest pleasure is to keep it. For instance, Miss Laura, whatever she sees worth a shilling in any shop, might be hers if she pleases; so then it is quite as good as her own. We shall look in at the bazaar every morning, to fix upon something that she would like to have, and then consider of it for two or three days."

Laura thought this plan so very unsatisfactory, that she lost no time in getting her shilling changed into two sixpences, one of which she immediately presented to Harry, who positively refused for a long time to accept of it, insisting that Laura should rather buy some pretty plaything for herself; but she answered that it was much pleasanter to divide her fortune with Harry, than to be selfish, and spend it all alone. "I am sure, Harry," added she, "if this money had been yours, you would have said the same thing, and given the half of what you got to me; so now let us say no more about that, but tell me what would be the best use to make of my sixpence?"

"You might buy that fine red morocco purse we saw in the shop-window yesterday," observed Harry, looking very serious and anxious, on being consulted. "Do you remember how much we both wished to have it?"

"But what is the use of a purse, with no money to keep in it?" answered Laura, looking earnestly at Harry for more advice. "Think again of something else."

"Would you like a new doll?"

"Yes; but I have nothing to dress her with."

"Suppose you buy that pretty geranium in a red flower-pot at the gardener's!"

"If it would only live for a week, I might be tempted to try; but flowers will always die with me. They seem to wither when I so much as look at them. Do you remember that pretty fuchsia that I almost drowned the first day grandmama gave it me; and we forgot for a week afterwards to water it at all. I am not a good flower doctor."

"Then buy a gold watch at once," said Harry, laughing; "or a fine pony, with a saddle, to ride on."

"Now, Harry, pray be quite in earnest. You know I might as well attempt to buy the moon as a gold watch; so think of something else."

"It is very difficult to make a good use of money," said Harry, pretending to look exceedingly wise. "Do you know, Laura, I once found out that you could have twelve of those large ship-biscuits we saw at the baker's shop for sixpence. Only think! you could feed the whole town, and make a present to everybody in the house besides! I daresay Mrs Crabtree might like one with her tea. All the maids would think them a treat. You could present one to Frank, another to old Andrew, and there would still be some left for these poor children at the cottage."

"Oh! that is the very thing!" cried Laura, running out of the room to send Andrew off with a basket, and looking as happy as possible. Not long afterwards, Frank, who had returned from school, was standing at the nursery-window, when he suddenly called out with a voice of surprise and amusement,

"Come here, Harry! look at old Andrew! he is carrying something tied up in a towel, as large as his own head! what can it be?"

"That is all for me! These are my biscuits!" said Laura, running off to receive the parcel, and though she heard Frank laughing, while Harry told all about them, she did not care, but brought her whole collection triumphantly into the nursery.

"Oh, fancy! how perfect!" cried Harry, opening the bundle; "this is very good fun!"

"Here are provisions for a siege!" added Frank. "You have at least got enough for your money, Laura!"

"Take one yourself, Frank!" said she reaching him the largest, and then with the rest all tied in her apron, Laura proceeded up and down stairs, making presents to every person she met, till her whole store was finished; and she felt quite satisfied and happy because everybody seemed pleased and returned many thanks, except Mrs Crabtree, who said she had no teeth to eat such hard things, which were only fit for sailors going to America or the West Indies.

"You should have bought me a pound of sugar, Miss Laura, and that might have been a present worth giving."

"You are too sweet already, Mrs Crabtree!" said Frank, laughing. "I shall send you a sugar-cane from the West Indies, to beat Harry and Laura with, and a whole barrel of sugar for yourself from my own estate."

"None of your nonsense, Master Frank! Get out of the nursery this moment! You with an estate, indeed! You will not have a place to put your foot upon soon except the top-mast in a man-of-war, where all the bad boys in a ship are sent."

"Perhaps, as you are not to be the captain, I may escape, and be dining with the officers, sometimes! I mean to send you home a fine new India shawl, Mrs Crabtree, the very moment I arrive at Madras, and some china tea-cups from Canton."

"Fiddlesticks and nonsense!" said Mrs Crabtree, who sometimes enjoyed a little jesting with Frank. "Keep all them rattle-traps till you are a rich nabob, and come home to look for Mrs Frank,—a fine wife she will be! Ladies that get fortunes from India are covered all over with gold chains, and gold muslins, and scarlet shawls. She will eat nothing but curry and rice, and never put her foot to the ground, except to step into her carriage."

"I hope you are not a gipsy, to tell fortunes!" cried Harry, laughing. "Frank would die rather than take such a wife."

"Or, at least I would rather have a tooth drawn than do it," added Frank, smiling. "Perhaps I may prefer to marry one of those old wives on the chimney-tops; but it is too serious to say I would rather die, because nobody knows how awful it is to die, till the appointed day comes."

"Very true and proper, Master Frank," replied Mrs Crabtree; "you speak like a printed book sometimes, and you deserve a good wife."

"Then I shall return home some day with chests of gold, and let you choose one for me, as quiet and good-natured as yourself, Mrs Crabtree," said Frank, taking up his books and hastening off to school, running all the way, as he was rather late, and Mr Lexicon, the master, had promised a grand prize for the boy who came most punctually to his lessons, which everybody declared that Frank was sure to gain, as he had never once been absent at the right moment.

Major Graham often tried to tease Frank, by calling him " the Professor,"—asking him questions which it was impossible to answer, and then pretending to be quite shocked at his ignorance; but no one ever saw the young scholar put out of temper by those tricks and trials, for he always laughed more heartily than any one else at the joke.

" Now shew me, Frank," said uncle David, one morning, " how do you advance three steps backwards ?"

" That is quite impossible, unless you turn me into a crab."

" Tell me, then, which is the principal town in Caffraria ?"

" Is there any town there ? I do not recollect it."

" Then so much the worse!—how are you ever to get through life without knowing the chief town in Caffraria! I am quite ashamed of your ignorance. Now, let us try a little arithmetic! Open the door of your understanding and tell me, when wheat is six shillings a bushel, what is the price of a penny loaf? Take your slate and calculate that."

"Yes, uncle David, if you will find out when

gooseberries are two shillings a pint, what is the price of a three-penny tart. You remind me of my old nursery song—

> 'The man in the wilderness asked me,
> How many strawberries grew in the sea?
> I answered him, as I thought it good,
> As many red herrings as grew in the wood.'"

Some days after Laura had distributed the biscuits, she became very sorry for having squandered her shilling, without attending to Lady Harriet's good advice, about keeping it carefully in her pocket for at least a week, to see what would happen. A very pleasant way of using money now fell in her way, but she had been a foolish spendthrift, so her pockets were empty when she most wished them to be full. Harry came that morning after breakfast into the nursery, looking in a great bustle, and whispering to Laura, "What a pity your sixpence is gone! but as Mrs Crabtree says, 'We cannot both eat our cake and have it!'"

"No!" answered Laura, as seriously as if she had never thought of this before; "but why do you so particularly wish my money back to-day?"

"Because such a very nice, funny thing is to be done this morning. You and I are asked to join the party, but I am afraid we cannot afford it! All our little cousins and companions intend going with Mr Harwood, the tutor, at twelve o'clock, to climb up to the very top of Arthur Seat, where they are to dine and have a dance. There will be about twenty boys and girls of the party, but everybody is to carry a basket filled with provisions for dinner, either cakes, or fruit, or biscuits, which are to be eat on the great rock at the top of the hill. Now grandmama says we ought to have had money enough to supply what is necessary, and then we might have gone; but no one can be admitted who has not at least sixpence to buy something."

"Oh! how provoking!" said Laura, sadly. "I wonder when we shall learn always to follow grandmama's advice, for that is sure to turn out best in the end. I never take my own way without being sorry for it afterwards, so I deserve now to be disappointed and remain at home; but, Harry, your sixpence is still safe; so pray join this delightful party, and tell me all about it afterwards."

"If it could take us both, I should be very happy; but I will not go without you, Laura, after you were so good to me, and gave me this in a present. No, no! I only wish we could do like the poor madman grandmama mentioned, who planted sixpences in the ground that they might grow into shillings."

"Pray, what are you two looking so solemn about?" asked Frank, hurrying into the room at that moment, on his way to school. "Are you talking of some mischief that has been done already, or only about some mischief you are intending to do soon?"

"Neither the one nor the other," answered Laura. "But oh! Frank, I am sure you will be sorry for us, when we tell you of our sad disappointment."

She then related the whole story of the party to Arthur Seat, mentioning that Mr Harwood had kindly offered to take charge of Harry and herself, but as her little fortune had been so foolishly squandered, she could not go, and Harry said it would be impossible to enjoy the fun without her, though Lady Harriet had given them both leave to be of the party.

All the time that Laura spoke, Frank stood with his hands in his pockets, where he seemed evidently searching for something, and when the whole history was told, he said to Harry, "Let me see this poor little sixpence of yours! I am a very clever conjuror, and could perhaps turn it into a shilling!"

"Nonsense, Frank!" said Laura, laughing; "you might as well turn Harry into uncle David!"

"Well! we shall see!" answered Frank, taking up the sixpence. "I have put the money into this box!—rattle it well!—once! twice! thrice!—

there, peep in!—now it is a shilling! I told you so?"

Frank ran joyously out of the room, being much amused with the joke, for he had put one of his own shillings into the box for Harry and Laura, who were excessively surprised at first, and felt really ashamed to take this very kind present from Frank, when he so seldom had money of his own, but they knew how generous he was, for he often repeated that excellent maxim, "It is more blessed to give than to receive."

After a few minutes, they remembered that nothing could prevent them now from going with Mr Harwood to Arthur Seat, which put Laura into such a state of ecstacy, that she danced round the room for joy, while Harry jumped upon the tables and chairs, tumbled head over heels, and called Betty to come immediately, that they might get ready.

When Mrs Crabtree heard such an uproar, she hastened also into the room, asking what had happened to cause this riot, and she became very angry indeed, to hear that Harry and Laura had both got leave to join in this grand expedition.

"You will be spoiling all your clothes, and getting yourselves into a heat! I wonder her ladyship allows this! How much better you would be taking a quiet walk with me in the gardens! I shall really speak to Lady Harriet about it! The air must be very cold on the top of them great mountains! I am sure you will both have colds for a month after this tomfoolery."

"Oh no, Mrs Crabtree! I promise not to catch cold!" cried Harry, eagerly; "and, besides, you can scarcely prevent our going now, for grandmama has set out on her long airing in the carriage, so there is nobody for you to ask about keeping us at home except uncle David."

Mrs Crabtree knew from experience, that Major Graham was a hopeless case, as he always took part with the children, and liked nothing so much for old and young as "a ploy;" so she grumbled on to herself, while her eyes looked as sharp as a pair of scissors, with rage. "You will come back turned into scarecrows, with all your nice, clean clothes in tatters," said she, angrily; "but if there is so much as a speck upon this best new jacket and trousers, I shall know the reason why."

"What a comfort it would be, if there were no such things in the world as 'new clothes,' for I am always so much happier in the old ones," said Harry. "People at the shops should sell clothes that will never either dirty or tear."

"You ought to be dressed in fur, like Robinson Crusoe; or sent out naked, like the little savages," said Mrs Crabtree; " or painted black and blue like them wild old Britons that lived here long ago!"

" I am black and blue sometimes, without being painted," said Harry, escaping to the door. "Goodbye, Mrs Crabtree! I hope you will not die of weariness without us! On our return we shall tell you all our delightful adventures."

About half an hour afterwards, Harry and Laura were seen hurrying out of Mrs Weddel's pastry-shop, bearing little covered baskets in their hands, but nobody could guess what was in them. They whispered and laughed together with merry faces, looking the very pictures of happiness, and running along as fast as they could to join the noisy party of their cousins and companions, almost fearing that Mr Harwood might have set off without them. Frank often called him "Mr Punctuality," as he was so very particular about his scholars being in good time on all occasions; and certainly Mr Harwood carried his watch more in his hand than in his pocket, being in the habit of constantly looking to see that nobody arrived too late. Mail-coaches or steam-boats could hardly keep the time better, when an hour had once been named; and the last words that Harry heard when he was invited were, "Remember! sharp twelve."

The great clock of St Andrew's Church was

busy striking that hour, and every little clock in the town was saying the same thing, when Mr Harwood himself, with his watch in his hand, opened the door, and walked out, followed by a dozen of merry-faced boys and girls, all speaking at once, and vociferating louder than the clocks, as if they thought everybody had grown deaf.

"I shall reach the top of Arthur Seat first," said Peter Grey. "All follow me, for I know the shortest way. It is only a hop, step, and a jump!"

"Rather a long step!" cried Robert Fordyce. "But I could lead you a much better way, though I shall shew it to nobody but myself."

"We must certainly drink water at St Anthony's Well," observed Laura; "because whatever any one wishes for when he tastes it, is sure to happen immediately."

"Then I shall wish that some person may give me a new doll," said Mary Forrester. "My old one is only fit for being lady's maid to a fine new doll."

"I am in ninety-nine minds what to wish for," exclaimed Harry; "we must take care not to be like the foolish old woman in the fairy tale, who got only a yard of black pudding."

"I shall ask for a piebald pony, with a whip, a saddle, and a bridle!" cried Peter Grey; "and for a week's holidays,—and a new watch,—and a spade,—and a box of French plums,—and to be first at the top of Arthur Seat,—and—and—"

"Stop, Peter! stop! you can only have one wish at St Anthony's Well," interrupted Mr Harwood. "If you ask more, you lose all."

"That is very hard; for I want everything," replied Peter. "What are you wishing for, Sir?"

"What shall I ask for?" said Mr Harwood, reflecting to himself. "I have not a want in the world!"

"O yes, Sir! you must wish for something!" cried the whole party, eagerly. "Do invent something to ask, Mr Harwood!"

"Then I wish you may all behave well till we reach the top of Arthur Seat, and all come safely down again."

"You may be sure of that already!" said Peter, laughing. "I set such a very good example to all my companions, that they never behave ill when I am present,—no! not even by accident! When Dr Algebra examined our class to-day, he asked Mr Lexicon, 'What has become of the best boy in your school this morning?' and the answer was, 'Of course you mean Peter Grey! He is gone to the top of Arthur Seat with that excellent man, Mr Harwood!'"

"Indeed!—and pray, Master Peter, what bird whispered this story into your ear, seeing it has all happened since we left home?—but people who are praised by nobody else, often take to praising themselves!"

"Who knows better?—and here is Harry Graham, the very ditto of myself,—so steady he might be fit to drill a whole regiment. We shall lead the party quite safely up the hill, and down again, without any ladders."

"And without wings," added Harry, laughing; "but what are we to draw water out of the well with?—here are neither buckets, nor tumblers, nor glasses!"

"I could lend you my thimble!" said Laura, searching her pocket. "That will hold enough of water for one wish, and every person may have the loan of it in turn."

"This is the very first time your thimble has been of use to anybody!" said Harry, slyly; "but I daresay it is not worn into holes with too much sewing, therefore it will make a famous little magical cup for St Anthony's Well. You know the fairies who dance here by moonlight, lay their table-cloth upon a mushroom, and sit round it, to be merry, but I never heard what they use for a drinking-cup."

Harry now proceeded briskly along to the well, singing, as he went, a song which had been taught him by uncle David, beginning,

> I wish I were a brewer's horse,
>   Five quarters of a year,
> I'd place my head where was my tail,
>   And drink up all the beer.

Before long the whole party seated themselves in a circle on the grass round St Anthony's Well, while any stranger who chanced to pass might have supposed, from the noise and merriment, that the saint had filled his well with champagne and punch for the occasion, as everybody seemed perfectly tipsy with happiness. Mr Harwood laughed prodigiously at some of the jokes, and made a few of his own, which were none of the best, though they caused the most laughter, for the boys thought it very surprising that so grave and great a man should make a joke at all.

When Mary Forrester drank her thimbleful of water, and wished for a new doll, Peter and Harry privately cut out a face upon a red-cheeked apple, making the eyes, nose, and mouth, after which, they hastily dressed it up in pocket handkerchiefs, and gave her this present from the fairies, which looked so very like what she had asked for that the laugh which followed was loud and long. Afterwards Peter swallowed his draught, calling loudly for a piebald pony, when Harry, in his white trousers and dark jacket, went upon all-fours, and let Peter mount on his back. It was very difficult, however, to get Peter off again, for he enjoyed the fun excessively, and stuck to his seat like Sinbad's old man of the sea, till at last Harry rolled on his back, tumbling Peter head over heels into St Anthony's Well, upon seeing which, Mr Harwood rose, saying, he had certainly lost his own wish, as they had behaved ill, and met with an accident already. Harry laughingly proposed that Peter should be carefully hung upon a tree to dry, till they all came down again; but the mischievous boy ran off so fast, he was almost out of sight in a moment, saying, "Now for the top of Arthur Seat, and I shall grow dry with the fatigue of climbing."

The boys and girls immediately scattered themselves all over the hill, getting on the best way they could, and trying who could scramble up fastest, but the grass was quite short, and as slippery as ice, therefore it became every moment more difficult to stand, and still more difficult to climb. The whole party began sliding whether they liked it or not, and staggered and tried to grasp the turf, but there was nothing to hold, while occasionally a shower of stones and gravel came down from Peter, who pretended they fell by accident.

"Oh, Harry!" cried Laura, panting for breath,

while she looked both frightened and fatigued. " if this were not a party of pleasure, I think we are sometimes quite as happy in our own gardens! People must be very miserable at home, before they come here to be amused! I wish we were cats, or goats, or anything that can stand upon a hill without feeling giddy."

" I think this is very good fun!" answered Harry, gasping, and trying not to tumble for the twentieth time; " you would like, perhaps, to be back in the nursery with Mrs Crabtree."

" No! no! I am not quite so bad as that! But Harry! do you ever really expect to reach the top? for I never shall; so I mean to sit down quietly here, and wait till you all return."

" I have a better plan than that, Laura! You shall sit upon the highest point of Arthur Seat as well as anybody, before either of us is an hour older! Let me go first, because I get on famously, and you must never look behind, but keep tight hold of my jacket, so then every step I advance will pull you up also."

Laura was delighted with this plan, which succeeded perfectly well, but they ascended rather slowly, as it was exceedingly fatiguing to Harry, who looked quite happy all the time to be of use; for he always felt glad when he could do anything for anybody, more particularly for either Laura or

Frank. Now, the whole party was at last safely assembled on the very highest point of Arthur Seat, so the boys threw their caps up in the air, and gave three tremendous cheers, which frightened the very crows over their heads, and sent a flock of sheep scampering down the mountain side. After that, they planted Mr Harwood's walking-stick in the ground, for a staff, while Harry tore off the blue silk handkerchief which Mrs Crabtree had tied about his neck, and without caring whether he caught cold or not, he fastened it on the pole for a flag, being quite delighted to see how it waved in the wind most triumphantly, looking very like what sailors put up when they take possession of a desert island.

"Now, for business!" said Mr Harwood, sitting down on the rock, and uncovering a prodigious cake, nearly as large as a cheese, which he had taken the trouble to carry, with great difficulty, up the hill. "I suppose nobody is hungry after our long walk! Let us see what all the baskets contain!"

Not a moment was lost in seating themselves on the grass, while the stores were displayed, amidst shouts of laughter and applause which generally followed whatever came forth. Sandwiches, or, as Peter Grey called them, "savages," gingerbread, cakes, and fruit, all appeared in turn. Robert Fordyce brought a dozen of hard-boiled eggs, all dyed different colours, blue, green, pink, and yellow, but not one was white. Edmund Ashford produced a collection of very sour-looking apples, and Charles Forrester shewed a number of little gooseberry tarts ; but when it became time for Peter's basket to be opened, it contained nothing except a knife and a fork to cut up whatever his companions would give him !

"Peter! Peter! you shabby fellow!" said Charles Forrester, reaching him one of his tarts, " you should be put in the tread-mill as a sturdy beggar!"

" Or thrown down from the top of this precipice," added Harry, giving him a cake. "I wonder you can look any of us in the face, Peter!"

" I have heard," said Mr Harwood, "that a stone is shewn in Ireland, called 'the stone of Blarney,' and whoever kisses it, is never afterwards ashamed of anything he does. Our friend Peter has probably passed that way lately!"

" At any rate, I am not likely to be starved to death amongst you all!" answered the impudent boy, demolishing every thing he could get; and it is believed that Peter ate, on this memorable occasion, three times more than any other person, as each of the party offered him something, and he never was heard to say, " No!"

"I could swallow Arthur Seat, if it were turned into a plum-pudding," said he, pocketing buns, apples, eggs, walnuts, biscuits, and almonds, till his coat stuck out all round like a balloon. "Has any one anything more to spare?"

"Did you ever hear," said Mr Harwood, "that a pigeon eats its own weight of food every day? Now, I am sure, you and I know one boy in the world, Peter, who could do as much."

"What is to be done with that prodigious cake you carried up here, Mr Harwood?" answered Peter, casting a devouring eye upon it; "the crust seems as hard as a rhinoceros' skin, but I daresay it is very good. One could not be sure, however, without tasting it! I hope you are not going to take the trouble of carrying that heavy load back again?"

"How very polite you are become all on a sudden, Peter!" said Laura, laughing. "I should be very sorry to attempt carrying that cake to the bottom of the hill, for we would both roll down the shortest way together."

"I am not over-anxious to try it either," observed Charles Forrester, shaking his head.— "Even Peter, though his mouth is constantly ajar, would find that cake rather heavy to carry, either as an inside or an outside passenger."

"I can scarcely lift it at all!" continued Laura,

when Mr Harwood had again tied it up in the towel; "What can be done?"

"Here is the very best plan!" cried Harry, suddenly seizing the prodigious cake; and before any body could hinder him, he gave it a tremendous push off the steepest part of Arthur Seat, so that it rolled down like a wheel, over stones and precipices, jumping and hopping along with wonderful rapidity, amidst the cheers and laughter of all the children, till at last it reached the bottom of the hill, when a general clapping of hands ensued.

"Now for a race!" cried Harry, becoming more and more eager. "The first boy or girl who reaches that cake shall have it all to himself!"

Mr Harwood tried with all his might to stop the commotion, and called out that they must go quietly down the bank, for Harry had no right to give away the cake, or to make them break their legs and arms with racing down such a hill. But he might as well have spoken to the east wind, and asked it not to blow. The whole party dispersed, like a hive of bees that has been upset; and in a moment they were in full career after the cake.

Some of the boys tried to roll down, hoping to get on more quickly. Others endeavoured to slide, and several attempted to run, but they all fell; and many of them might have been tumblers at

Sadler's Wells, they tumbled over and over so cleverly. Peter Grey's hat was blown away, but he did not stop to catch it. Charlie Hume lost his shoe. Robert Fordyce sprained his ankle, and every one of the girls tore her frock. It was a frightful scene; such devastation of bonnets and jackets as had never been known before; while Mr Harwood looked like the general of a defeated army, calling till he became hoarse, and running till he was out of breath, vainly trying thus to stop the confusion, and to bring the stragglers back in better order.

Meantime Harry and Peter were far before the rest, though Edward Ashford was following hard after them in desperate haste, as if he still hoped to overtake their steps. Suddenly, however, a loud cry of distress was heard overhead; and when Harry looked up, he saw so very alarming a sight, that he could scarcely believe his eyes, and almost screamed out himself with the fright it gave him, while he seemed to forget in a moment, the race, Peter Grey, and the prodigious cake.

Laura had been very anxious not to trouble Harry with taking care of her in coming down the bank again; for she saw that during all this fun about the cake, he perfectly forgot that she was not accustomed every day to such a scramble on the hills, and would have required some help.

After looking down on every side of the descent, and thinking that each appeared steeper than another, while they all made her equally giddy, Laura determined to venture on a part of the hill which seemed rather less precipitous than the rest; but it completely cheated her, being the most difficult and dangerous part of Arthur Seat. The slope became steeper and steeper at every step; but Laura always tried to hope her path might grow better, till at last she reached a place where it was impossible to stop herself. Down she went! down! down! whether she or would not, screaming and sliding on a long slippery bank, till she reached the very edge of a dangerous precipice, which appeared higher than the side of a room. Laura then grappled hold of some stones and grass, calling loudly for help, while scarcely able to keep from falling into the deep ravine, which would probably have killed her. Her screams were echoed all over the hill, when Harry, seeing her frightful situation, clambered up the bank faster than any lamplighter, and immediately flew to Laura's assistance, who was now really hanging over the chasm, quite unable to help herself. At last he reached the place where poor Laura lay, and seized hold of her by the frock; but for some time it seemed an equal chance whether she dragged him into the hole, or he pulled her away from it.

Luckily, however, by a great effort, Harry succeeded in delivering Laura, whom he placed upon a secure situation, and then, having waited patiently till she recovered from the fright, he led her carefully and kindly down to the bottom of Arthur Seat.

Now, all the boys had already got there, and a violent dispute was going on about which of them first reached the cake. Peter Grey had pushed down Edward Ashford, who caught hold of Robert Fordyce, and they all three rolled to the bottom together, so that nobody could tell which had won the race; while Mr Harwood laboured in vain to convince them that the cake belonged neither to the one nor the other, being his own property.

They all laughed at Harry for being distanced, and arriving last; while Mr Harwood watched him coming down, and was pleased to observe how carefully he attended to Laura, though, still being annoyed at the riot and confusion which Harry had occasioned, he determined to appear exceedingly angry, and put on a very terrible voice, saying,

"Hollo! young gentleman! what shall I do to you for beginning this uproar? As the old proverb says, 'One fool makes many.' How dare you roll my fine cake down the hill in this way, and send everybody rolling after it? Look me in the face, and say you are ashamed of yourself!"

Harry looked at Mr Harwood—and Mr Harwood looked at Harry. They both tried to seem very grave and serious, but somehow Harry's eyes glittered very brightly, and two little dimples might be seen in his cheeks. Mr Harwood had his eye-brows gathered into a terrible frown, but still his eyes were likewise sparkling, and his mouth seemed to be pursed up in a most comical manner. After staring at each other for several minutes, both Mr Harwood and Harry burst into a prodigious fit of laughing, and nobody could tell which began first or laughed longest.

"Master Graham! you must send a new frock to every little girl of the party, and a suit of clothes to each of the boys, for having caused theirs to be all destroyed. I really meant to punish you severely for beginning such a riot, but something has made me change my mind. In almost every moment of our lives, we either act amiably or unamiably; and I observed you treat Miss Laura so kindly and properly all this morning, that I shall say not another word about

"THE PRODIGIOUS CAKE."

CHAPTER V

THE LAST CLEAN FROCK.

" For," said she, in spite of what grandmama taught her,
" I'm really remarkably fond of the water."

  *   *   *   *

She splashed, and she dashed, and she turned herself round.
And heartily wished herself safe on the ground.

ONCE upon a time Harry and Laura had got into so many scrapes, that there seemed really no end to their misconduct. They generally forgot to learn any lessons—often tore their books—drew pictures on their slates, instead of calculating sums—and made the pages of their copy-books into boats; besides which, Mrs Crabtree caught them one day, when a party of officers dined at Lady Harriet's, with two of the captains' sword-belts buckled round their waists, and cocked hats upon their heads, while they beat the crown of a gentleman's hat with a walking-stick, to sound like a drum.

Still it seemed impossible to make uncle David feel sufficiently angry with them, though Mrs Crabtree did all she could to put him in a passion, by telling the very worst; but he made fifty excuses a-minute, as if he had been the naughty person himself, instead of Harry or Laura; and, above all, he said that they both seemed so exceedingly penitent when he explained their delinquencies, and they were both so ready to tell upon themselves, and to take all the blame of whatever mischief might be done, that he was determined to shut his eyes and say nothing, unless they did something purposely wrong.

One night, when Mrs Crabtree had gone out, Major Graham felt quite surprised on his return home from a late dinner-party, to find Laura and Harry still out of bed. They were sitting in his library when he entered, both looking so tired and miserable that he could not imagine what had happened; but Harry lost no time in confessing that he and Laura feared that they had done some dreadful mischief, so they could not sleep without asking pardon, and mentioning whose fault it was, that the maids might not be unjustly blamed.

"Well, you little imps of mischief! what have I to scold you for now?" asked uncle David, not looking particularly angry. "Is it something that I shall be obliged to take the trouble of punishing you for? We ought to live in the Highlands, where there are whole forests of birch ready for use! Why are your ears like a bell-rope, Harry? because they seem made to be pulled. Now, go on with your story. What is the matter?"

"We were playing about the room, uncle David, and Laura lost her ball, so she crept under that big table, which has only one large leg. There is a brass button below, so we were trying if it would come off, when all on a sudden, the table fell quite to one side, as you see it now, tumbling down those prodigious books and tin boxes on the floor! I cannot think how this fine, new table could be so easily broken; but whenever we even look at anything it seems to break!"

"Yes, Harry! you remind me of Meddlesome Matty, in the nursery rhymes,

> 'Sometimes she'd lift the teapot lid,
> To peep at what was in it,
> Or tilt the kettle, if you did
> But turn your back a minute.
> In vain you told her not to touch,
> Her trick of meddling grew so much.'

You have scarcely left my poor table a leg to stand upon. How am I ever to get it mended?"

"Perhaps the carpenter could do it to-morrow!"

"Or, perhaps uncle David could do it this moment," said Major Graham, raising the fallen side with a sudden jerk, when Harry and Laura heard a click under the table like the locking of a door, after which the whole affair was rectified.

"Did I ever—!" exclaimed Harry, staring with astonishment. "So we have suffered all our fright for nothing, and the table was not really broken! I shall always run to you, uncle David, when we are in a scrape, for you are sure to get us off."

"Do not reckon too certainly on that, Master Harry; it is easier to get into one than to get out of it, any day; but I am not so seriously angry at the sort of scrapes Laura and you get into, because you would not willingly and deliberately do wrong. If any children commit a mean action, or get into a passion, or quarrel with each other, or omit saying their prayers and reading their Bibles, or tell a lie, or take what does not belong to them, then it might be seen how extremely angry I could be; but while you continue merely thoughtless and forgetful, I mean to have patience a little longer, before turning into a cross old uncle, with a pair of tawse."

Harry sprung upon uncle David's knee, quite delighted to hear him speak so very kindly, and Laura was soon installed in her usual place there also, listening to all that was said, and laughing at his jokes.

"As Mrs Crabtree says," continued Major

Graham, "'we cannot put an old head on young shoulders;' and it would certainly look very odd if you could."

So uncle David took out his pencil, and drew a funny picture of a cross, old, wrinkled face upon young shoulders like Laura's; and after they had all laughed at it together for about five minutes, he sent the children both to bed, quite merry and cheerful.

A long time elapsed afterwards without anything going wrong; and it was quite pleasant to see such learning of lessons, such attention to rules, and such obedience to Mrs Crabtree, as went on in the nursery during several weeks. At last, one day, when Lady Harriet and Major Graham were preparing to set off on a journey, and to pay a short visit at Holiday House, Laura and Harry observed a great deal of whispering and talking in a corner of the room, but they could not exactly discover what it was all about, till Major Graham said, very earnestly, "I think we might surely take Laura with us."

"Yes," answered Lady Harriet, "both the children have been invited, and are behaving wonderfully well of late, but Lord Rockville has such a dislike to noise, that I dare not venture to take more than one at a time. Poor Laura has a very severe cough, so she may be recovered by change of air. As for Harry, he is quite well, and therefore he can stay at home."

Now, Harry thought it very hard that he was to be left at home, merely because he felt quite well, so he immediately wished to be very ill indeed, that he might have some chance of going to Holiday House; but then he did not exactly know how to set about it. At all events, Harry determined to catch a cold like Laura's, without delay. He would not for the whole world have pretended to suffer from a cough if he really had none, because uncle David had often explained that making any one believe an untruth was the same as telling a lie; but he thought that there might be no harm in really getting such a terrible cold, that nothing could possibly cure it except change of air, and a trip to Holiday House with Laura. Accordingly Harry tried to remember everything that Mrs Crabtree had forbid him to do " for fear of catching cold." He sprinkled water over his shirt-collar in the morning before dressing, that it might be damp; he ran violently up and down stairs to put himself in a heat, after which he sat between the open window and door till he felt perfectly chilled; and when going to bed at night, he washed his hair in cold water, without drying it. Still, all was in vain! Harry had formerly caught cold a hundred times when he did not want one but now, such a thing was not to be had for love or money. Nothing seemed to give him the very slightest attempt at a cough; and when the day at last arrived for Lady Harriet to begin her journey, Harry still felt himself most provokingly well. Not so much as a finger ached, his cheeks were as blooming as roses, his voice as clear as a bell; and when uncle David accidentally said to him in the morning, "How do you do?" Harry was obliged, very much against his will, to answer, "Quite well, I thank you!"

In the mean time, Laura would have felt too happy if Harry could only have gone with her; and even as it was, being impatient for the happy day to arrive, she hurried to bed an hour earlier than usual the night before, to make the time of setting out appear nearer; and she could scarcely sleep or eat, for thinking of Holiday House, and planning all that was to be done there.

"It is pleasant to see so joyous a face," said Major Graham. "I almost envy you, Laura, for being so happy."

"Oh! I quite envy myself! but I shall write a long letter every day to poor Harry, telling him all the news, and all my adventures."

"Nonsense! Miss Laura! wait till you come home," said Mrs Crabtree. "Who do you think is going to pay postage for so many foolish letters!"

"I shall!" answered Harry. "I have got sixpence, and twopence, and a halfpenny; so I shall buy every one of Laura's letters from the postman, and write her an answer immediately afterwards. She will like to hear, Mrs Crabtree, how very kind you are going to be, when I am left by myself here. Perhaps you will play at nine-pins with me, and Laura can lend you her skipping rope."

"You might as well offer uncle David a hobby-horse," said Frank, laughing, and throwing his satchel over his shoulders. "No, Harry! you shall belong to me now. Grandmama says you may go every day to my play-ground, where all the school-boys assemble, and you can have plenty of fun till Laura comes back. We shall jump over the moon, every morning, for joy."

Harry brightened up amazingly, thinking he had never heard of such good news before, as it was a grand piece of promotion to play with really big school-boys; so he became quite reconciled to Laura's going away for a short time without him; and when the hour came for taking leave, instead of tears being shed on either side, it would have been difficult to say, as they kissed each other, and said a joyous goodbye, which face looked the most delighted.

All Laura's clothes had been packed the night before, in a large chaise-seat, which was now put into the carriage along with herself, and everything seemed ready for departure, when Lady Harriet's maid was suddenly taken so very ill as to be quite unfit for travelling; therefore she was left behind, and a doctor sent for to attend her; while Lady Harriet said she would trust to the maids at Holiday House, for waiting upon herself and Laura.

It is seldom that so happy a face is seen in this world as Laura wore during the whole journey. It perfectly sparkled and glittered with delight, while she was so constantly on a broad grin, laughing, that Major Graham said he feared her mouth would grow an inch wider on the occasion.

"You will tire of sitting so long idle! It is a pity we did not think of bringing a few lesson-books in the carriage, to amuse you, Laura," said the Major, slyly. "A piece of needle-work might have beguiled the way. I once knew an industrious lady who made a ball-dress for herself in the carriage during a journey."

"How very stupid of her to miss seeing all the pretty trees, and cottages, and farm-houses! I do like to watch the little, curly-headed, dirty children, playing on the road, with brown faces, and hair bleached white in the sun; and the women hanging out their clothes on the hedges to dry; and the blacksmith shoeing horses, and the ducks swimming in the gutters, and the pigs thrusting their noses out of the sty, and the old women knitting stockings, and the workmen sitting on a wall, to eat their dinners! It looks all so pretty and so pleasant!"

"What a picture of rural felicity! You ought to be a poet or a painter, Laura!"

"But I believe poets always call this a miserable world; and I think it the happiest place I have ever been in, uncle David! Such fun during the holidays! I should go wild altogether, if Mrs Crabtree were not rather cross sometimes."

"Or very cross always," thought Major Graham.

"But here we are, Laura, near our journey's end. Allow me to introduce you to Holiday House! Why, you are staring at it like a dog looking at a piece of cold beef! My dear girl, if you open your eyes so wide, you will never be able to shut them again."

Holiday House was not one of those prodigious places, too grand to be pleasant, with the garden a mile off in one direction, and the farm a mile off in another, and the drawing-room a mile off from the dining-room; but it was a very cheerful, modern mansion, with rooms large enough to hold as many people as any one could desire to see at once, all very comfortably furnished. A lively, dashing river streamed past the windows; a small park, sprinkled with sheep, and shaded by fine trees, surrounded the house; and beyond were beautiful gardens, filled with a superabundance of the gayest and sweetest common flowers. Roses, carnations, wallflowers, hollyhocks, dahlias, lilies, and violets, were assembled there in such crowds, that Laura might have plucked nosegays all day, without making any visible difference; and she was also made free of the gooseberry bushes and cherry-trees, with leave to gather, if she pleased, more than she could eat.

Every morning, Laura entered the breakfast-room with cheeks like the roses she carried, bringing little bouquets for all the ladies, which she had started out of bed early in order to gather; and her great delight was to see them worn and admired all the forenoon, while she was complimented on the taste with which they had been selected and arranged. She filled every ornamental jar, basin, and tea-cup in the drawing-room, with groups of roses, and would have been the terror of any gardener but the one at Holiday House, who liked to see his flowers so much admired, and was not keeping up any for a horticultural show.

Laura's chief delight, however, was in the dairy, which seemed the most beautiful thing she had ever beheld, being built of rough, transparent spar, which looked exactly like crystal, and reminded her of the ice palace built by the Empress of Russia.

The windows were of painted glass; the walls and shelves were of Dutch tiles, and in the centre rose a beautiful jet d'eau of clear, bright water.

Laura thought it looked like something built for the fairies; but within she saw a most substantial room, the floor and tables in which were so completely covered with cheeses, that they looked like some old Mosaic pavement. Here the good-natured dairymaid shewed Laura how to make cheese, and afterwards manufactured a very small one, about the size of a soup plate, entirely for the young lady herself, which she promised to take home after her visit was over; and a little churn was also filled full of cream, which Laura one morning churned into butter, and breakfasted upon, after having first practised printing it into a variety of shapes. It was altered about twenty times from a swan into a cow, and from a cow into a rose, and from a rose back to a swan again, before she could be persuaded to leave off her amusement.

Laura continued to become more and more delighted with Holiday House; and she one day skipped about Lady Harriet's room, saying,

"Oh! I am too happy! I scarcely know what to do with so much happiness. How delightful it would be to stay here all my life, and never to go to bed, nor say any more lessons, as long as I live!"

"What a useless, stupid girl you would soon become," observed Lady Harriet. "Do you think, Laura, that lessons were invented for no other purpose but to torment little children?"

"No, grandmama; not exactly! They are of use also to keep us quiet."

"Come here, little madam, and listen to me. I shall soon be very old, Laura, and not able to read my Bible, even with spectacles; for, as the Scriptures told us, in that affecting description of old age which I read to you yesterday, 'The keepers of the house shall tremble, and the grinders cease, because they are few, and those that look out of the windows be darkened;' what, then, do you think I can do, because the Bible now is my best comfort, which I shall need more and more every day, to tell me all about the eternal world, where I am going, and to shew me the way?"

"Grandmama! you promised long ago to let me attend on you when you grow old and blind! I shall be very careful, and very—very—very kind. I almost wish you were old and blind now, to let you feel how much I love you, and how anxious I am to be as good to you as you have always been to me. We shall read the Bible together every morning, and as often afterwards as you please."

"Thank you, my dear child! but you must take the trouble of learning to read well, or we shall be sadly puzzled with the difficult words. A friend of mine once had nobody that could read to her when she was ill but the maid, who bargained that she might leave out every word above two syllables long, because they were too hard for her; and you could hardly help laughing at the nonsense it sometimes made; but I hope you will manage better."

"O certainly, grandmama! I can spell chrononhotonthologos, and all the other five-cornered words in my 'Reading Made Easy,' already."

"Besides that, my dear Laura! unless you learn to look over my bills, I may be sadly cheated by servants and shopkeepers. You must positively study to find out how many cherries make five."

"Ah! grandmama! nobody knows better than I do, that two and two make four. I shall soon be quite able to keep your accounts."

"Very well! but you have not yet heard half the trouble I mean to give you. I am remarkably fond of music, and shall probably at last be obliged to hire every old fiddler as he passes in the street, by giving him sixpence, in order to enjoy some of my favourite tunes."

"No, grandmama! you shall hear them all from me. I can play Malbrook, and Auld Robin Gray, already; and Frank says if I practise two hours every day for ten years, I shall become a very tolerable player, fit for you and uncle David to hear, without being disagreeable."

"Then that will be more than seven thousand hours of musical lessons which you have yet to endure, Laura! There are many more things of still greater importance to learn also, if you wish to be any better than a musical snuff-box. For instance, when visitors come to see me, they are often from France or Italy; but perhaps you will not mind sitting in the room as if you were deaf and dumb, gazing at those foreigners, while they gaze at you, without understanding a syllable they say, and causing them to feel strange and uncomfortable as long as they remain in the house."

"No! I would not for the world seem so unkind and uncivil. Pray, let me learn plenty of languages."

"Very well! but if you study no geography, what ridiculous blunders you will be falling into! asking the Italians about their native town Madrid, and the Americans if they were born at Petersburgh. You will be fancying that travellers go by steam-boats to Moscow, and travel in a day from

Paris, through Stockholm to Naples. How ashamed I should be of such mistakes!"

"So should I, grandmama, still more than you; for it would be quite a disgrace."

"Do you remember, Laura, your uncle David laughing, when he last went to live at Leamington, about poor Mrs Marmalade coming up stairs to say, she did not wish to be troublesome, but she would feel greatly obliged if he would call at Portsmouth occasionally to see her son Thomas? And when Captain Armylist's regiment was ordered last winter to the village of Bathgate, near this, he told me they were to march in the course of that morning all the way to Bagdad!"

"Yes, grandmama! and Mrs Crabtree said some weeks ago, that if her brother went to Van Diemen's Land, she thought he would of course, in passing, take a look of Jerusalem; and Frank was amused lately to hear Peter Grey maintain, that Gulliver was as great a man as Columbus, because he discovered Liliput!"

"Quite like him! for I heard Peter ask one day lately, what side Bonaparte was on at the battle of Leipsic! We must include a little history, I think, Laura, in our list of studies, or you will fancy that Lord Nelson fought at the battle of Blenheim, and that Henry VIII. cut off Queen Mary's head."

"Not quite so bad as that, grandmama! I seem to have known all about Lord Nelson and Queen Mary, ever since I was a baby in long frocks! You have shewn me, however, that it would be very foolish not to feel anxious for lessons, especially when they are to make me a fit companion for you at last."

"Yes, Laura! and not only for me, but for many whose conversation will entertain and improve you more than any books. The most delightful accomplishment that a young person can cultivate, is that of conversing agreeably; and it is less attended to in education than in any other. You cannot take a harp or piano about with you; but our minds and tongues are always portable, and accompany us wherever we go. If you wish to be loved by others, and to do good to your associates, as well as to entertain them, take every opportunity of conversing with those who are either amiable or agreeable; not only attending to their opinions, but also endeavouring to gain the habit of expressing your own thoughts with ease and fluency; and then rest assured, that if the gift of conversation be rightly exercised, it is the most desirable of all, as no teaching can have greater influence in leading people to think and act aright, than the incidental remarks of an enlightened

Christian, freely and unaffectedly talking to his intimate friends."

"Well, grandmama! the moral of all this is, that I shall become busier than anybody ever was before, when we get home; but in the mean time, I may take a good dose of idleness now at Holiday House, to prepare me for setting to very hard labour afterwards," said Laura, hastily tying on her bonnet. "I wonder if I shall ever be as merry and happy again!"

Most unfortunately, all the time of Laura's visit at Holiday House, she had been, as usual, extremely heedless, in taking no care whatever of her clothes! consequently her blue merino frock had been cruelly torn; her green silk dress became frightfully soiled; four white frocks were utterly ruined; her Swiss muslin seemed a perfect object; and her pink gingham was both torn and discoloured. Regularly every evening Lady Harriet told her to take better care, or she would be a bankrupt in frocks altogether; but whatever her grandmama said on that subject, the moment she was out of sight it went out of mind, till another dress had shared the same deplorable fate.

At last, one morning, as soon as Laura got up, Lady Harriet gravely led her towards a large table on which all the ill-used frocks had been laid out in a row; and a most dismal sight they were! Such a collection of stains and fractures was probably never seen before! A beggar would scarcely have thanked her for her blue merino; and the green silk frock looked like the tattered cover of a worn-out umbrella.

"Laura," said Lady Harriet, "in Switzerland a lady's wardrobe descends to many generations; but nobody will envy your successor! One might fancy that a wild beast had torn you to pieces every day! I wonder what an old clothesman would give for your whole baggage! It is only fit for being used as rags in a paper manufactory!"

Poor Laura's face became perfectly pink when she saw the destruction that a very short time had occasioned; and she looked from one tattered garment to another, in melancholy silence, thinking how lately they had all been fresh and beautiful; but now not a vestige of their former splendour remained. At last her grandmama broke the awful silence, by saying,

"My dear girl! I have warned you very often lately, that we are not at home, where your frocks could be washed and mended as soon as they were spoiled; but without considering this, you have every day destroyed several; so now the maid finds, on examining your drawers, that there is only one clean frock remaining!"

Laura looked gravely at the last clean frock,

and wondered much what her grandmama would say next.

"I do not wish to make a prisoner of you at home during this very fine weather; yet in five minutes after leaving the house, you will, of course, become unfit to be seen, which I should very much regret, as a number of fine people are coming to dinner, whom you would like to see. The great General Courtenoy, and all his aides-de-camp, intend to be here on their way from a review, besides many officers and ladies who know your papa very well, and wish to see my little granddaughter; but I would not on any account allow you to appear before them, looking like a perfect tatterdemalion, as you too often do. They would suppose you had been drawn backwards through a hedge! Now my plan is, that you shall wear this old pink gingham for romping all morning in the garden, and dress in your last clean frock for dinner; but remember to keep out of sight till then. Remain within the garden walls, as none of the company will be walking there, but be sure to avoid the terraces and shrubberies till you are made tidy; for I shall be both angry and mortified if your papa's friends see you for the first time looking like rag-fair."

Laura promised to remember her grandmama's injunctions, and to remain invisible all morning so off she set to the garden, singing and skipping with joy, as she ran towards her pleasant hiding-place, planning twenty ways in which the day might be delightfully spent alone. Before long she had strung a long necklace of daisies—she had put many bright leaves in a book to dry—she had made a large ball of cowslips to toss in the air—she had watered the hyacinths with a watering-pot, till they were nearly washed away—she had plucked more roses than could possibly be carried, and ate as many gooseberries and cherries as it was convenient to swallow,—but still there were several hours remaining to be enjoyed, and nothing very particular, that Laura could think of, to do.

Meanwhile, the miserable pink frock was torn worse than ever, and seemed to be made of nothing but holes, for every gooseberry-bush in the garden had got a share of it. Laura wished pink gingham frocks had never been invented, and wondered why nothing stronger could be made. Having become perfectly tired of the garden, she now wished herself anywhere else in the world, and thought she was no better off, confined in this way within four walls, than a canary bird in a cage.

"I should like so much to go, if it were only for five minutes, on the terrace!" said she to herself. " How much pleasanter it is than this! Grandmama did not care where I went, provided nobody saw me! I may at least take a peep, to see if any one is there!"

Laura now cautiously opened the garden-door, and put her head out, intending only to look for a moment; but the moment grew longer and longer, till it stretched into ten minutes.

" What crowds of fine people are walking about on the terrace!" thought she. " It looks as gay as a fair! Who can that officer be in a red coat, and cocked hat with white feathers? Probably General Courteney paying attention to Lady Rockville. There is a lady in a blue cloak and blue flowers! how very pretty! Everybody is so exceedingly smart! and I see some little boys too! Grandmama never told me any children were coming! I wonder how old they are, and if they will play with me in the evening! It would be very amusing to venture a little nearer, and get a better glimpse of them all!"

If Laura's wishes pointed one way and her duty pointed the other, it was a very sad thing how often she forgot to pause and consider which she ought to follow; and on this occasion, as usual, she took the naughty side of the question, and prepared to indulge her curiosity, though very anxious that nothing might happen to displease her grandmama. She observed at some distance on the terrace a remarkably thick holly-bush, near which the great procession of company would probably pass before long; therefore, hoping nobody could possibly see her there, she stole hastily out of the garden and concealed herself behind it; but when children do wrong, in hopes of not being found out, they generally find themselves mistaken, as Laura soon discovered to her cost. It is very lucky, however, for the culprits, when they are detected, that they may learn never to behave foolishly again, because the greatest misfortune that can happen to any child is, not to be found out and punished when he does wrong.

A few minutes after Laura had taken her station behind the holly-bush, crowds of ladies and officers came strolling along, so very near her hiding-place, that she saw them all distinctly, and felt excessively amused and delighted at first, to be perched like a bird in a tree, watching this grand party, while nobody saw her, nor guessed that she was there. Presently, however, Laura became sadly frightened when an officer in a scarlet coat happened to look towards the holly-bush, and exclaimed, with some surprise,

"There is surely something very odd about that plant! I see large pink spots between the leaves!"

"Oh no, Captain Digby, you are quite mistaken,"

answered one of the ladies, dressed in a bright yellow bonnet and green pelisse. "I see nothing particular there! Only a common ugly bush of holly! I wonder you ever thought of noticing it!"

"But, Miss Perceval! there certainly is something very curious behind! I would bet five to one there is!" replied Captain Digby, stepping up close to the holly-bush, and peeping over: "What have we here? a ragged little girl, I do believe! in a pink frock!"

Poor Laura was now in a terrible scrape! she started up immediately to run away. Probably she never ran so fast in her life before, but Captain Digby was a person who enjoyed a joke; so he called out,

"Tally-ho! a race for a thousand pounds!"

Off set the Captain, and away flew Laura. At any other time she would have thought it capital fun, but now she was frightened out of her wits, and tore away at the very top of her speed. The whole party of ladies and gentlemen stood laughing and applauding, to see how fast they both cleared the ground, while Laura, seeing the garden-gate still wide open, hoped she might be able to dart in, and close it; but alas! when she arrived within four steps of the threshold, feeling almost certain of escape, Captain Digby seized hold of her pink frock behind. It instantly began tearing, so she had great hopes of leaving the piece in his hand and getting off; but he was too clever for that, as he grasped hold of her long sash, which was floating far out behind, and led Laura a prisoner before the whole company.

When Lady Harriet discovered that this was really Laura advancing, her head hanging down, her hair streaming about her ears, and her face like a full moon, she could scarcely credit her own eyes, and held her hands up with astonishment while uncle David shrugged his shoulders, till they almost met over his head, but not a word was said on either side until they got home, when Lady Harriet at last broke the awful silence by saying,

"My dear girl! you must, of course, be severely punished for this act of disobedience; and it is not so much on account of feeling angry at your misconduct that I mean to correct you, but because I love you, and wish to make you behave better in future. Parents are appointed by God to govern their children as He governs us, not carelessly indulging their faults, but wisely correcting them; for we are told that our Great Father in heaven chastens those whom He loves, and only afflicts us for great and wise purposes. I have suffered many sorrows in the world, but they always made me better in the end ; and whatever discipline you meet with from me, or from that Great Being who loves you still more than I do, let it teach you to consider your ways, to repent of your wilfulness, and to pray that you may be enabled to act more properly in future."

"Yes, grandmama," replied Laura, with tears in her eyes, "I am quite willing to be punished; for it was very wrong indeed to make you so vexed and ashamed, by disobeying your orders."

"Then here is a long task which you must study before dinner, as a penalty for trespassing bounds. It is a beautiful poem on the death of Sir John Moore, which every school-girl can repeat; but being rather long you will scarcely have time to learn it perfectly, before coming down to dessert; therefore, that you may be quite ready, I shall ring now for Lady Rockville's maid, and have you washed and dressed immediately. Remember this is your last clean frock, and be sure not to spoil it."

When Laura chose to pay attention, she could learn her lessons wonderfully fast, and her eyes seemed nailed to the book for some time after Lady Harriet went away, till at last she could repeat the whole poem perfectly well. It was neither "slowly nor sadly" that Laura "laid down" her book, after practising it all, in a sort of jig time, till she could rattle over the poem like a railroad, and she walked to the window, still murmuring the verses to herself with prodigious glee, and giving little thought to their melancholy subject.

A variety of plans suggested themselves to her mind for amusing herself within doors, as she had been forbidden to venture out, and she lost no time in executing them. First, she tried on all her grandmama's caps at a looking-glass, none of which were improved by being crushed and tumbled in such a way. Then she quarrelled with Lady Rockville's beautiful cockatoo, till it bit her finger violently, and after that, she teased the old cat till it scratched her; but all these diversions were not sufficiently entertaining, so Laura began to grow rather tired, till at last she went to gaze out at the portico of Holiday House, being perfectly determined, on no account whatever, to go one single step farther.

Here Laura saw many things which entertained her extremely; for she had scarcely ever seen more of the country than was to be enjoyed with Mrs Crabtree in Charlotte Square. The punctual crows were all returning home at their usual hour for the evening, and looked like a black shower over her head, while hundreds of them seemed trying to make a concert at once; the robins hopped close to her feet, evidently accustomed to be fed; a tame pheasant, as fat as a London alderman, came up the steps to keep her company; and the peacock spreading his tail, and strutting about, looked the very picture of silly pride and vanity.

Laura admired and enjoyed all this extremely, and crumbled down nearly a loaf of bread, which she scattered on the ground, in order to be popular among her visitors, who took all they could get from her, and quarrelled among themselves about it, very much as boys and girls would perhaps have done in the same circumstances.

It happened at this moment that a large flock of geese crossed the park, on their way towards the river, stalking along in a slow, majestic manner, with their heads high in the air. Laura observed them at a distance, and thought they were the prettiest creatures in the world, with their pure white feathers and yellow stockings; so she wondered what kind of birds these were, having never seen a goose before, except when roasted for dinner, though indeed, she was a sad goose herself, as will very soon be told.

"How I should like to examine those large, white, beautiful birds, a little nearer," thought Laura to herself. "I wonder if they could swim or fly!—oh! how perfect they would look floating like water-lilies on the river, and then I might take a bit of bread to throw in, and they would all rush after it!"

Laura, as usual, did not wait to reflect what her grandmama might be likely to think! Indeed it is to be feared Laura forgot at the moment that she had a grandmama at all; for her mind was never large enough to hold more than one thing at a time, and now it was entirely filled with the flock of geese. She instantly set off in pursuit of them, and began chasing the whole party across the park, making all sorts of dreadful noises, in hopes they might fly; but, on the contrary, they held up their heads, as if she had been a dancing-master, and marched slowly on, cackling loudly to each other, and evidently getting extremely angry.

Laura was now quite close to her new acquaintances, and even threw a pebble to hurry them forward, when suddenly an old gander stopped, and turned round in terrible rage. The whole flock of geese then did the same, after which they flew towards Laura, with their bills wide open, hissing furiously, and stretching out their long necks in an angry, menacing way, as if they wished to tear her in pieces.

Poor Laura became frightened out of any wits she ever had, and ran off, with all the geese after her! Anybody must have laughed into fits, could they have heard what a triumphant cackle the geese set up, and had they seen how fast she flew away. If Laura had borrowed a pair of wings from her pursuers, she could scarcely have got more quickly on.

In the hurry of escaping, she always looked back to see if the enemy followed, and scarcely observed which way she ran herself, till suddenly her foot stumbled upon a large stone, and she fell headlong into the river! Oh, what a scream Laura gave! it terrified even the old gander himself, and sent the whole flock of geese marching off, nearly as fast as they had come; but Laura's cries also reached, at a great distance, the ears of somebody, who she would have been very sorry to think had heard them.

Lady Harriet, and all her friends at Holiday House, were taking a delightful walk under some fine old fir-trees, on the banks of the river, admiring the beautiful scenery, while Miss Perceval was admiring nothing but her own fine pocket-handkerchief, which had cost ten guineas, being worked with her name, trimmed with lace, and perfumed with eau-de-Cologne; and Captain Digby was admiring his own scarlet uniform, reflected in the bright, clear water, and varying his employment occasionally by throwing pebbles into the stream, to see how far they would go. Suddenly, however, he stopped, with a look of surprise and alarm, saying, "What noise can that be?—a loud scream in the water!"

"Oh dear, no! it was only one of those horrid peacocks," answered Miss Perceval, waving her fine pocket-handkerchief. "They are the most disagreeable, noisy creatures in the world! If mama ever keeps one, I shall get him a singing-master, or put a muzzle on his mouth!"

"But surely there is something splashing in the river at a great distance. Do you see that!—what can that be!"

"Nothing at all, depend upon it! I could bet the value of my pocket-handkerchief, ten guineas, that it is nothing. Officers who live constantly in the barracks are so unaccustomed to the country, that they seem to expect something wonderful shall happen every minute! That is probably a salmon or a minnow."

"I am determined, however, to see. If you are quite sure this is a salmon, will you promise to eat for your dinner whatever we find, provided I can catch it?"

"Certainly! unless you catch a whale! Oh! I have dropped my pocket-handkerchief,—pray pick it up!"

Captain Digby did so; but without waiting to examine the pattern, he instantly ran forward, and to his own very great astonishment, saw Laura up to her knees in the river, trying to scramble out, while her face was white with terror, and her limbs trembled with cold, like a poodle dog newly washed.

"Why, here you are again!—the very same little girl that I caught in the morning," cried he, laughing heartily, while he carefully pulled Laura towards the bank, though, by doing so, he splashed his beautiful uniform most distressingly. "We have had a complete game at bo-peep to-day, my friend! but here comes a lady who has promised to eat you up, therefore I shall have no more trouble."

Laura would have consented to be eaten up with pleasure, rather than encounter Lady Harriet's eye, who really did not recognise her for the first minute, as no one can suppose what a figure she appeared. The last clean frock had been covered entirely over with mud—her hair was dripping with water—and her new yellow sash might be any colour in the world. Laura felt so completely ashamed, she could not look up from the ground, and so sorry, she could not speak, while hot tears mingled themselves with the cold water which trickled down her face.

"What is the matter? Who is this?" cried Lady Harriet, hurrying up to the place where they stood. "Laura!! impossible!!!"

"Let me put on a pair of spectacles, for I cannot believe my eyes without them!" said Major Graham.

"Ah! sure enough it is Laura, and such a looking Laura as I never saw before. You must have had a nice cold bath!"

"I have heard," continued Lady Harriet, "that naughty people are often ducked in the water as a punishment, and in that respect I am sure Laura deserves what she has got, and a great deal more."

"She reminds me," observed Captain Digby, "of the Chinese bird which has no legs, so it constantly flies about from place to place, never a moment at rest."

"Follow me, Laura," said Lady Harriet, "that I may hear whether you have anything to say for yourself on this occasion. It is scarcely possible that there can be any excuse, but nobody should be condemned unheard."

When Laura had been put into dry clothes, she told her whole history, and entreated Lady Harriet to hear how very perfectly she had first learned her task before venturing to stir out of the room; upon which her grandmama consented, and amidst tears and sobs, the monody of Sir John Moore was repeated without a single mistake. Lady Rockville then came in, to entreat that, as this was the last day of the visit to Holiday House, Laura might be forgiven and permitted to appear at dessert, as all the company were anxious to see her, and particularly Captain Digby, who regretted that he had been the means at first of getting her into a scrape.

"Indeed, my dear Lady Rockville! I might perhaps have agreed to your wishes," answered Lady Harriet, "particularly as Laura seems sincerely sorry, and did not premeditate her disobedience; but she actually has not a tolerable frock to appear in now!"

"I must lend her one of my velvet dresses to destroy next," said Lady Rockville, smiling.

"Uncle David's Mackintosh cloak would be the fittest thing for her to wear," replied Lady Harriet, rising to leave the room. "Laura, you must learn a double task now! Here it is! and at Lady Rockville's request I excuse you this once; though I am sorry that, for very sufficient reasons, we cannot see you at dessert, which otherwise I should have been most happy to do."

Laura sat down and cried during a quarter of an hour after Lady Harriet had gone to dinner. She felt very sorry for having behaved ill, and sorry to have vexed her good grandmama; and sorry not to see all the fine party at dessert; and sorry to think that next day she must leave Holiday House; and sorry, last of all, to consider what Mrs Crabtree would say when all her ruined frocks were brought home. In short, poor Laura felt perfectly overwhelmed with the greatness and variety of her griefs, and scarcely believed that any one in the world was ever more miserable than herself.

Her eyes were fixed on her task, while her thoughts were wandering fifty miles away from it, when a housemaid, who had frequently attended upon Laura during her visit, accidentally entered the room, and seemed much surprised, as well as concerned, to find the young lady in such a way; for her sobbing could be heard in the next room. It was quite a relief to see any one; so Laura told over again all the sad adventures of the day, without attempting to conceal how naughty she had been; and most attentively was her narrative listened to, till the very end.

"You see, Miss!" observed Nelly, "when people doesn't behave well, they must expect to be punished."

"So they should!" sobbed Laura; "and I daresay it will make me better! I would not pass such a miserable day as this again, for the world; but I deserve to be more punished than I am."

"That's right, Miss!" replied Nelly, pleased to see the good effect of her admonitions. "Punishment is as sure to do us good when we are naughty, as physic when we are ill. But now you'll go down to dessert, and forget it all."

"No! grandmama would have allowed me, and Lady Rockville and everybody was so very kind about inviting me down; but my last clean frock is quite unfit to be seen, so I have none to put on. Oh, dear! what a thousand million of pities!"

"Is that all, Miss! Then dry your eyes, and I can wash the frock in ten minutes. Give it to me, and learn your lesson, so as to be ready when I come back."

Laura sprang off her seat with joy at this proposal, and ran—or rather flew—to fetch her miserable object of a frock, which Nelly crumpled under her arm, and walked away with, in such haste that she was evidently determined to return very soon; while Laura took her good advice, and sat down to learn her task, though she could hardly look at the book during two minutes at a time—she watched so impatiently for her benefactress from the laundry.

At length the door flew open, and in walked Nelly, whose face looked as red and hot as a beef-steak; but in her hand she carried a basket, on which was laid out, in great state, the very cleanest frock that ever was seen! It perfectly smelled of soap and water, starch and hot irons, and seemed still almost smoking from the laundry; while Laura looked at it with such delight and admiration, it might have been supposed she had never seen a clean frock before.

When Lady Harriet was sitting after dinner

that day, sipping her wine, and thinking about nothing very particular, she became surprised to feel somebody gently twitching her sleeve to attract notice. Turning instantly round to ascertain what was the matter, and who it could be, what was her astonishment to see Laura at her elbow, looking rather shy and frightened.

"How did you get here, child!" exclaimed Lady Harriet, in accents of amazement, though almost laughing. "Am I never to see the last of you to-day? Where did you get that frock? It must have dropped from the clouds! Or did some good fairy give you a new one?"

"That good fairy was Nelly the housemaid," whispered Laura. "She first tossed my frock into a washing-tub; and then at the great kitchen fire she toasted it, and —— ——"

"—— And buttered it, I hope," added Major Graham. "Come here, Laura! I can read what is written in your grandmama's face at this moment; and it says, 'you are a tiresome little puss, that nobody can keep in any order except uncle David;' therefore sit down beside him, and eat as many almonds and raisins as he bids you."

"You are a nice, funny uncle David!" whispered Laura, crushing her way in between his chair and Miss Perceval's; "nobody will need a tongue now, if you can read so exactly what we are all thinking."

"But here is Miss Perceval, still more wonderful; for she knows by the bumps on your head, all that is contained inside. Let me see if I could do so! There is a large bump of reading, and a small one of writing and arithmetic. Here is a terrible organ of breaking dolls and destroying frocks. There is a very small bump of liking uncle David, and a prodigious one of liking almonds and raisins!"

"No! you are quite mistaken! It is the largest bump for loving uncle David, and the small one for every thing else," interrupted Laura, eagerly. "I shall draw a map of my head some day, to shew you how it is all divided."

"And leave no room for any thing naughty or foolish! Your head should be swept out, and put in order every morning, that not a single cobweb may remain in your brains. What busy brains they must be for the next ten years! But in the mean time let us hope that you will never again be reduced to your

"LAST CLEAN FROCK."

CHAPTER VI

—·—

THE LONG LADDER

There was a young pickle, and what do you think!
He lived upon nothing but victuals and drink;
Victuals and drink were the chief of his diet,
And yet this young pickle could never be quiet.

ONE fine, sultry day in the month of August, Harry and Laura stood at the breakfast-room window, wondering to see the large, broken, white clouds, looking like curds and whey, while the sun was in such a blaze of heat, that everything seemed almost red-hot. The street door had become blistered by the sunbeams. Jowler the dog lay basking on the pavement; the green blinds were closed at every opposite house; the few gentlemen who ventured out, were fanning themselves with their pocket handkerchiefs; the ladies were strolling lazily along, under the umbrageous shade of their green parasols; and the poor people who were accustomed in winter to sell matches for lighting a fire, now carried about gaudy paper-hangings for the empty grates. Lady Harriet found the butter so melted at breakfast, that she could scarcely lift it on her knife! and uncle David complained that the sight of hot smoking tea put him in a fever, and said he wished it could be iced.

"I wonder how iced porridge would taste!" said Harry. "I put mine at the open window to cool, but that made it seem hotter. We were talking of the gentleman you mentioned yesterday, who toasted his muffins at a volcano; and certainly yours might almost be done at the drawing-room window this morning."

"Wait till you arrive at the countries I have visited, where, as somebody remarked, the very salamanders die of heat. At Agra, which is the hottest part of India, we could scarcely write a letter, because the ink dries in the pen before you can get it to the paper. I was obliged, when our regiment was there, to lie down in the middle of the day, during several hours, actually gasping for breath; and to make up for that we all rose at midnight. An officer of ours, who lived long in India, got up always at three in the morning, after we returned home, and walked about the streets of Portsmouth, wondering what had become of everybody."

"I shall try not to grumble about the weather

any more," said Laura. "We seem no worse off than other people."

"Or rather we are a great deal better off! At Bermuda, where my regiment stopped on its way to America, the inhabitants are so tormented with high winds, that they build 'hurricane houses'— low, flat rooms, where the families must retire when a storm comes on, as trees, houses, people, and cattle, are all whirled about with such violence, that not a life is safe on the island while it lasts."

"That reminds me," said Lady Harriet, "of a droll mistake made yesterday by the African camel, when he landed at Leith. His keepers were leading him along the high road to be made a show of in Edinburgh, at a time when the wind was particularly high, and the poor animal, encountering such clouds of dust, thought this must be a simoom of the desert, and threw himself flat down, burying his nose in the ground, according to custom on those occasions. It was with great difficulty that he could at last be induced to face the danger, and proceed."

"Quite a compliment to our dust," observed Laura. "But really, in such a hot day, the kangaroos and tigers might feel perfectly at home here. Oh! how I should like to visit the Zoological Gardens in London!"

"Then suppose we set off immediately!" said

Major Graham, pretending to rise from his chair. "Your grandmama's donkey-carriage holds two."

"Ah! but you could carry the donkey-carriage more easily than it could carry you!"

"Shall I try? Well, if we go, who is to pay the turnpikes, for I remember the time, not a hundred years ago, when Harry and you both thought that paying the gates was the only expense of travelling. You asked me then how poor grandmama could afford so many shillings and sixpences."

"We know all about every thing now, though!" said Harry, nodding in a very sagacious manner. "I can tell exactly how much time it takes going by the public coach to London, and it sleeps only one night on the road."

"Sleeps!" cried uncle David. "What? it puts on a nightcap, and goes to bed?"

"Yes! and it dines and breakfasts too, Mr uncle David; for I heard Mrs Crabtree say so."

"Never name anybody, unless you wish to see her immediately," said Major Graham, hearing a well-known tap at the door. "As sure as you mention an absent person, if he is supposed to be fifty miles off at the time, it is rather odd, but he instantly appears!"

"Then there is somebody that I shall speak about very often."

"Who can this Mr Somebody be?" asked uncle

David, smiling. "A foolish person that spoils you both I daresay, and gives you large slices of bread and jelly like this. Hold them carefully! Now, goodbye, and joy be with you."

But it was with rather rueful faces that Harry and Laura left the room, wishing they might have remained another hour to talk nonsense with uncle David, and dreading to think what new scrapes and difficulties they would get into in the nursery, which always seemed to them a place of torture and imprisonment.

Major Graham used to say that Mrs Crabtree should always have a thermometer in her own room when she dressed, to tell her whether the weather was hot or cold, for she seemed to feel no difference, and scarcely ever made any change in her own attire, wearing always the same pink gown and scarlet shawl, which made her look like a large red flower-pot, while she was no more annoyed with the heat than a flower-pot would have been. On this oppressive morning she took as much pains in suffocating Harry with a silk handkerchief round his neck, as if it had been Christmas; and though Laura begged hard for leave to go without one of her half-a-dozen wrappings, she might as well have asked permission to go without her head, as Mrs Crabtree seemed perfectly deaf upon the subject.

"This day is so very cold, and so very shivering, said Harry, slyly, "that I suppose you will make Laura wear at least fifty shawls."

"Not above twenty," answered Mrs Crabtree, dryly. "Give me no more of your nonsense, Master Harry! This is no business of yours! I was in the world long before you were born, and must know best; so hold your tongue. None but fools and beggars need ever be cold."

At last Mrs Crabtree had heaped as many clothes upon her two little victims as she was pleased to think necessary; so she sallied forth with them, followed by Betty, and proceeded towards the country, taking the sunny side of the road, and raising clouds of dust at every step, till Harry and Laura felt as if they had been made of wax, and were melting away.

"Mrs Crabtree!" said Harry, "did you hear uncle David's funny story yesterday? One hot morning a gentleman was watching an ant's nest, when he observed, that every little insect, as it came out, plucked a small leaf, to hold over its head, as a parasol! I wish we could find leaves large enough for us."

"You must go to the Botanical Gardens, where one leaf of a palm-tree was shewn to grandmama, which measured fourteen feet long," observed Laura. "How horrid these very warm countries must be, when the heat is all the year like this!"

"You may well say that," answered Mrs Crabtree. "I would not go to them East Indies—no! not if I were Governess-General,—to be running away with a tiger at your back, and sleeping with real live serpents twisted round the bed-post, and scorpions under your pillow. Catch me there! I'm often quite sorry for Master Frank, to think that his ship is maybe going that way! I'm told the very rats have such a smell in that outlandish place, that if they touch the outside of a bottle with their tails, it tastes of musk ever after; and when people are sitting comfortably down, expecting to enjoy their dinner, a swarm of great ants will come, and fall an inch thick, on all the side-dishes. I've no desire whatever to see foreign parts!"

"But I wish to see every country in the universe," said Harry; "and I hope there will be a railroad all round the world before I am grown up. Only think, Mrs Crabtree, what fun lion-hunting must be, and catching dolphins, and riding on elephants."

The pedestrians had now arrived at the pretty village of Corstorphine, when they were unexpectedly met by Peter Grey, who joined them without waiting to ask leave. Here the hills are so beautifully wooded, and the villas so charming, that Harry, Peter, and Laura stopped a moment, to consider what house they would like best to live in. Near one side of the road stood a large cart of hay, on the top of which were several men, forking it in at the window of a high loft, which could only be entered by a long ladder that leaned against the wall. It was a busy, joyous scene, and soon attracted the children's whole attention, who were transfixed with delight, seeing how rapidly the people ran up and down, with their pitchforks in their hands, and tilted the hay from the cart into the loft, while they had many jokes and much laughter among themselves. At last their whole business was finished, and the workmen drove away for another supply, to the neighbouring fields, where they had been raking and tossing it all morning, as merry as crickets.

"What happy people!" exclaimed Harry, looking wistfully after the party, and wishing he might have scrambled into the cart beside them. "I would be a haymaker for nothing, if anybody would employ me; would not you, Peter?"

"It is very strange," said Master Grey, "why little ladies and gentlemen seem always obliged to endure a perfectly useless walk every day, as you and Laura are doing now. You never saw animals set out to take a stroll for the good of their healths! How odd it would be to see a couple of dogs set off for a country walk!"

"Miss Laura!" said Mrs Crabtree, "Master Harry may rest here for a minute or two with Master Peter, and let them count their fingers, while you come with Betty and me to visit a sick old aunt of mine who lives round the corner; but be sure, boys, you do not presume to wander about, or I shall punish you most severely We are coming back in two minutes."

Mrs Crabtree had scarcely disappeared into a small shabby-looking cottage, before Peter turned eagerly to Harry, with a face of great joy and importance, exclaiming, "Only see how very lucky this is! The haymakers have left their long ladder standing on purpose for us! The window of that loft is wide open, and I must climb up immediately to peep in, because never in all my life, did I see the inside of a hay-loft before!"

"Nor I," added Harry "Uncle David says, that all round the floor there are deep holes, called mangers, down which food is thrown for the horses, so that they can thrust their heads in, to take a bite, whenever they choose."

"How I should hate to have my dinner hung up always before my nose in that way! Suppose the kitchen were placed above your nursery, and that Mrs Marmalade showered down tarts and puddings, which were to remain there till you eat them, you would hate the sight of such things at last. But now, Harry, for the hay-loft."

Peter scrambled so rapidly up the ladder that he soon reached the top, and instantly vanished in at the window, calling eagerly for Harry to follow. "You never saw such a nice, clean, funny place as this, in all your life!—make haste!—come faster!—never mind crushing your hat or tearing your jacket,—I'll put it all to rights. Ah! there!—that's the thing!—walk up, gentlemen! walk up!—the grand show!—sixpence each, and children half price!"

All this time, Harry was slowly, and with great difficulty, picking his steps up the ladder, but a most troublesome business it was! First, his foot became entangled in a rope,—then his hat got squeezed so out of shape, it looked perfectly tipsy,—next, one of his shoes nearly came off,—and afterwards he dropped his gloves; but at last he stumbled up in safety, and stood beside Peter in the loft, both laughing with delight at their own enterprise.

The quantity of hay piled up on all sides, astonished them greatly, while the nice, wide floor between seemed larger than any drawing-room, and was certainly made on purpose for a romp. Harry rolled up a large ball of hay to throw at Peter, while he, in return, aimed at him; so they ran after each other, round and round the loft, raising such a riot, that "the very rafters dirled."

The hay now flew about in clouds, while they jumped over it, or crept under it, throwing handfuls about in every direction, and observing that this was the best play-room they had ever been in.

"How lucky that we came here!" cried Peter. "I should like to stay an hour at least!"

"Oh! two hours,—or three,—or all day," added Harry. "But what shall we do about Mrs Crabtree? She has not gone to settle for life with that old sick aunt, so I am afraid we must be really hurrying back, in case she may find out our expedition, and that, you know, Peter, would be dreadful!"

"Only fancy, Harry, if she sees you and me clinging to the ladder, about half way down! what a way she would be in!"

"We had better make haste," said Harry, looking around. "What would grandmama say?—I wish we had never come up!"

At this moment Harry was still more brought to his senses, by hearing Mrs Crabtree's voice, exclaiming in loud angry accents, "Where in all the world can those troublesome boys be gone! I must tether them to a tree the next time they are left together! Why, sure! they would not venture up that long ladder into the hay-loft! If they have, they had better never come down again; for I shall shew who is master here."

"Peter Grey would run up a ladder to the stars, if he could find one," replied Betty. "Here are Master Harry's gloves lying at the bottom of it. They can be gone nowhere else, for I have searched every other place. We must send the town-crier with his bell after them, if they are not found up there!"

Mrs Crabtree now seemed fearfully angry, while Laura began to tremble with fright for Harry, who was listening overhead, and did not know very well what to do, but foolishly thought it best to put off the evil hour of being punished as long as possible; so he and Peter silently crept in below a great quantity of hay, and hid themselves so cunningly, that even a thief-catcher could scarcely have discovered their den. In this dark corner, Harry had time to reflect and to feel more and more alarmed and sorry for his misconduct; so he said in a very distressed voice, "Oh Peter! what a pity it is ever to be naughty, for we are always found out, and are always so much happier when we are good!"

"I wonder how Mrs Crabtree will get up the long ladder!" whispered Peter, laughing. "I would give my little finger, and one of my ears, to see her and Betty scrambling along!"

Harry had to pinch Peter's arm almost black and blue before he would be quiet; and by the time he stopped talking, Mrs Crabtree and Betty were both standing in the hay-loft, exceedingly out of breath with climbing so unusually high, while Mrs Crabtree very nearly fell, having stumbled over a step at the entrance.

"Why, sure! there's nobody here!" exclaimed she, in a disappointed tone. "And what a disorderly place this is! I thought a hay-loft was always kept in such nice order, with the floor all swept! but here is a fine mess! Those two great lumps of hay in the corner look as if they were meant for people to sleep upon!"

Harry gave himself up for lost when Mrs Crabtree noticed the place where he and Peter had buried themselves alive; but to his great relief, no suspicion seemed to have been excited, and neither of the two searchers was anxious to venture beyond the door, after having so nearly tripped upon the threshold.

"They must have been stolen by a gipsy, or perhaps fallen into a well," said Betty, who rather liked the bustle of an accident. "I always thought Master Peter would break his neck, or something of that kind. Poor thing! how distressed his papa will be!"

"Hold your tongue," interrupted Mrs Crabtree, angrily. "I wish people would either speak sense, or not speak at all! Did you hear a noise among the hay?"

"Rats, I daresay! or perhaps a dog!" answered Betty, turning hastily round and hurrying down the ladder faster than she had come up. "I certainly thought something moved in yon far corner."

"Where can that little shrimp of a boy be hid?" added Mrs Crabtree, following. "He must have obedience knocked like a nail into his head, with a few good severe blows. I shall beat him to powder when once we catch him."

"You may depend upon it," persisted Betty, "that some gipsy has got the boys for the sake of their clothes. It will be a great pity, because Master Harry had on his best blue jacket and trousers."

No sooner was the loft cleared of these unwelcome visitors, than Harry and Peter began to recover from their panic, and jumped out of the hay, shaking themselves free from it, and skipping about in greater glee than ever.

While they played about as they had done before, and tumbled as if they had been tumblers at Ducrow's, poor Harry got into such spirits, that he completely forgot about the deep holes called mangers, for containing the horses' food, till all at once, when Peter was running after him, he fell, with a loud crash, headlong into one of them! Oh! what a scream he gave!—it echoed through the stable, terrifying a whole team of horses that were feeding there, more particularly Snowball, into whose manger he had fallen. The horse gave a tremendous start when Harry plunged down close to his nose, and not being able to run away, he put back his ears, opened his mouth, and kicked and struggled in the most frightful manner; while Harry, who could not make his escape any more than the horse, shouted louder and louder for help.

Peter did all he could to assist Harry in this extraordinary predicament, but finding it impossible to be of any use, he forgot their terror of Mrs Crabtree in his fears about Harry, and rushed to the window, calling back their two pursuers, who were walking away at a great distance. He screamed and hallooed, and waved his handkerchief, without ceasing, till at last Mrs Crabtree heard him, and turned round; but never was anybody more astonished than she on seeing him there, so she scolded, stormed, and raged, back to the very foot of the ladder.

"Now, you are the besiegers, and I am the garrison!" cried Peter, when he saw Mrs Crabtree panting and toiling in her ascent. "We must make a treaty of peace together, for I could tumble you over in a minute, by merely pushing this end a very little more to one side!"

"Do not touch it, Master Peter!" cried Mrs Crabtree, almost afraid he was in earnest. "There is a good boy,—be quiet!"

"A good boy!!" whispered Peter to himself. "What a fright Mrs Crabtree must be in, before she said that!"

The next moment Mrs Crabtree snatched Harry out of the manger, and shook him with rage. She then scolded and beat him, till he was perfectly stupified with fright and misery, after which, the whole party proceeded towards home, while Harry stumbled along the road, and hung down his head, wishing, fifty times over, that he and Peter Grey had never gone up

"THE LONG LADDER."

CHAPTER VII.

THE MAD BULL.

> There's something in a noble boy,
> A brave, free-hearted, careless one
> With his uncheek'd, unbidden joy,
> His dread of books, and love of fun
> And in his clear and ready smile,
> Unshaded by a thought of guile,
> And unrepress'd by sadness,—
> Which brings me to my childhood back,
> As if I trod its very track,
> And felt its very gladness.
> WILLIS.

ONE evening when Harry and Laura came down to dessert, they were surprised to observe the two little plates usually intended for them, turned upside down, while uncle David pretended not to notice anything, though he stole a glance to see what would happen next. On lifting up these mysterious plates, what did they see lying underneath, but two letters with large red seals, one directed to "Master Harry Graham," and the other to "Miss Laura Graham."

"A letter for me!!" cried Harry, in a tone of delightful astonishment, while he tore open the seal, and his hand shook with impatience, so that he could hardly unfold the paper. "What can it be about! I like getting a letter very much! Is it from papa? Did the postman bring it?"

"Yes he did," said uncle David; "and he left a message that you must pay a hundred pounds for it to-morrow"

"Very likely, indeed," said Laura; "you should pay that for telling me such a fine story; but my letter is worth more than a hundred pounds, for it is inviting me to spend another delightful week at Holiday House."

"I am asked too! and not Mrs Crabtree!" cried Harry, looking at his letter, and almost screaming out for joy, whilst he skipped about the room, rubbing his hands together, and ended by twirling Laura round and round, till they both fell prostrate on the floor.

"If that be meant as a specimen of how you intend to behave at Holiday House, we had better send your apology at once," observed Lady Harriet, smiling. "Lord Rockville is very particular about never hearing any noise, and the slamming of a door, or even the creaking of a pair of unruly shoes, would put him distracted."

"Yes!" added uncle David, "Holiday House is as quiet as Harry's drum with a hole in it. If a pin drops in any part of the mansion, Lord Rockville becomes annoyed, and the very wasps scarcely dare to buzz at his window so loud as at any other person's. You will feel quite fish-out-of-water-ish, trying to be quiet and humdrum for a whole week; so let me advise you not to go."

"The meaning of advice always is something that one would rather wish not to do," observed Laura, gravely "I never in my life was advised to enjoy anything pleasant! Taking physic—or learning lessons—or staying at home, are very often advised, but never playing, or having a holiday, or amusing ourselves!"

"You know, Laura, that Harry's little Shetland pony, Tom Thumb, in my field, is of no use at present, but kicks, and capers, and runs about all day! yet presently he will be led out fastened to a rope, and made to trot round and round in a circle, day after day, till he has no longer a will of his own, —that is education. Afterwards he shall have a bridle put in his mouth, which some little girls would be much the better of also, when he shall be carefully guided ever afterwards in the best ways;

and you likewise will go much more steadily for all the reining-in and whipping you have got from Mrs Crabtree and me, which may, perhaps, make you keep in the road of duty more easily hereafter."

"Uncle David!" said Harry, laughing, "we have read, in the Arabian Nights, about people being turned into animals, but I never thought you would turn Laura into a horse! What shall we do with my little Shetland pony if I go away next week?"

"I have thought of a capital plan for making Tom Thumb useful during the whole winter! Your grandmama wants a watch-dog in the country, so we shall build him a kennel—put a chain round his neck, and get some one to teach him to bark."

"Uncle David should be Professor of Nonsense at the University," said Lady Harriet, smiling. "But my dear children, if you are allowed to pay this visit at Holiday House, I hope you will endeavour to behave creditably!"

"Yes," added Major Graham, "I understand that Lord Rockville wished to have some particularly quiet children there, for a short time, so he fixed upon Harry and Laura! Poor, mistaken Lord Rockville! But my good friends, try not to break all his china ornaments the first day—spare a few jars and tea cups—leave a pane or two of glass in the windows, and throw none of your marbles at the mirrors."

"I remember hearing," said Lady Harriet, "that when Miss Pelham was married last year, her old aunt, Mrs Bouverie, sent for her, and said, that as she could not afford to give baubles or trinkets, she would give her a valuable piece of advice; and what do you think it was, Laura?"

"I have no idea! Do tell me!"

"Then I shall bestow it on you, as the old lady did on her niece—'Be careful of china, paper, and string, for they are all very transitory possessions in this world!'"

"Very true! and most judicious!" observed Major Graham, laughing. "I certainly know several persons who must have served an apprenticeship under that good lady: many gentlemen, who despatch all their epistles from the club, because there the paper costs them nothing; and a number of ladies, who, for the same good reason, never write letters till they are visiting in a country house."

Having received so many warnings and injunctions about behaving well, Harry and Laura became so quiet during the first few days at Holiday House, that they were like shadows flitting through the rooms, going almost on tiptoe, scarcely speaking above a whisper, and observing that valuable rule for children, to let themselves be seen, but not heard. Lord Rockville was quite charmed with such extreme good conduct, for they were both in especial awe of him, and thought it a great condescension if he even looked at them, he was so tall, so grand, and so grave, wearing a large, powdered wig and silver spectacles, which gave him a particularly venerable appearance, though Harry was one day very nearly getting into disgrace upon that subject. His Lordship had a habit of always carrying two pairs of spectacles in his pocket, and often, after thrusting one pair high upon his forehead, he forgot where they were, and put others on his nose, which had such a droll appearance, that the first time Harry saw it, he felt quite taken by surprise, and burst into a fit of laughter, upon which Lord Rockville gave him such a comical look of surprise and perplexity, that Harry's fit of laughing got worse and worse. The more people know they are wrong, and try to stop, the more convulsive it becomes, and the more difficult to look grave again; so at last, after repeated efforts to appear serious and composed, Harry started up, and, in his hurry to escape, very nearly slammed the door behind him, which would have given the last finish to his offences.

Both the little visitors found Lady Rockville so extremely indulgent and kind, that she seemed like another grandmama; therefore they gradually ventured to talk some of their own nonsense before her, and even to try some of their old ways, and frolicsome tricks, which she seldom found any fault with, except when Harry one day eloped with Lord Rockville's favourite walking-stick, to be used as a fishing-rod among the minnows, with a long thread at the end for a line, and a crooked pin to represent the hook; while, on the same day, Laura privately mounted the ass that gave Lord Rockville ass's milk, and rode it all round the park, while he sat at home expecting his usual refreshing tumbler. Still they both passed muster for being very tolerable children; and his Lordship was heard once to say, in a voice of great approbation, that Master and Miss Graham were so punctual at dinner, and so perfectly quiet, he really often forgot they were in the house. Indeed, Harry's complaisance on the day after he had laughed so injudiciously about the spectacles, was quite unheard of, as he felt anxious to make up for his misconduct; and when Lord Rockville asked if he would like a fire in the playroom, as the evening was chilly, he answered very politely, "Thank you, my Lord! We are ready to think it hot or cold just as you please!"

All this was too good to last! One morning when Harry and Laura looked out of the window, it was a most deplorably wet day. The whole sky looked like a large, grey cotton umbrella, and the clouds were so low that Harry thought he could almost have touched them. In short, as Lord Rockville remarked, "it rained cats and dogs;" so his Lordship knitted his brows, and thrust his hands into his waistcoat pockets, walking up and down the room in a perfect fume of vexation, for he was so accustomed to be obeyed, that it seemed rather a hardship when even the weather contradicted his wishes. To complete his vexation, as "single misfortunes never come alone," his valet, when carelessly drying the Morning Post at a large kitchen fire, had set it in flames, so that all the wonderful news it contained was reduced to ashes; therefore Lord Rockville might well have given notice, that, for this day at least, he had a right to be in extremely bad humour.

Lady Rockville privately recommended Harry and Laura to sit quietly down and play at cat's cradle, which accordingly they did, and when that became no longer endurable, some dominoes were produced. Thus the morning wore tediously away till about two o'clock, when suddenly the rain stopped, the sun burst forth with prodigious splendour, every leaf in the park glittered, as if it had been sprinkled with diamonds, and a hundred birds seemed singing a chorus of joy, while bees and butterflies fluttered at the windows, and flew away rejoicing.

Harry was the first to observe this delightful change, and with an exclamation of delight, he sprung from his seat, pulled Laura from hers, upset the domino-table, and rushed out of the room, slamming the door with a report like twenty cannons. Away they both flew to the forest, Laura swinging her bonnet in her hand, and Harry tossing his cap in the air, while Lord Rockville watched them angrily from the drawing-room window, saying, in a tone of extreme displeasure, "That boy has a voice that might do for the town-crier! He laughs so loud it is enough to crack every glass in the room! I wish he were condemned to pass a week in those American prisons where no one is allowed to speak. In short he would be better anywhere than here; for I might as well live with a hammer and tongs as with the two children together. They are more restless than the quicksilver figures from China, and I wish they were as quiet; but my only comfort is, that at any rate they come home punctually to dinner at five. Nothing is so intolerable as people dropping in too late, and disordering the table."

Meantime the woods at Holiday House rung with sounds of mirth and gaiety, while Harry scrambled up the trees like a squirrel, and swung upon the branches, gathering walnuts and crab-apples for Laura, after which they both cut their names upon the bark of Lord Rockville's favourite beech, so that every person who passed that way must observe the large distinct letters. They were laughing and chatting over this exploit, both talking at once, as noisy and happy as possible, and expecting nothing particular to happen, when, all on a sudden, Laura turned pale, and grasped hold of Harry's arm, saying, in a low, frightened voice,

"Hush, Harry!—hush!—I hear a very strange noise. It sounds like some wild beast! What can that be?"

Harry listened as if he had ten pairs of ears, and nearly cracked his eye-balls staring round him, to see what could be the matter. A curious, deep, growling sound might be heard at some distance, while there was the noise of something trampling heavily on the ground, and of branches breaking off the trees, as if some large creature were forcing his way through. Harry and Laura now stood like a couple of little statues, not daring to breathe, they felt so terrified! The noise grew louder and louder, while it gradually became nearer and nearer, till at length a large, black bull burst into view, with his tail standing high in the air, while he tore up the ground with his horns, bellowing as loudly as he could roar, and galloping straight towards the place where they stood.

Laura's knees tottered under her, and she instantly dropped on the ground with terror, feeling as if she would die the next minute of fright, while, as for attempting to escape, it never entered her head to think that possible. Harry felt quite differently; for he was a bold boy, not easily scared out of his senses, and instantly saw that something must be done, or they would both be lost. Many selfish people would have run away alone, without caring for the safety of any one but themselves, which was not at all the case with Harry, who thought first of his poor, frightened companion. "Hollo, Laura! are you hiding in a cart-rut?" he exclaimed, pulling her hastily off the ground. "The bull will soon find you here! Come! come! as fast as possible! we must have a race for it yet! That terrible beast can scarcely make his way through the branches, they grow so closely! Perhaps we may get on as fast as he!"

All this time, Harry was dragging Laura along, and running himself into the thickest part of the plantation; but it was very difficult to make any progress, as she had become quite faint and bewildered with fright.

"Oh, Harry!" cried she, trembling all over, "you must get on alone! I am so weak with terror, it is impossible to run a step farther."

"Do not waste your breath with talking," answered Harry, still pushing on at full speed. "How can you suppose I would be so shabby as to make my escape without you? No! no! we must either both be caught or both get off!"

Laura felt so grateful to Harry when he said this, that she seemed for a moment almost to forget the bull, which was still coming furiously on behind, while she now made a desperate exertion to run faster than she had been able to do before, clearing the ground almost as rapidly as Harry could have done, though he still held her firmly by the hand, to encourage her.

The trampling noise continued, the breaking of branches, and the frightful bellowing of this dreadful animal, when at last Harry caught sight of a wooden paling, which he silently pointed out to Laura, being quite unable now to speak. Having rushed forward to it, with almost frantic haste, Harry threw himself over the top, after which he helped Laura to squeeze herself underneath, when they proceeded rather more leisurely onwards.

"That fence will puzzle Mr Bull," said Harry, triumphantly, yet gasping for breath. "We can push through places where his great hoof could scarcely be thrust! I saw him coming along, with his heels high in the air, and his head down, like an enormous wheelbarrow."

Scarcely had Harry spoken, before the infuriated animal advanced at full gallop towards the fence, and after running along the side a little way, he suddenly tore up the paling with his horns, as if it had been made of paper, and rushed forward more rapidly than ever.

Harry now began to fear that indeed all was over, for his strength had become nearly exhausted, when, to his great joy, he espied a large, rough stone-wall, not very far off, which was as welcome a sight as land to a shipwrecked sailor.

"Run for your life, Laura!" he cried, pointing it out, to encourage her. "There is safety if we reach it."

On they both flew faster than the wind, and Harry having scrambled up the wall, like a grasshopper, pulled Laura up beside him, and there they both stood at last, encamped quite beyond the reach of danger, though the enemy arrived a few minutes afterwards, pawing the air, and foaming and bellowing with disappointment.

"Laura!" said Harry, after she had a little recovered from her fright, and was walking slowly homewards, while she cast an alarmed glance frequently behind, thinking she still heard the bull in pursuit, "you see, as uncle David says, whatever danger people are in, it is foolish to be quite in despair, but we should rather think what is best to do, and do it directly."

"Yes, Harry! and I shall never forget that you

would not forsake me, but risked your own life, like a brave brother, in my defence. I should like to do as much for you another time!"

" Thank you, Laura, as much as if you had; but I hope we shall never be in such a scrape again! If Frank were here, he would put us both in mind to thank a merciful God for taking so much care of us, and bringing us safely home!"

" Yes, Harry! It is perhaps a good thing being in danger sometimes, to remind us that we cannot be safe or happy an hour without God's care; so in our prayers to-night we must remember what has happened, and return thanks very particularly."

It was long past five before Harry and Laura reached Holiday House, where Lord Rockville met them at the drawing-room door, looking taller, and grander, and graver than ever, while Lady Rockville rose from her sofa, and came up to them, saying, in a tone of gentle reproach, " My dear children! you ought to return home before the dinner hour, and not keep his Lordship waiting!"

The very idea of Lord Rockville waiting dinner was too dreadful ever to have entered their heads till this minute; but Harry and Laura immediately explained how exceedingly sorry they were for what had occurred, and to shew that it was their misfortune rather than their fault, they told the whole frightful story of the mad bull, to which

Lady Rockville listened, as if her very wig was standing upon end, to hear of such doings. she even turned up her eyes with astonishment to think of what a wonderful escape they had made but his Lordship frowned through his spectacles, and leaned his chin upon his stick, looking, as Harry thought, very like a bear upon a pole.

"Pshaw!—nonsense!" exclaimed Lord Rockville, impatiently "The bull would have done you no harm! He is a most respectable, quiet, well-disposed animal, and brought an excellent character from his last place! I never heard a complaint of him before!"

"It is curious," observed Laura, "that all bulls are reckoned perfectly peaceable and tame, till they have tossed two or three people, and killed them!"

"I thought," added Lord Rockville, looking very grand and contemptuous, "that Harry was grown more a man than to be so easily put to flight. When a bull, another time, threatens to toss you, my boy, seize hold of his tail,—or toss him!—or, in short, do anything rather than run away the first time an animal looks at you. This is a mere cock-and-a-bull story, to excuse your keeping me waiting almost a quarter of an hour for dinner!—you should be made a guard of a mail-coach for a month, to teach you punctuality, Master Graham."

Lord Rockville gravely looked at his watch, while Harry luckily considered how often his grandmama had recommended him to make no answer when he was scolded; so he nearly bit off the tip of his tongue to keep it quiet, while he could not but wish, in his own mind, that my Lord himself had seen how very fierce the bull looked.

Laura felt more vexed on Harry's account than her own, and the dinner went on as uncomfortably as possible; for even if a French cook has dressed it, if ill-humour be the sauce, any dish becomes unpalatable. Nothing was to be seen reflected on the surface of many fine silver covers, but very cross, or very melancholy faces; while Lady Rockville tried to make her own countenance look both cheerful and good-natured. She told Harry and Laura, to divert them, that old Mrs Bouverie had once been pursued by a furious milch-cow, along a lane flanked on both sides by such very high walls that escape seemed impossible, so the good lady, who was fat and breathless, became so desperate, that without a hope of getting off, she seized the enraged animal by the horns, and screamed in its face, till the cow herself became frightened. The creature stared, stepping backwards and backwards, with increasing alarm, till at last, to the old lady's great relief and surprise, she fairly turned tail and ran off.

In the evening, Lord Rockville, not having yet recovered his equanimity, went out, rather in bad humour, to take his usual walk before supper. Without once remembering about Harry and the bull, he strolled a great way into the woods, marking several trees to be cut down, and admiring a fine forest which he planted himself long ago, but without particularly considering which way he turned. It was beginning, at last, to grow very dark and gloomy, so Lord Rockville had some thoughts of returning home, when he became suddenly startled by hearing a loud roar not far off, and a moment afterwards the furious bull dashed out of a neighbouring thicket, raging and foaming, and tearing the ground with his horns, exactly as Harry had described in the morning, while poor Lord Rockville, who seldom moved faster than a very dignified walk, instantly quickened his pace, in an opposite direction, striding away faster and faster, till at last,—it must be confessed,—his Lordship ended by running!!!

In spite of all Lord Rockville's exertions, the bull continued rapidly to gain upon him, for his Lordship, being rather corpulent and easily fatigued, stopped every now and then to gasp for breath; till at last, feeling it impossible to get on faster, though the stables were now within sight, he seized the branch of a large oak tree which swept nearly to the ground, and contrived with great difficulty to scramble out of reach.

The enraged bull gazed up into the tree and bellowed with fury, when he saw Lord Rockville so judiciously perched overhead, and he remained for half-an-hour, watching to see if his Lordship would venture down again. At last the tormenting animal began leisurely eating grass under the tree, but gradually he moved away, turning his back while he fed, till Lord Rockville vainly deluded himself with the hope of stealing off unobserved. Being somewhat rested and refreshed, while the enemy was looking in another direction, he descended cautiously, as if he had been going to tread upon needles and pins; but, unaccustomed to such movements, he jumped so heavily upon the ground, that the bull, hearing a noise, turned round, and set up a loud, furious roar, when he saw his intended victim again within reach.

Now the race began once more with redoubled agility! The odds seemed greatly in favour of the bull, and Lord Rockville thought he already felt the animal's horns in his side, when a groom, who saw the party approaching, instantly seized a pitchfork, and flew to the rescue of his master. Lord Rockville never stopped his career till he reached the stable, and ran up into a loft, from the window of which he gave the alarm, and called for more assistance, when several ploughmen and stable-boys assembled, who drove the animal, with great difficulty, into a stall, where he continued so ungovernable, that iron chains were put round his neck, and some days afterwards, seeing no one could manage him, Lord Rockville ordered the bull to be shot, and his carcass turned into beef for the poor of the parish, who all, consequently, rejoiced at his demise; though the meat turned out so tough, that it required their best teeth to eat it with.

Meantime, on that memorable evening of so many adventures, Harry, Laura, and Lady Rockville, wondered often what had become of his Lordship; and, at last, when supper appeared at the usual hour, his absence became still more unaccountable!

"What can be the matter?" exclaimed Lady Rockville, anxiously. "This is very odd! His Lordship is as punctual as the postman in general! especially for supper; and here is Lord Rockville's favourite dish of sago and wine, which will become uneatably cold in ten minutes, if he does not return home to enjoy it!"

Scarcely had she finished speaking, when the door opened, and Lord Rockville walked majestically into the room. There was something so different from usual in his manner and appearance, however, that Harry and Laura exchanged looks of astonishment; his neckcloth was loose—his face excessively red—and his hand shook, while he breathed so hard, that he might have been heard at the porter's lodge. Lady Rockville gazed with amazement at all she saw, and then asked what he chose for supper; but when Lord Rockville tried to speak, the words died on his lips, so he could only point in silence to the sago and wine.

"What, in all the world, has happened to you this evening, my Lord?" exclaimed Lady Rockville, unable to restrain her curiosity a moment longer. "I never saw you in such a way before! Your eyes are perfectly blood-shot—your dress strangely disordered—and you seem so hot and so fatigued? Tell me!—what is the matter?"

"Nothing," answered Lord Rockville, drawing himself up, while he tried to look grander and graver than ever, though his Lordship could not help panting for breath—putting his hands to his sides—and wiping his forehead with his pocket-handkerchief in an agony of fatigue. Harry observed all this for some time, as eagerly and intently as a cat watches a bird on a tree. He saw that something extraordinary had occurred, and he began to have hopes that it really was the very thing he wished; because, seeing Lord Rockville now perfectly safe, he would not have grudged him a pretty considerable fright from his friend the bull.

At last, unable any longer to control his impatience, Harry started off his chair, gazing so earnestly at Lord Rockville, that his eyes almost sprung out of their sockets, while he rubbed his hands with ecstacy, saying,

"I guess you've seen the bull! Oh! I am sure you did! Pray tell us if you have! Did he run after you,—and did you run away?"

Lord Rockville tried more than he had ever done in his life to look grave, but it would not do. Gradually his face relaxed into a smile, till at last he burst into loud peals of laughter, joined most heartily by Harry, Laura, and Lady Rockville. Nobody recovered any gravity during the rest of that evening, for whenever they tried to think or talk quietly about anything else, Harry and Laura were sure to burst forth again upon the subject, and even after being safely stowed in their beds for the night, they both laughed themselves to sleep at the idea of Lord Rockville himself having been obliged, after all, to run away from that "most respectable, quiet, well-disposed animal,

"THE MAD BULL!"

CHAPTER VIII.

THE BROKEN KEY

> First he moved his right leg,
> Then he moved his left leg,
> Then he said, " I pardon beg,"
>   And sat upon his seat.

"OH! uncle David! uncle David!" cried Laura, when they arrived from Holiday House, "I would jump out of the carriage-window with joy to see you again, only the persons passing in the street might be surprised!"

"Not at all! They are quite accustomed to see people jumping out of the windows with joy, whenever I appear."

"We have so much to tell you," exclaimed Harry and Laura, each seizing hold of a hand, "we hardly know where to begin!"

"Ladies and gentlemen! If you both talk at once, I must get a new pair of ears! So you have not been particularly miserable at Holiday House?"

"No! no! uncle David! we did not think there had been so much happiness in the world," answered Laura, eagerly. The last two days we could do nothing but play, and laugh, and"——

"And grow fat! Why! you both look so well fed, you are just fit for killing! I shall be obliged to shut you up two or three days, without anything to eat, as is done to pet lap-dogs, when they are getting corpulent and gouty."

"Then we shall be like bears living on our paws," replied Harry; "and uncle David! I would rather do that than be a glutton like Peter Grey. He went to a cheap shop lately, where old cheese-cakes were sold at half-price, and greedily devoured nearly a dozen, thinking that the dead flies scattered on the top were currants, till Frank shewed him his mistake!"

"Frank should have let him eat in peace! There is no accounting for tastes. I once knew a lady who liked to swallow spiders! She used to crack and eat them with the greatest delight, whenever she could catch one."

"Oh! what a horrid woman! That is even worse than grandmama's story about Dr Manvers having dined on a dish of mice, fried in crumbs of bread!"

"You know the old proverb, Harry, 'One man's meat is another man's poison.' The Persians are disgusted at our eating lobsters; and the Hindoos think us scarcely fit to exist, because we live on beef; while we are equally amazed at the Chinese, for devouring dog-pies, and bird's nest soup. You turn up your nose at the French for liking frogs; and they think us ten times worse, with our singed sheep's head, oat cakes, and haggis."

"That reminds me," said Lady Harriet, "that when Charles X. lived in what he called the 'dear Canongate,' his majesty was heard to say, that he tried every sort of Scotch goose, 'the solan goose, the wild goose, and the tame goose, but the best goose of all was the hag-goose.'"

"Very polite, indeed, to adopt our national taste so completely," observed uncle David, smiling. "When my regiment was quartered in Spain, an officer of ours, a great epicure, and not quite so complaisant, used to say that the country was scarcely fit to live in, because there it is customary to dress almost every dish with sugar. At last, one day in a rage, he ordered eggs to be brought up in their shells for dinner, saying 'That is the only thing the cook cannot possibly spoil.' We played him a trick, however, which was very like what you would have done, Harry, on a similar occasion. I secretly put pounded sugar into the salt-cellar, and when he tasted his first mouthful, you should have seen the look of fury with which he sprung off his seat, exclaiming, 'The barbarians eat sugar even with their eggs!'"

"That would be the country for me to travel in," said Harry. "I could live in a barrel of sugar; and my little pony, Tom Thumb, would be happy to accompany me there, as he likes anything sweet."

"All animals are of the same opinion. I remember the famous rider, Ducrow, telling a brother-officer of mine, that the way in which he gains so much influence over his horses, is merely by bribing them with sugar. They may be managed in that way like children, and are quite aware if it be taken from them as a punishment for being restive."

"Oh! those beautiful horses at Ducrow's! How often I think of them since we were there!" exclaimed Harry. "They are quite like fairies, with fine arched necks and long tails!"

"I never heard before of a fairy with a long tail, Master Harry; but perhaps in the course of your travels you may have seen such a thing."

"How I should like to ride upon Tom Thumb in Ducrow's way, with my toe on the saddle!"

"Fine doings, indeed!" exclaimed Mrs Crabtree, who had entered the room at this moment. "Have you forgotten already, Master Harry, how many of the nursery plates you broke one day I was out, in trying to copy that there foolish Indian juggler, who tossed his plates in the air, and twirled them on his thumb! There must be no more such nonsense; for if once your neck is broke by a fall off Tom Thumb, no doctor that I know of can mend it again. Remember what a terrible tumble you had off Jessy last year!"

"You are always speaking about that little overturn, Mrs Crabtree; and it was not worth recollecting above a week! Did you never see a man thrown off his horse before?"

"A man and horse, indeed!" said uncle David, laughing when he looked at Harry. "You and your charger were hardly large enough then for a toy-shop; and you must grow a little more, Captain Gulliver, before you will be fit for a dragoon regiment."

Harry and Laura stayed very quietly at home for several weeks after their return from Holiday House, attending so busily to lessons, that uncle David said he felt much afraid they were going to be a pair of little wonders, who would die of too much learning.

"You will be taken ill of the multiplication table some day, and confined to bed with a violent fit of geography! Pray take care of yourselves, and do not devour above three books at once," said Major Graham, one day, entering the room with a note in his hand. "Here is an invitation that I suppose you are both too busy to accept, so perhaps I might as well send an apology; eh, Harry?"

Down dropped the lesson-books upon the floor, and up sprung Harry in an ecstacy of delight ' An invitation! Oh! I like an invitation so very much? Pray tell us all about it!"

"Perhaps it is an invitation to spend a month with Dr Lexicon. What would you say to that? They breakfast upon Latin grammars at school, and have a dish of real French verbs, smothered in onions, for dinner every day."

"But in downright earnest, uncle David! where are we going?"

"Must I tell you! Well! that good-natured old lady, Mrs Darwin, intends taking a large party of children next week, in her own carriage, to pass ten days at Ivy Lodge, a charming country house about twenty miles off, where you are all to enjoy perfect happiness. I wish I could be ground down into a little boy myself, for the occasion! Poor, good woman! what a life she will lead! There is only one little drawback to your delight, that I am almost afraid to announce."

"What is that, uncle David?" asked Harry, looking as if nothing in nature could ever make him grave again. "Are we to bite off our own noses before we return?"

"Not exactly; but somebody is to be of the party who will do it for you. Mrs Darwin has heard that there are certain children who become occasionally rather unmanageable! I cannot think who they can be, for it is certainly nobody we ever saw; so she has requested that Mrs Crabtree will follow in the mail-coach."

Harry and Laura looked as if a glass of cold water had been thrown in their faces, after this was mentioned; but they soon forgot every little vexation, in a burst of joy, when, some days afterwards, Mrs Darwin stopped at the door to pick them up, in the most curious-looking carriage they had ever seen. It was a very large open car, as round as a bird's nest, and so perfectly crowded with children, that nobody could have supposed any room left even for a doll; but Mrs Darwin said that whatever number of people came in, there was always accommodation for one more; and this really proved to be the case, for Harry and Laura soon elbowed their way into seats, and set off, waving their handkerchiefs to Major Graham, who had helped to pack them in, and who now stood smiling at the door.

As this very large vehicle was drawn by only one horse, it proceeded very slowly; but Mrs Darwin amused the children with several very diverting stories, and gave them a grand luncheon in the carriage; after which, they threw what was left, wrapped up in an old newspaper, to some people breaking stones on the road, feeling quite delighted to see the surprise and joy of the poor labourers when they opened the parcel. In short, everybody became sorry when this diverting journey was finished, and they drove up, at last, to the gate of a tall, old house, that looked as if it had been built in the year one. The walls were very thick, and quite mouldy with age. Indeed, the only wonder was, that Ivy Lodge had still a roof upon its head, for everything about it looked so tottering and decayed. The very servants were all old; and a white-headed butler opened the door, who looked as frail and gloomy as the house; but before long, the old walls of Ivy Lodge rung and echoed again with sounds of mirth and joy. It seemed to have been built on purpose for hide-and-seek; there were rooms with invisible doors, and closets cut in the walls, and great old chests, where people might have been buried alive for a year without being found out. The gardens, too, were perfectly enchanting. Such arbours to take strawberries and cream in! and such summer-houses, where they drank tea out of doors every evening! Here they saw a prodigious eagle fastened to the ground by a chain, and looking the most dull, melancholy creature in the world; while Harry wished the poor bird might be liberated, and thought how delightful it would be to stand by and see him soaring away to his native skies.

"Yes! with a large slice of raw meat in his beak!" said Peter Grey, who was always thinking of eating. "I daresay he lives much better here, than he would do killing his own mutton up in the clouds there, or taking his chance of a dead horse on the sea-shore occasionally."

Harry and Peter were particularly amused with Mrs Darwin's curious collection of pets. There were black swans with red bills swimming gracefully in a pond close to the window, and ready to rush forward on the shortest notice for a morsel of bread. The lop-eared rabbits also surprised them, with their ears hanging down to the ground; and they were interested to see a pair of carrier-pigeons which could carry letters as well as the postman. Mrs Darwin shewed them tumbler-pigeons, too, that performed a summersault in the air when they flew, and horsemen and dragoon pigeons, trumpeters and pouters, till Peter Grey at last begged to see the pigeons that made the pigeon-pies, and the cow that gave the butter-milk; he was likewise very anxious for leave to bring his fishing-rod into the drawing-room, to try whether he could catch one of the beautiful gold-fish that swam about in a large glass-globe, saying he thought it might perhaps be a very good red herring to eat at breakfast. Mrs Darwin had a pet lamb that she was exceedingly proud of, because it followed her everywhere, and Harry, who was very fond of the little creature, said he wished some plan could be invented to hinder its ever growing into a great, fat, vulgar sheep; and he thought the white mice were old animals that had grown grey with years.

There were donkeys for the children to ride upon, and Mrs Darwin had a boat that held the whole party, to sail in, round the pond; and she hung up a swing that seemed to fly about as high as the house, which they swung upon; after which they were allowed to shake the fruit-trees, and to eat whatever came down about their ears; so it very often rained apples and pears in the gardens at Ivy Lodge, for Peter seemed never to tire of that joke; indeed the apple-trees had a sad life of it as long as he remained.

Peter told Mrs Darwin that he had "a patent appetite," which was always ready on every occasion; but the good lady became so fond of stuffing the children at all hours, that even he felt a little puzzled sometimes how to dispose of all she heaped upon his plate, while both Harry and Laura, who were far from greedy, became perfectly wearied of hearing the gong. The whole party assembled at eight every morning, to partake of porridge and butter-milk, after which, at ten, they breakfasted with Mrs Darwin, on tea, muffins, and sweetmeats. They then drove in the round open car, to bathe in the sea, on their return from which, luncheon was always ready; and after concluding that, they might pass the interval till dinner among the fruit-trees. They never could eat enough to please Mrs Darwin at dinner; tea followed, on a most substantial plan; their supper consisted of poached eggs, and the maid was desired to put a biscuit under every visitor's pillow, in case the young people should be hungry in the night; for Mrs Darwin said she had been starved at school herself when she was a little girl, and wished nobody ever to suffer as she had done, from hunger.

The good lady was so anxious for everything to be exactly as the children liked it, that sometimes Laura felt quite at a loss what to say or do. One day having cracked her egg-shell at breakfast, Mrs Darwin peeped anxiously over her shoulder, saying,

" I hope, my dear! your egg is all right?"

" Most excellent, indeed!"

" Is it quite fresh?"

" Perfectly! I daresay it was laid only a minute before it was boiled!"

" I have seen the eggs much larger than that!"

" Yes! but then I believe they are rather coarse,

—at least we think so, when Mrs Crabtree gives us a turkey-egg at dinner."

"If you prefer them small, perhaps you would like a guinea-fowl's egg!"

"Thank you! but this one is just as I like them."

"It looks rather over-done! If you think so, we could get another in a minute!"

"No! they are better well boiled!"

"Then probably it is not enough done. Some people like them quite hard, and I could easily pop it into the slop-basin for another minute."

"I am really obliged to you, but it could not be improved."

"Do you not take any more salt with your egg?"

"No, I thank you!"

"A few more grains would improve it!"

"If you say so, I daresay they will."

"Ah! now I am afraid you have put in too much! Pray do get another!"

This long-continued attack upon her egg was too much for Laura's gravity, who appeared for some minutes to have a violent fit of coughing, and ended in a burst of laughter, after which she hastily finished all that remained of it, and thus the discussion closed.

In the midst of all their happiness, while the children thought that every succeeding day had no fault but being too short, and Harry even planned with Peter to stop the clock altogether, and see whether time itself would not stand still, nobody ever thought for a moment of anything but joy; and yet a very sad and sudden distress awaited Mrs Darwin. One forenoon she received a letter that seemed very hastily and awkwardly folded,—the seal was all to one side, and surrounded with stray drops of red wax,—the direction seemed sadly blotted, and at the top was written, in large letters, the words " To be delivered immediately."

When Mrs Darwin hurriedly tore open this very strange-looking letter, she found that it came from her own housekeeper in town, to announce the dreadful event that her sister Lady Barnet had been that day seized with an apoplectic fit, and was thought to be at the point of death, therefore it was hoped that Mrs Darwin would not lose an hour in returning to town, that she might be present on the melancholy occasion. The shock of hearing this news was so very great, that poor Mrs Darwin could not speak about it, but after trying to compose herself for a few minutes, she went into the play-room, and told the children that, for reasons she could not explain, they must get ready to return home in an hour, when the car would be at the door for their journey.

Nothing could exceed their surprise on hearing Mrs Darwin make so unexpected a proposal. At first Peter Grey thought she was speaking in jest, and said he would prefer if she ordered out a balloon to travel in, this morning; but when it appeared that Mrs Darwin was really in earnest about their pleasant visit being over so soon, Harry's face grew perfectly red with passion, while he said, in a loud, angry voice,

"Grandmama allowed me to stay here till Friday! —and I was invited to stay,—and I will not leave this nice, pretty house!"

"Oh, fie, Master Harry!" said Mrs Crabtree. "Do not talk so! You ought to know better! I shall soon teach you, however, to do as you are bid!"

Saying these words, she stretched out her hand to seize violent hold of him, but Harry dipped down and escaped. Quickly opening the door, he ran, half in joke, and half in earnest, at full speed, up two pairs of stairs, followed closely by Mrs Crabtree, who was now in a terrible rage, especially when she saw what a piece of fun Harry thought this fatiguing race. A door happened to be standing wide open on the second landing-place, which, having been observed by Harry, he darted in, and slammed it in Mrs Crabtree's face, locking and double-locking it, to secure his own safety, after which he sat down in the empty apartment to enjoy his victory in peace. When people once begin to grow self-willed and rebellious, it is impossible to guess where it will all end! Harry might have been easily led to do right at first, if any one had reasoned with him and spoken kindly, but now he really was in a sort of don't-care-a-button humour and scarcely minded what he did next.

As long as Mrs Crabtree continued to scold and rave behind the door, Harry grew harder and harder; but at length the good old lady Mrs Darwin herself arrived up stairs, and represented how ungrateful he was, not doing all in his power to please her, when she had taken so much pains to make him happy. This brought the little rebel round in a moment, as he became quite sensible of his own misconduct, and resolved immediately to submit. Accordingly, Harry tried to open the door, but what is very easily done cannot sometimes be undone, which turned out the case on this occasion, as, with all his exertions, the key would not turn in the lock! Harry tried it first one way, then another. He twisted with his whole strength, till his face became perfectly scarlet with the effort, but in vain! At last he put the poker through the handle of the key, thinking this a very clever plan, and quite sure to succeed, but after a desperate struggle, the unfortunate key broke in two; so then nobody could possibly open the door!

After this provoking accident happened, Harry

felt what a very bad boy he had been, so he burst into tears, and called through the key-hole to beg Mrs Darwin's pardon, while Mrs Crabtree scolded him through the key-hole in return, till Harry shrunk away as if a cannonading had begun at his ear.

Meantime, Mrs Darwin hurried off, racking her brains to think what had best be done to deliver the prisoner, since no time could be lost, or she might perhaps not get to town at all that night, and the car was expected every minute to come round for the travellers. The gardener said he thought it might be possible to find a few ladders, which, being tied one above another, would perhaps reach as high as the window, where Harry had now appeared, and by which he could easily scramble down; so the servants made haste to fetch all they could find, and to borrow all they could see, till a great many were collected. These they joined together very strongly with ropes, but when it was at last reared against the wall, to the great disappointment of Mrs Darwin, the ladder appeared a yard and a half too short!

What was to be done?

The obliging gardener mounted to the very top of his ladder, and Harry leaned so far over the window, he seemed in danger of falling out, but still they did not reach one another, so not a single person could guess what plan would be tried next. At length Harry called out very loudly to the gardener,

"Hollo! Mr King of Spades! if I were to let myself drop very gently down from the window, could you catch me in your arms?"

"Master Harry! Master Harry! if you dare!" cried Mrs Crabtree, shaking her fist at him. "You'll be broken in pieces like a tea-pot; you'll be made as flat as a pan-cake! Stay where you are! Do ye hear?"

But Harry seemed suddenly grown deaf, and was now more than half out—fixing his fingers very firmly on the ledge of the window, and slowly dropping his legs downwards.

"Oh, Harry! you will be killed!" screamed Laura. "Stop! stop! Harry, are you mad? can nobody stop him?"

But nobody could stop him; for, being so high above everybody's head, Harry had it all his own way, and was now hanging altogether out of the window, but he stopped a single minute, and called out, "Do not be frightened, Laura! I have behaved very ill, and deserve the worst that can happen. If I do break my head it will save Mrs Crabtree the trouble of breaking it for me, after I come down."

The gardener now balanced himself steadily on

the upper step of the ladder, and spread his arms out, while Harry slowly let himself drop. Laura tried to look on without screaming out, as that might have startled him, but the scene became too frightful, so she closed her eyes, put her hands over her face, and turned away, while her heart beat so violently, that it might almost have been heard. Even Mrs Crabtree clasped her hands in an agony of alarm, while Mrs Darwin put up her pocket-handkerchief, and could not look on another moment. An awful pause took place, during which a feather falling on the ground would have startled them, when suddenly a loud shout from Peter Grey and the other children, which was gaily echoed from the top of the ladder, made Laura venture to look up, and there was Harry safe in the gardener's arms, who soon helped him down to the ground, where he immediately asked pardon of everybody for the fright he had given them.

There was no time for more than half a scold from Mrs Crabtree, as Mrs Darwin's car had been waiting some time; so Harry said she might be owing him the rest, on some future occasion.

"Yes! and a hundred lashes besides!" added Peter Grey, laughing. "Pray touch him up well, Mrs Crabtree, when you are about it. There is no law against cruelty to boys!"

This put Mrs Crabtree into such a rage, that she

followed Peter with a perfect hail-storm of angry words, till at last, for a joke, he put up Mrs Darwin's umbrella to screen himself, and immediately afterwards the car drove slowly off.

When uncle David heard all the adventures at Ivy Lodge, he listened most attentively to " the confessions of Master Harry Graham," and shook his head in a most serious manner after they were concluded, saying, " I have always thought that boys are like cats, with nine lives at least! You should be hung up in a basket, Harry, as they do with unruly boys in the South Sea Islands, where such young gentlemen as you are left dangling in the air for days together, without a possibility of escape!"

" I would not care for that, compared with being teased and worried by Mrs Crabtree. I really wish, uncle David, that Dr Bell would order me never to be scolded any more! It is very bad for me! I generally feel an odd sort of over-all-ish-ness as soon as she begins; and I am getting too big now for anything but a birch-rod like Frank. How pleasant it is to be a grown-up man, uncle David, as you are, sitting all day at the club with your hat on your head, and nothing to do but look out of the window. That is what I call happiness!"

" But once upon a time, Harry," said Lady Harriet, "when I stopped in the carriage for your uncle

David at the club, he was in the middle of such a yawn at the window that he very nearly dislocated his jaw! It was quite alarming to see him, and he told me in a great secret, that the longest and most tiresome hours of his life are, when he has nothing particular to do."

"Now, at this moment, I have nothing particular to do," said Major Graham, "therefore I shall tell you a wonderful story, children, about liking to be idle or busy, and you must find out the moral for yourselves."

"A story! a story!" cried Harry and Laura, in an ecstacy of delight; and as they each had a knee of uncle David's, which belonged to themselves, they scrambled into their places, exclaiming, "Now let it be all about very bad boys, and giants, and fairies!"

CHAPTER IX.

UNCLE DAVID'S NONSENSICAL STORY ABOUT GIANTS AND FAIRIES.

"Pie-crust, and pastry-crust, that was the wall;
The windows were made of black-puddings and white,
And slated with pancakes—you ne'er saw the like!"

In the days of yore, children were not all such clever, good, sensible people as they are now! Lessons were then considered rather a plague—sugar-plums were still in demand—holidays continued yet in fashion—and toys were not then made to teach mathematics, nor story-books to give instruction in chemistry and navigation. These were very strange times, and there existed at that period, a very idle, greedy, naughty boy, such as we never hear of in the present day. His papa and mama were—no matter who,—and he lived, no matter where. His name was Master No-book, and he seemed to think his eyes were made for nothing but to stare out of the windows, and his mouth for no other purpose but to eat. This young gentleman hated lessons liked mustard, both of which brought tears into his eyes, and during school-hours he sat gazing at his books, pretending to be busy, while his mind wandered away to wish impatiently for dinner, and to consider where he could get the nicest pies, pastry, ices, and jellies, while he smacked his lips at the very thoughts of them. I think he must have been first cousin to Peter Grey; but that is not perfectly certain.

Whenever Master No-book spoke, it was always to ask for something, and you might continually hear him say, in a whining tone of voice, "Papa! may I take this piece of cake? Aunt Sarah! will you give me an apple? Mama! do send me the whole of that plum-pudding!" Indeed, very frequently, when he did not get permission to gormandize, this naughty glutton helped himself without leave. Even his dreams were like his waking hours, for he had often a horrible night-mare about lessons, thinking he was smothered with Greek Lexicons, or pelted out of the school with a shower of English Grammars; while one night he fancied himself sitting down to devour an enormous plum-cake, and all on a sudden it became transformed into a Latin Dictionary!

One afternoon, Master No-book, having played truant all day from school, was lolling on his mama's best sofa in the drawing-room, with his leather boots tucked up on the satin cushions, and nothing to do but to suck a few oranges, and nothing to think of but how much sugar to put upon them, when suddenly an event took place, which filled him with astonishment.

A sound of soft music stole into the room, becoming louder and louder the longer he listened, till at length, in a few moments afterwards, a large hole burst open in the wall of his room, and there stepped into his presence two magnificent fairies, just arrived from their castles in the air, to pay him a visit. They had travelled all the way on purpose to have some conversation with Master No-book, and immediately introduced themselves in a very ceremonious manner.

The fairy Do-nothing was gorgeously dressed with a wreath of flaming gas round her head, a robe of gold tissue, a necklace of rubies, and a bouquet in her hand of glittering diamonds. Her cheeks were rouged to the very eyes,—her teeth were set in gold, and her hair was of a most brilliant purple; in short, so fine and fashionable-looking a fairy never was seen in a drawing-room before.

The fairy Teach-all, who followed next, was

simply dressed in white muslin, with bunches of natural flowers in her light brown hair, and she carried in her hand a few neat small books, which Master No-book looked at with a shudder of aversion.

The two fairies now informed him, that they very often invited large parties of children to spend some time at their palaces, but as they lived in quite an opposite direction, it was necessary for their young guests to choose which it would be best to visit first; therefore now they had come to inquire of Master No-book, whom he thought it would be most agreeable to accompany on the present occasion.

"In my house," said the fairy Teach-all, speaking with a very sweet smile, and a soft, pleasing voice, "you shall be taught to find pleasure in every sort of exertion; for I delight in activity and diligence. My young friends rise at seven every morning, and amuse themselves with working in a beautiful garden of flowers,—rearing whatever fruit they wish to eat,—visiting among the poor, —associating pleasantly together,—studying the arts and sciences,—and learning to know the world in which they live, and to fulfil the purposes for which they have been brought into it. In short, all our amusements tend to some useful object, either for our own improvement or the good of others, and you will grow wiser, better, and happier every day you remain in the palace of Knowledge."

"But in Castle Needless, where I live," interrupted the fairy Do-nothing, rudely pushing her companion aside, with an angry, contemptuous look, "we never think of exerting ourselves for anything. You may put your head in your pocket, and your hands in your sides as long as you choose to stay. No one is ever even asked a question, that he may be spared the trouble of answering. We lead the most fashionable life imaginable, for nobody speaks to anybody! Each of my visitors is quite an exclusive, and sits with his back to as many of the company as possible, in the most comfortable arm-chair that can be contrived. There, if you are only so good as to take the trouble of wishing for anything, it is yours, without even turning an eye round to look where it comes from. Dresses are provided of the most magnificent kind, which go on themselves, without your having the smallest annoyance with either buttons or strings,—games which you can play without an effort of thought,—and dishes dressed by a French cook, smoking hot under your nose, from morning till night,—while any rain we have, is either made of sherry, brandy lemonade, or lavender water, and in winter it generally snows iced-punch for an hour during the **forenoon.**"

Nobody need be told which fairy Master No-book preferred; and quite charmed at his own good fortune in receiving so agreeable an invitation, he eagerly gave his hand to the splendid new acquaintance who promised him so much pleasure and ease, and gladly proceeded in a carriage lined with velvet, stuffed with downy pillows, and drawn by milk-white swans, to that magnificent residence, Castle Needless, which was lighted by a thousand windows during the day, and by a million of lamps every night.

Here Master No-book enjoyed a constant holiday and a constant feast, while a beautiful lady covered with jewels was ready to tell him stories from morning till night, and servants waited to pick up his playthings if they fell, or to draw out his purse or his pocket-handkerchief when he wished to use them.

Thus Master No-book lay dozing for hours and days on rich embroidered cushions, never stirring from his place, but admiring the view of trees covered with the richest burned almonds, grottoes of sugar-candy, a jet d'eau of champagne, a wide sea which tasted of sugar instead of salt, and a bright clear pond, filled with gold fish, that let themselves be caught whenever he pleased. Nothing could be more complete; and yet, very strange to say, Master No-book did not seem particularly happy! This appears exceedingly unreasonable, when so much trouble was taken to please him but the truth is, that every day he became more fretful and peevish. No sweetmeats were worth the trouble of eating, nothing was pleasant to play at, and in the end he wished it were possible to sleep all day, as well as all night.

Not a hundred miles from the fairy Do-nothing's palace, there lived a most cruel monster called the giant Snap-'em-up, who looked, when he stood up, like the tall steeple of a great church, raising his head so high that he could peep over the loftiest mountains, and was obliged to climb up a ladder to comb his own hair!

Every morning regularly, this prodigiously-great giant walked round the world before breakfast for an appetite, after which he made tea in a large lake, used the sea as a slop-basin, and boiled his kettle on Mount Vesuvius. He lived in great style, and his dinners were most magnificent, consisting very often of an elephant roasted whole, ostrich patties, a tiger smothered in onions, stewed lions, and whale soup; but for a side dish his greatest favourite consisted of little boys, as fat as possible, fried in crumbs of bread, with plenty of pepper and salt.

No children were so well fed, or in such good condition for eating as those in the fairy Do-nothing's garden, who was a very particular friend of the giant Snap-'em-up's, and who sometimes laughingly said she would give him a licence, and call her own garden his " preserve," because she allowed him to help himself, whenever he pleased, to as many of her visitors as he chose, without taking the trouble even to count them, and in return for such extreme civility, the giant very frequently invited her to dinner.

Snap-em-up's favourite sport was, to see how many brace of little boys he could bag in a morning; so in passing along the streets, he peeped into all the drawing-rooms without having occasion to get upon tiptoe, and picked up every young gentleman who was idly looking out of the windows, and even a few occasionally who were playing truant from school ; but busy children seemed always somehow quite out of his reach.

One day, when Master No-book felt even more lazy, more idle, and more miserable than ever, he lay beside a perfect mountain of toys and cakes, wondering what to wish for next, and hating the very sight of everything and everybody. At last he gave so loud a yawn of weariness and disgust, that his jaw very nearly fell out of joint, and then he sighed so deeply, that the giant Snap-'em-up heard the sound as he passed along the road after breakfast, and instantly stepped into the garden, with his glass at his eye, to see what was the matter. Immediately on observing a large, fat, over-grown boy, as round as a dumpling, lying on a bed of roses, he gave a cry of delight, followed by a gigantic peal of laughter, which was heard three miles off, and picking up Master No-book between his finger and thumb, with a pinch that very nearly broke his ribs, he carried him rapidly towards his own castle, while the fairy Do-nothing laughingly shook her head as he passed, saying "That little man does me great credit!—he has only been fed for a week, and is as fat already as a prize ox! What a dainty morsel he will be When do you dine to-day, in case I should have time to look in upon you?"

On reaching home the giant immediately hung up Master No-book by the hair of his head, on a prodigious hook in the larder, having first taken some large lumps of nasty suet, forcing them down his throat to make him become still fatter, and then stirring the fire, that he might be almost melted with heat, to make his liver grow larger. On a shelf quite near, Master No-book perceived the dead bodies of six other boys, whom he remembered to have seen fattening in the fairy Do-nothing's garden, while he recollected how some of them had rejoiced at the thoughts of leading a long, useless, idle life, with no one to please but themselves.

The enormous cook now seized hold of Master No-book, brandishing her knife, with an aspect of horrible determination, intending to kill him, while he took the trouble of screaming and kicking in the most desperate manner, when the giant turned gravely round and said, that as pigs were considered a much greater dainty when whipped to death than killed in any other way, he meant to see whether children might not be improved by it also; therefore she might leave that great hog of a boy till he had time to try the experiment, especially as his own appetite would be improved by the exercise. This was a dreadful prospect for the unhappy prisoner; but meantime it prolonged his life a few hours, as he was immediately hung up again in the larder, and left to himself. There, in torture of mind and body,—like a fish upon a hook,—the wretched boy began at last to reflect seriously upon his former ways, and to consider what a happy home he might have had, if he could only have been satisfied with business and pleasure succeeding each other, like day and night, while lessons might have come in as a pleasant sauce to his play-hours, and his play-hours as a sauce to his lessons.

In the midst of many reflections, which were all very sensible, though rather too late, Master No-book's attention became attracted by the sound of many voices laughing, talking, and singing, which caused him to turn his eyes in a new direction, when, for the first time, he observed that the fairy Teach-all's garden lay upon a beautiful sloping bank not far off. There a crowd of merry, noisy, rosy-cheeked boys were busily employed, and seemed happier than the day was long; while poor Master No-book watched them during his own miserable hours, envying the enjoyment with which they raked the flower-borders, gathered the fruit, carried baskets of vegetables to the poor, worked with carpenter's tools, drew pictures, shot with bows and arrows, played at cricket, and then sat in the sunny arbours learning their tasks, or talking agreeably together, till at length, a dinner-bell having been rung, the whole party sat merrily down with hearty appetites, and cheerful good humour, to an entertainment of plain roast meat and pudding, where the fairy Teach-all presided herself, and helped her guests moderately, to as much as was good for each.

Large tears rolled down the cheeks of Master

No-book while watching this scene; and remembering that if he had known what was best for him, he might have been as happy as the happiest of these excellent boys, instead of suffering ennui and weariness, as he had done at the fairy Do-nothing's, ending in a miserable death; but his attention was soon after most alarmingly roused by hearing the giant Snap-'em-up again in conversation with his cook; who said, that if he wished for a good large dish of scolloped children at dinner, it would be necessary to catch a few more, as those he had already provided would scarcely be a mouthful.

As the giant kept very fashionable hours, and always waited dinner for himself till nine o'clock, there was still plenty of time; so, with a loud grumble about the trouble, he seized a large basket in his hand, and set off at a rapid pace towards the fairy Teach-all's garden. It was very seldom that Snap-'em-up ventured to think of foraging in this direction, as he never once succeeded in carrying off a single captive from the enclosure, it was so well fortified and so bravely defended; but on this occasion, being desperately hungry, he felt as bold as a lion, and walked, with outstretched hands, straight towards the fairy Teach-all's dinner-table, taking such prodigious strides, that he seemed almost as if he would trample on himself

A cry of consternation arose the instant this tremendous giant appeared; and as usual on such occasions, when he had made the same attempt before, a dreadful battle took place. Fifty active little boys bravely flew upon the enemy, armed with their dinner knives, and looked like a nest of hornets, stinging him in every direction, till he roared with pain, and would have run away, but the fairy Teach-all, seeing his intention, rushed forward with the carving-knife, and brandishing it high over her head, she most courageously stabbed him to the heart!

If a great mountain had fallen to the earth, it would have seemed like nothing in comparison of the giant Snap-'em-up, who crushed two or three houses to powder beneath him, and upset several fine monuments that were to have made people remembered for ever; but all this would have seemed scarcely worth mentioning, had it not been for a still greater event which occurred on the occasion, no less than the death of the fairy Do-nothing, who had been indolently looking on at this great battle, without taking the trouble to interfere, or even to care who was victorious; but being also lazy about running away, when the giant fell, his sword came with so violent a stroke on her head, that she instantly expired.

Thus, luckily for the whole world, the fairy

Teach-all got possession of immense property, which she proceeded without delay to make the best use of in her power.

In the first place, however, she lost no time in liberating Master No-book from his hook in the larder, and gave him a lecture on activity, moderation, and good conduct, which he never afterwards forgot; and it was astonishing to see the change that took place immediately in his whole thoughts and actions. From this very hour, Master No-book became the most diligent, active, happy boy in the fairy Teach-all's garden; and on returning home a month afterwards, he astonished all the masters at school by his extraordinary reformation. The most difficult lessons were a pleasure to him,—he scarcely ever stirred without a book in his hand,—never lay on a sofa again,—would scarcely even sit on a chair with a back to it, but preferred a three-legged stool,—detested holidays, —never thought any exertion a trouble,—preferred climbing over the top of a hill to creeping round the bottom,—always ate the plainest food in very small quantities,—joined a Temperance Society!—and never tasted a morsel till he had worked very hard and got an appetite.

Not long after this, an old uncle, who had formerly been ashamed of Master No-book's indolence and gluttony, became so pleased at the won

derful change, that, on his death, he left him a
magnificent estate, desiring that he should take his
name; therefore, instead of being any longer one
of the No-book family, he is now called Sir Timothy Bluestocking,—a pattern to the whole country
round, for the good he does to every one, and especially for his extraordinary activity, appearing as
if he could do twenty things at once. Though generally very good-natured and agreeable, Sir Timothy
is occasionally observed in a violent passion, laying
about him with his walking-stick in the most ter-
rific manner and beating little boys within an inch
of their lives; but on inquiry, it invariably appears, that he has found them out to be lazy, idle,
or greedy, for all the industrious boys in the parish
are sent to get employment from him, while he
assures them that they are far happier breaking
stones on the road, than if they were sitting idly
in a drawing-room with nothing to do. Sir Timothy cares very little for poetry in general; but the
following are his favourite verses, which he has
placed over the chimney-piece at a school that he
built for the poor, and every scholar is obliged, the
very day he begins his education, to learn them

> Some people complain they have nothing to do,
> And time passes slowly away;
> They saunter about with no object in view,
> And long for the end of the day

In vain are the trifles and toys they desire,
  For nothing they truly enjoy;
Of trifles, and toys, and amusements they tire,
  For want of some useful employ.

Although for transgression the ground was accursed,
  Yet gratefully man must allow,
'Twas really a blessing which doom'd him, at first,
  To live by the sweat of his brow.

"Thank you a hundred times over uncle David!" said Harry, when the story was finished. "I shall take care not to be found hanging any day, on a hook in the larder! Certainly, Frank, you must have spent a month with the good fairy; and I hope she will some day invite me to be made a scholar of too, for Laura and I still belong to the No-book family"

"It is very important, Harry, to choose the best course from the beginning," observed Lady Harriet. "Good or bad habits grow stronger and stronger every minute, as if an additional string were tied on daily, to keep us in the road where we walked the day before; so those who mistake the path of duty at first, find hourly increasing difficulty in turning round."

"But Grandmama!" said Frank, "you have put up some finger-posts to direct us right; and whenever I see 'No passage this way,' we shall all wheel about directly."

"As Mrs Crabtree has not tapped at the door yet, I shall describe the progress of a wise and a foolish man, to see which Harry and you would prefer copying," replied Lady Harriet, smiling. "The fool begins when he is young, with hating lessons, lying long in bed, and spending all his money on trash. Any books he will consent to read, are never about what is true or important; but he wastes all his time and thoughts on silly stories that never could have happened. Thus he neglects to learn what was done and thought by all the great and good men who really lived in former times; while even his Bible, if he has one, grows dusty on the shelf. After so bad a beginning, he grows up with no useful or interesting knowledge; therefore his whole talk is to describe his own horses, his own dogs, his own guns, and his own exploits; boasting of what a high wall his horse can leap over, the number of little birds he can shoot in a day, and how many bottles of wine he can swallow without tumbling under the table. Thus 'glorying in his shame,' he thinks himself a most wonderful person, not knowing that men are born to do much better things than merely to find selfish pleasure and amusement for themselves. Presently he grows old, gouty, and infirm—no longer able to do such prodigious achievements; therefore now his great delight is, to sit with his feet upon the fender, at a club, all day, telling what a famous rider, shooter, and drinker he was long ago: but nobody cares to hear such old stories; therefore he is called a 'proser,' and every person avoids him. It is no wonder a man talks about himself, if he has never read or thought about any one else. But at length his precious time has all been wasted, and his last hour comes, during which he can have nothing to look back upon, but a life of folly and guilt. He sees no one around who loves him, or will weep over his grave; and when he looks forward, it is towards an eternal world, which he has never prepared to enter, and of which he knows nothing."

"What a terrible picture, grandmama!" said Frank, rather gravely. "I hope there are not many people like that, or it would be very sad to meet with them. Now pray let us have a pleasanter description of the sort of persons you would like Harry and me to become."

"The first foundation of all is, as you already know, Frank, to pray that you may be put in the right course, and kept in it; for of ourselves we are so sinful and weak, that we can do no good thing. Then feeling a full trust in the Divine assistance, you must begin and end every day with studying your Bible; not merely reading it, but carefully endeavouring to understand and obey what it contains. Our leisure should be bestowed on reading of wiser and better people than ourselves, which will keep us humble while it instructs our understandings, and thus we shall be fitted to associate with persons whose society is even better than books. Christians who are enlightened and sanctified in the knowledge of all good things, will show us an example of carefully using our time, which is the most valuable of all earthly possessions. If we waste our money, we may perhaps get more—if we lose our health, it may be restored—but time squandered on folly must hereafter be answered for, and can never be regained. Whatever be your station in life, waste none of your thoughts upon fancying how much better you might have acted in some other person's place, but see what duties belong to that station in which you live, and do what that requires with activity and diligence. When we are called to give an account of our stewardship, let us not have to confess at the last that we wasted our one talent, because we wished to have been trusted with ten; but let us prepare to render up what was given to us with joy and thankfulness, perfectly satisfied that the best place in life is where God appoints, and where He will guide us to a safe and peaceful end."

"Yes!" added Major Graham. "We have two eyes in our minds as well as in our bodies. With one of these we see all that is good or agreeable in our lot—with the other we see all that is unpleasant or disappointing; and you may generally choose which eye to keep open. Some of my friends always peevishly look at the troubles and vexations they endure, but they might turn them into good, by considering that every circumstance is sent from the same hand, with the same merciful purpose—to make us better now, and happier hereafter."

"Well! my dear children," said Lady Harriet, "it is time now for retiring to Bedfordshire; so good night."

"If you please, grandmama! not yet," asked Harry, anxiously. "Give us five minutes longer!"

"And then in the morning you will want to remain five minutes more in bed. That is the way people learn to keep such dreadfully late hours at last, Harry! I knew one very rich old gentleman formerly, who always wished to sit up a little later every night, and to get up a little later in the morning, till at length, he ended by hiring a set of servants to rise at nine in the evening, as he did himself, and to remain in bed all day"

"People should regulate their sleep very conscientiously," added Major Graham, " so as to waste as little time as possible; and our good king George III. set us the example, for he remarked, that six hours in the night were quite enough for a man, seven hours for a woman, and eight for a fool. Or perhaps, Harry, you might like to live by Sir William Jones' rule :

' Six hours to read, to soothing slumber seven,
 Ten to the world allot—and all to Heaven ' '

CHAPTER X.

THE ILLUMINATION.

*A neighbour's house he'd slyly pass,
And throw a stone to break the glass.*

ONE fine morning, Peter Grey persuaded a party of his companions to spend all the money that they had on cakes and sugar-plums, and to make a splendid entertainment under the trees in Charlotte Square, where they were to sit like a horde of gipsies, and amuse themselves with telling fortunes to each other. Harry and Laura had no one with them but Betty, who gladly joined a group of nursery-maids at a distance, leaving them to their own devices; upon which they rushed up to Peter and offered their assistance, subscribing all their pocket-money, and begging him to set forth and obtain provisions for them as well as for himself. Neither Harry nor Laura cared for eating the trash that was collected on this occasion, and would have been quite as well pleased to distribute it among their companions but they both enjoyed extremely the bustle of arranging this elegant déjeuné, or "*disjune*," as Peter called it. Harry gathered leaves off the trees to represent plates, on each of which Peter arranged some of the fruit or sweetmeats he had purchased, while they placed benches together as a table, and borrowed Laura's white India shawl for a table-cloth.

"It looks like that grand public dinner we saw at the Assembly Room. one day!" exclaimed Harry, in an ecstacy of admiration. " We must have speeches and toasts like real gentlemen and officers. Peter! if you will make a fine oration, full of compliments to me, I shall say something wonderful about you, and then Laura must beat upon the table with a stick, to show that she agrees to all that we observe in praise of each other."

"Or suppose we all take the names of some great personages," added Peter; " I shall be the Duke of Wellington, and Laura, you must be Joseph Hume, and Harry, you are Sir Robert Peel, that we may seem as different as possible; but here comes the usher of the black rod to disperse us all! Mrs Crabtree hurrying into the square, her very gown flaming with rage! what can be the matter! she must have smelled the sugar-plums a mile off! One comfort is, if Harry and Laura are taken away, we shall have the fewer people to divide these cakes among, and I could devour every one of them for my own share."

Before Peter finished speaking, Mrs Crabtree had come close up to the table, and without waiting to utter a word, or even to scold, she twitched up Laura's shawl in her hand, and thus scattered the whole feast in every direction on the ground, after which she trampled the sugar-plums and cakes into the earth, saying,

"I knew how it would be, as soon as I saw whose company you were in, Master Harry! Peter Grey is the father of mischief! he ought to be put into the monkey's cage at the Geological gardens! I would not be your maid, Master Grey, for a hundred a-year."

"You would need to buy a thrashing machine immediately," said Peter, laughing; "what a fine time I should have of it! you would scarcely allow me, I suppose, to blow my porridge! How long would it take you, Mrs Crabtree, to make quite a perfectly good boy of me? Perhaps a month, do you think? or, to make me as good as Frank, it might possibly require six weeks?"

"Six weeks!" answered Mrs Crabtree; "six years, or sixty would be too short. You are no more like Master Frank than a shilling is to a guinea, or a wax light is to a dip. If the news were told that you had been a good boy for a single day, the very *statutes* in the streets would come running along to see the wonder. No! no! I have seen many surprising things in my day, but them great pyramuses in Egypt will turn upside down before you turn like Master Frank."

Some days after this adventure of Harry and Laura's, there arrived newspapers from London containing accounts of a great battle which had been fought abroad. On that occasion the British troops of course performed prodigies of valour, and completely conquered the enemy, in consequence of which, it was ordered by government, that, in every town, and every village, and every house throughout the whole kingdom, there should be a grand illumination.

Neither Harry nor Laura had ever heard of such a thing as an illumination before, and they were full of curiosity to know what it was like; but their very faces became lighted up with joy, when Major Graham described that they would see crowds of candles flaming in every window, tar-barrels blazing on every hill, flambeaux glaring at the doors, and transparencies, fireworks, and coloured lamps, shining in all the streets.

"How delightful! and walking out in the dark to see it," cried Harry, " that will be best of all! oh! and a whole holiday! I hardly know whether

I am in my right wits, or my wrong wits for joy! I wish we gained a victory every day!"

"What a warrior you would be, Harry! Cæsar was nothing to you," said Frank. "We might be satisfied with one good battle in a year, considering how many are killed and wounded."

"Yes, but I hope all the wounded soldiers will recover."

"Or get pensions," added uncle David. "It is a grand sight, Frank, to see a whole nation rejoicing at once! In general, when you walk out and meet fifty persons in the street, they are all thinking of fifty different things, and each intent on some business of his own, but on this occasion all are of one mind and one heart."

Frank and Harry were allowed to nail a dozen little candlesticks upon each window in the house, which delighted them exceedingly; and then before every pane of glass they placed a tall candle, impatiently longing for the time when these were to be illuminated. Laura was allowed to carry a match, and assist in lighting them, but in the excess of her joy, she very nearly made a bonfire of herself, as her frock took fire, and would soon have been in a blaze, if Frank had not hastily seized a large rug and rolled it round her.

In every house within sight, servants and children were to be seen hurrying about with burning matches, while hundreds of lights blazed up in a moment, looking as if all the houses in town had taken fire.

"Such a waste of candles!" said Mrs Crabtree, angrily; "can't people be happy in the dark?"

"No, Mrs Crabtree," answered Frank, laughing. "They cannot be happy in the dark! People's spirits are always in exact proportion to the number of lights. If you ever feel dull with one candle, light another; and if that does not do, try a third, or a fourth, till you feel merry and cheerful. We must not let you be candle-snuffer to-night, or you will be putting them all out. You would snuff out the sun itself, to save a shilling."

"The windows might perhaps be broken," added Laura; "for whatever pane of glass does not exhibit a candle, is to have a stone sent through it. Harry says the mob are all glaziers, who break them on purpose to mend the damage next day, which they will be paid handsomely for doing."

There were many happy, joyous faces to be seen that evening in the streets, admiring the splendid illumination; but the merriest party of all was composed of Frank, Harry, and Laura, under the command of uncle David, who had lately suffered from a severe fit of the gout; but it seemed to have left him this night, in honour of the great victory, when he appeared quite as much a boy as either of his two companions. For many hours they walked about in the streets, gazing up at the glittering windows, some of which looked as if a constellation of stars had come down for a night to adorn them; and others were filled with the most beautiful pictures of Britannia carrying the world on her shoulders; or Mars showering down wreaths of laurel on the Duke of Wellington, while victory was sitting at his feet, and fame blowing a trumpet at his ear. Harry thought these paintings finer than any he had ever seen before, and stood for some moments entranced with admiration, on beholding a representation in red, blue, yellow, and black, of Europe, Asia, Africa, and America, all doing homage to St George mounted on a dragon, which breathed out fire and smoke like a steam-boat. Nothing, however, occasioned the party such a burst of delightful surprise, as when they first beheld the line of blazing windows more than a mile long, from the bottom of the Canongate to the highest pinnacle of the Castle, where they seemed almost to meet the stars shining above, in their perpetual glory. "You see," remarked Major Graham, when he pointed them out to his young companions, "there is a fit emblem of the difference between earth and heaven. These lights are nearer and brighter to us at present, but when they have blazed and glittered for one little hour, they come to an end; while those above, which we see so dimly now, will continue to shine for ages and generations hereafter, till time itself is no more."

Occasionally, during their progress, Harry felt very indignant to observe a few houses perfectly dark; and whether the family were sick, or out of town, or whatever the reason might be, he scarcely became sorry when a frequent crash might be heard, as the mob, determined to have their own way this night, aimed showers of stones at the offending windows, till the very frames seemed in danger of being broken. At last uncle David led his joyous little party into Castle Street, in which not a light was to be seen, and every blind seemed carefully closed. A crowd had assembled, with an evident intention to attack these melancholy houses, when Major Graham suddenly caught hold of Harry's arm, on observing that he had privately picked up a large stone, which he was in the very act of throwing with his whole force at one of the defenceless windows. And now the whole party stood stock-still, while uncle David said in a very angry and serious voice,

"Harry! you heedless, mischievous boy! will you never learn to consider a moment before you do what is wrong? I am exceedingly displeased with you for this! What business is it of yours whether that house be lighted up or not?"

"But, uncle David! surely it is very wrong not to obey the government, and to be happy like everybody else! Besides, you see the mob will break those windows at any rate, so it is no matter if I help them."

"Then, for the same reason, if they were setting the house on fire, I suppose you would assist the conflagration, Harry. Your excuse is a bad one; when you hear what I have to say about this house let it be a lesson for the rest of your life, never to judge hastily, nor to act rashly. The officer to whom it belonged has been killed in the great battle abroad; and while we are rejoicing in the victory that his bravery helped to gain, his widow and children are weeping within those walls, for the husband and father who lies buried on a foreign shore. Think what a contrast these shouts of joy must be to their grief."

"Oh, uncle David! how sorry I am!" said Harry. "I deserve to go home this moment, and not to see a candle again for a week. It was very wrong of me indeed. I shall walk all the way home with my eyes shut, if you will only excuse me."

"No, no, Harry! that is not necessary! If the eyes of your mind are open, to see that you have acted amiss, then try to behave better in future. When people are happy themselves, they are too apt to forget that others may be in distress, and often feel quite surprised and provoked at those who appear melancholy; but our turn must come like theirs. Life is made up of sunshine and shadow, both of which are sent for our good, and neither of them last, in this world, for ever; but we should borrow part of our joys, and part of our sorrows, from sympathy with all those we see or know, which will moderate the excess of whatever is our portion in life."

At this moment, the mob, which had been gradually increasing, gave a tremendous shout, and were on the point of throwing a torrent of stones at the dark, mournful house, which had made so narrow an escape from Harry's vengeance, when Major Graham, forgetting his gout, hastily sprung upon a lamp-post, and calling for attention, he made a speech to the crowd, telling of the brave Captain D—— who had died for his country, covered with wounds, and that his mourning family was assembled in that house. Instantly the mob became as silent and motionless as if they had themselves been turned into stones; after which, they gradually stole away, with downcast eyes, and mournful countenances; while it is believed that some riotous people, who had been loudest and fiercest at first, afterwards stood at the top of the little street like sentinels, for more than an hour, to warn every one who passed, that he should go silently along, in respect for the memory of a brave and good officer. Not another shout was heard in the neighbourhood that night; and many a merry laugh was suddenly checked, from reverence for the memory of the dead, and the sorrow of the living; while some spectators remarked, with a sigh of melancholy reflection, that men must ever join trembling with their mirth, because even in the midst of life they are in death.

"If we feel so much sorrow for this one officer and his family, it shews," said Frank, "what a dreadful thing war is, which costs the lives of thousands and tens of thousands, in every campaign, by sickness and fatigue, and the other sources of misery that accompany every army."

"Yes, Frank! and yet there has scarcely been a year on earth, while the world has existed, without fighting in some country or another; for, since the time when Cain killed Abel, men have been continually destroying each other. Animals only fight in temporary irritation when they are hungry; but pride, ambition, and folly of every kind have caused men to hate and massacre each other. Even religion itself has caused the fiercest and most bloody conflicts, though, if that were only understood and obeyed as it ought to be, the great truths of Scripture would produce peace on earth, and good will among all the children of men."

The whole party had been standing for some minutes opposite to the Post-Office, which looked like a rainbow of coloured lamps, and Harry was beginning, for the twentieth time, to try if he could count how many there were, when Major Graham felt something twitching hold of his coat-pocket behind, and on wheeling suddenly round, he perceived a little boy, not much older than Harry, darting rapidly off in another direction, carrying his own purse and pocket-handkerchief in his hand. Being still rather lame, and unable to move very fast, Major Graham could only vociferate at the very top of his voice, "Stop thief! stop thief!" but not a constable appeared in sight, so the case seemed desperate, and the money lost for ever, when Frank observed also what had occurred, and being of an active spirit, he flew after the young thief, followed closely by Harry. An eager race ensued, up one street, and down another, with marvellous rapidity, while Frank was so evidently gaining ground, that the thief at last became terrified, and threw away the purse, hoping thus to end the chase; but neither of his pursuers paused a moment to pick it up, they were so intent upon capturing the little culprit himself At length Frank sprang forward and caught him by the collar, when a fierce conflict ensued, during which the young thief was so ingenious, that he nearly slipped his arms out of his coat, and would have made his escape, leaving a tattered garment in their hands, if Harry had not observed this trick, and held him by the hair, which, as it was not a wig, he could not so easily throw off.

At this moment a large, coarse, ruffianly-looking man hurried up to the party, evidently intending to rescue the little pickpocket from their custody; so Frank called loudly for help, while several police officers who had been sent by Major Graham, came racing along the street, springing their rattles, and vociferating "Stop thief!"

Now the boy struggled more violently than ever to disentangle himself, but Frank and Harry grasped hold of their prisoner, as if they had been a couple of Bow Street officers, till at length the tall, fierce man thought it time to be off, though not before he had given Harry a blow on the face, that caused him to reel back and fall prostrate on the pavement.

"There's a brave little gentleman!" said one of the constables, helping him up, while another secured the thief. "You ought to be knighted for fighting so well! This boy you have taken is a sad fellow! He broke his poor mother's heart a year since by his wicked ways, and I have long wished to catch him. A few weeks on the treadmill now, may save him from the gallows in future."

"He seems well practised in his business," observed Major Graham. "I almost deserved, however, to lose my pocket-book for bringing it out in a night of so much crowding and confusion. Some lucky person will be all the richer, though I fear it is totally lost to me."

"But here is your pocket-handkerchief, uncle David, if you mean to shed any tears for your misfortune," whispered Laura; "how very lucky that you felt it going!"

"Yes! and very surprising too, for the trick was so cleverly executed. That little rascal might steal the teeth out of one's head, without being noticed! When I was in India, the thieves there were so expert that they really could draw the sheets from under a person sleeping in bed, without disturbing his slumbers."

"With me, any person could do that, because I sleep so very soundly," observed Frank. "You might beat a military drum at my ear, as they do in the boys' sleeping-rooms at Sandhurst, and it would not have the smallest effect. I scarcely think that even a gong would do!"

"How very different from me," replied Laura. "Last night I was awakened by the scratching of a mouse nibbling in the wainscot, and soon after it ran across my face."

"Then pray sleep to-night with your mouth open, and a piece of toasted cheese in it to catch the mouse," said Major Graham. "That is the best trap I know!"

"Uncle David," asked Frank, as they proceeded along the street, "if there is any hope of that wicked boy being reformed, will you try to have him taught better? Being so very young he must have learned from older people to steal!"

"Certainly he must! It is melancholy to know how carefully mere children are trained to commit the very worst crimes, and how little the mind of any young boy can be a match for the cunning of old, experienced villains like those who lead him astray. When once a child falls into the snare of such practised offenders, escape becomes as impossible as that of a bird from a lime-twig."

"So I believe," replied Frank. "Grandmama told me that the very youngest children of poor people, when first sent to school in London, are often waylaid by those old women who sell apples in the street, and who pretend to be so good-natured that they make them presents of fruit. Of course they are very acceptable, but after some time, those wicked wretches propose that the child in return should bring them a book, or anything he can pick up at home, which shall be paid for in apples and pears. Few little boys have sufficient firmness not to comply, whether they like it or not, and after that the case is almost hopeless; because whenever the poor victim hesitates to steal more, those cruel women threaten to inform the parents of his misconduct, which terrifies the boy into doing anything rather than be found out."

"Oh, how dreadful!" exclaimed Laura. "It all begins so smoothly! No poor little boy could suspect any danger, and then he becomes a hardened thief at once!"

"Grandmama says, too, that pickpockets in London used to have the stuffed figure of a man hung from the roof of their rooms, and covered all over with bells, for the boys to practise upon, and no one was allowed to attempt stealing on the streets, till he could pick the pocket of this dangling effigy, without ringing one of the many bells with which it was ornamented."

"I think," said Harry, "when the young thieves saw that figure hanging in the air, it might have reminded them how soon they would share the same fate. Even crows take warning when they see a brother crow hanging dead in a field."

"It is a curious thing of crows, Harry, that they certainly punish thieves among themselves," observed Major Graham. "In a large rookery, some outcasts are frequently to be observed living apart from the rest, and not allowed to associate with their more respectable brethren. I remember hearing formerly that in the great rookery at Ashgrove, when all the other birds were absent, one solitary crow was observed to linger behind, stealing materials for his nest from those around; but next morning a prodigious uproar was heard among the trees,—the cawing became so vociferous, that evidently several great orators were agitating the crowd, till suddenly the enraged crows flew in a body upon the nest of their dishonest associate, and tore it in pieces."

'Bravo!" cried Frank. "I do like to hear about all the odd ways of birds and animals! Grandmama mentioned lately, that if you catch a crow and fasten him down with his back to the ground, he makes such an outcry, that all his black brothers come wheeling about the place, till one of them at last alights to help. Immediately the treacherous prisoner grapples hold of his obliging friend, and never afterwards lets him escape; so by fastening down one after another, we might entrap the whole rookery."

"I shall try it some day!" exclaimed Harry eagerly. "What fun to hear them a croaking and cawing!"

"We shall be croaking ourselves soon with

colds, if we do not hurry home," added uncle David. "There is not a thimbleful of light remaining, and your grandmama will be impatient to hear all the news. This has really been a most adventurous night, and I am sure none of us will soon forget it."

When the whole party entered the drawing-room, in a blaze of spirits, all speaking at once, to tell Lady Harriet what had occurred, Mrs Crabtree, who was waiting to take a couple of little prisoners off to bed, suddenly gave an exclamation of astonishment and dismay as she looked at Harry, who now, for the first time since the robber knocked him down, approached the light, when he did, to be sure, appear a most terrible spectacle! His jacket was bespattered with mud, his shirt frill torn and bloody, one eye almost swollen out of his head, and the side of his face quite black and blue.

"What mischief have you been in now, Master Harry?" cried Mrs Crabtree, angrily; "you will not leave a whole bone in your body, nor a whole shirt in your drawer!"

"These are honourable scars, Mrs Crabtree," interrupted Major Graham. "Harry has been fighting my battles, and gained a great victory! we must illuminate the nursery!"

Uncle David then told the whole story, with many droll remarks about his purse having been stolen, and said that, as Harry never complained of being hurt, he never supposed that anything of the kind could have occurred; but he felt very much pleased to observe how well a certain young gentleman was able to bear pain, as boys must expect hard blows in the world, when they had to fight their way through life, therefore it was well for them to give as few as they could, and to bear with fortitude what fell to their own share. Uncle David slyly added, that perhaps Harry put up with these things all the better for having so much practice in the nursery.

Mrs Crabtree seemed rather proud of Harry's manly spirit, and treated him with a little more respect than usual, saying, she would fetch him some hot water to foment his face, if he would go straight up stairs with Laura. Now it very seldom happened, that Harry went straight anywhere, for he generally swung down the bannisters again, or took a leap over any thing he saw on the way, or got on some of the tables and jumped off, but this night he had resolutely intended marching steadily to bed, and advanced a considerable way, when a loud shout in the street attracted his attention. Harry stopped, and it was repeated again, so seizing Laura by the hand, they flew eagerly into Lady Harriet's dressing-room, and throwing open a window, they picked up a couple of cloaks that were lying on a chair, and both stepped out on a balcony to find out what was going on; and in case any one should see them in this unusual place, Harry quietly shut down the window, intending to remain only one single minute. Minutes run very fast away when people are amused, and nothing could be more diverting than the sight they now beheld, for at this momenta grand crash exploded of squibs and rockets from the Castlehill, which looked so beautiful in the dark, that it seemed impossible to think of anything else. Some flew high in the air, and then burst into the appearance of twenty fiery serpents falling from the sky, others assumed a variety of colours, and dropped like flying meteors, looking as if the stars were all learning to dance, while many rushed into the air and disappeared, leaving not a trace behind. Harry and Laura stood perfectly entranced with admiration and delight, till the fireworks neither burst, cracked, nor exploded any more.

A ballad-singer next attracted their notice, singing the tune of "Meet me by moonlight," and afterwards Laura shewed Harry the constellation of Orion mentioned in the Bible, which, besides the Great Bear, was the only one she had the slightest acquaintance with. Neither of them had ever observed the Northern Lights so brilliant before, and now they felt almost alarmed to see them shooting like lances across the sky, and glittering with many bright colours, like a rainbow, while Laura remembered her grandmama mentioning some days ago, that the poor natives of Greenland believe these are the spirits of their fathers going forth to battle.

Meantime, Lady Harriet called Frank, as usual, to his evening prayers and reading in her dressing-room, where it was well known that they were on no account to be disturbed. After having read a chapter, and talked very seriously about all it was intended to teach, they had begun to discuss the prospect of Frank going abroad very soon to become a midshipman, and he was wondering much where his first great shipwreck would take place, and telling Lady Harriet about the loss of the Cabalvala, where the crew lived for eight days on a barren rock, with nothing to eat, but a cask of raspberry jam, which accidentally floated within their reach. Before Frank had finished his story, however, he suddenly paused, and sprang upon his feet with an exclamation of astonishment, while Lady Harriet, looking hastily round in the same direction, became terrified to observe a couple of faces looking in at the window. It was so dark, she could not see what they were like, but a moment afterwards, the sash began slowly and heavily opening, after which two figures leaped into the room, while Frank flew to ring a peal at the bell, and

Lady Harriet sank into her own arm-chair, covering her face with her hands, and nearly fainting with fright.

"Never mind, grandmama! do not be afraid! it is only us!" cried Harry; "surely you know me!"

"You!!!" exclaimed Lady Harriet, looking up with amazement. "Harry and Laura!! impossible! how in all the world did you get here! I thought you were both in bed half an hour ago! Tiresome boy! you will be the death of me some time or other! I wonder when you will ever pass a day without deserving the bastinado!"

"Do you not remember the good day last month, grandmama, when I had a severe toothache, and sat all morning beside the fire? Nobody found fault with me then, and I got safe to bed, without a single 'Oh fie!' from noon till night."

"Wonderful, indeed! what a pity I ever allowed that tooth to be drawn; but you behaved very bravely on the occasion of its being extracted. Now take yourselves off! I feel perfectly certain you will tell Mrs Crabtree the exact truth about where you have been, and if she punishes you, remember that it is no more than you deserve. People wh. behave ill are their own punishers, and should be glad that some one will kindly take the trouble to teach them better."

CHAPTER XI.

THE POOR BOY.

> Not all the fine things that fine people possess,
>   Should teach them the poor to despise;
> For 'tis in good manners, and not in good dress,
>   That the truest gentility lies.

THE following Saturday morning, Frank, Harry, and Laura were assembled before Lady Harriet's breakfast hour, talking over all their adventures on the night of the illumination; and many a merry laugh was heard while uncle David cracked his jokes and told his stories, for he seemed as full of fun and spirits as the youngest boy in a playground.

"Well, old fellow!" said he, lifting up Harry, and suddenly seating him on the high marble chimney-piece. "That is the situation where the poor little dwarf, Baron Borowloski, was always put by his tall wife, when she wished to keep him out of mischief, and I wonder Mrs Crabtree never thought of the same plan for you."

"Luckily there is no fire, or Harry would soon be roasted for the Giant Snap-'em-up's dinner," said Frank, laughing; "he looks up there like a Chinese mandarin. Shake your head, Harry, and you will do quite as well!"

"Uncle David!" cried Harry, eagerly, "pray let me see you stand for one moment as you do at the club on a cold day, with your feet upon the rug, your back to the fire, and your coat-tails under your arms! Pray do, for one minute!"

Uncle David did as he was asked, evidently expecting the result, which took place, for Harry sprang upon his back with the agility of a monkey, and they went round and round the room at full gallop, during the next five minutes, while Lady Harriet said she never saw two such noisy people, but it was quite the fashion now, since the king of France carried his grandchildren in the same way, every morning, a picture of which had lately been shewn to her.

"Then I hope his majesty gets as good an appetite with his romp as I have done," replied Major Graham, sitting down. "None of your tea and toast for me! that is only fit for ladies. Frank, reach me these beef-steaks, and a cup of chocolate."

Harry and Laura now planted themselves at the window, gazing at crowds of people who passed, while, by way of a joke, they guessed what everybody came out for, and who they all were.

"There is a fat cook with a basket under her arm, going to market," said Harry. "Did you ever observe when Mrs Marmalade comes home, she says to grandmama, ' I have desired a leg of mutton to come here, my lady! and I told a goose to be over also,' as if the leg of mutton and the goose walked here arm-in-arm of themselves."

"Look at those children, going to see the wild beasts," added Laura, "and this little girl is on her way to buy a new frock. I am sure she needs one! that old man is hurrying along because he is too late for the mail-coach; and this lady with a gown like a yellow daffodil, is going to take root in the Botanical Gardens!"

"Uncle David, there is the very poorest boy I ever saw!" cried Harry, turning eagerly round, "he has been standing in the cold here for ten minutes, looking the picture of misery! he wears no hat, and has pulled his long hair to make a bow about twenty times. Do come and look at him! he is very pale, and his clothes seem to have been made before he began to grow, for they are so much too small, and he is making us many signs to open the window. May I do it?"

"No! no! I never give to chance beggars of that kind, especially a young, able-bodied fellow like that, because there are so many needy, deserving people whom I visit, who worked as long as they could, and whom I know to be sober and honest. Most of the money we scatter to street beggars goes straight to the gin-shop, and even the very youngest children will buy or steal, to get the means of becoming intoxicated. Only last week, Harry, the landlord of an ale-house at Portobello was seen at the head of a long table, surrounded with ragged beggar boys about twelve or fourteen years of age, who were all perfectly drunk, and probably your friend might be of the party."

" Oh no ! uncle David ! this boy seems quite sober, and exceedingly clean, though he is so very poor !" replied Laura. " His black trousers are patched and repatched, his jacket has faded into fifty colours, and his shoes are mended in every direction, but still he looks almost respectable. His face is so thin you might use it for a hatchet; I wish you would take one little peep, for he seems so anxious to speak to us."

" I daresay that ! we all know what the youngster has to tell ! Probably a wife and six small children at home, or, if you like it better, he will be a shipwrecked sailor at your service. I know the whole affair already; but if you have sixpence to spare, Laura, come with me after breakfast, and we shall bestow it on poor, blind Mrs Wilkie, who has been bed-ridden for the last ten years; or old paralytic Jemmy Dixon the porter, who worked as long as he was able. If you had twenty more sixpences, I could tell you of twenty more people who deserve them as much."

"Very true," added Lady Harriet. "Street beggars, who are young and able to work, like that boy, it is cruelty to encourage. Parents bring up their children in profligate idleness, hoping to gain more money by lying and cheating than by honest industry; and they too often succeed, especially when the wicked mothers also starve and disfigure these poor creatures, to excite more compassion. We must relieve real distress, Harry, and search for it, as we would for hidden treasures, because thus we shew our love to God and man; but a large purse with easy strings will do more harm than good."

"Do you remember, Frank, how long I suspected that old John Davidson was imposing upon me!" said Major Graham. "He told such a dismal story always, that I never liked to refuse him some assistance; but yesterday, when he was here, the thought struck me by chance to say, ' What a fine supper you had last night, John!' You should have seen the start he gave, and his look of consternation, when he answered, ' Eh, Sir! how did ye hear of that? We got the turkey very cheap, and none of us took more than two glasses of toddy.'"

"That boy is pointing to his pockets, and making more signs for us to open the window!" exclaimed Laura. "What can it all mean! he seems so very anxious!"

Major Graham threw down his knife and fork—rose hastily from breakfast—and flung open the window, calling out in rather a loud, angry voice, "What do you want, you idle fellow? It is a perfect shame to see you standing there all morning! Surely you don't mean to say that an active youngster like you would disgrace yourself by begging?"

"No, Sir! I want nothing!" answered the boy respectfully, but colouring to the deepest scarlet. "I never asked for money in my life, and I never will."

"That's right, my good boy!" answered the Major, instantly changing his tone. "What brings you here, then?"

"Please, Sir, your servants shut the door in my face, and every body is so hasty like, that I don't know what to do. I can't be listened to for a minute, though I have got something very particular to say, that some one would be glad to hear."

Major Graham now looked exceedingly vexed with himself, for having spoken so roughly to the poor boy, who had a thoughtful, mild, but careworn countenance, which was extremely interesting, while his manner seemed better than his dress.

Frank was despatched, as a most willing messenger, to bring the young stranger up stairs, while uncle David told Harry that he would take this as a lesson to himself ever afterwards, not to judge hastily from appearances, because it was impossible for any one to guess what might be in the mind of another; and he began to hope this boy, who was so civil and well-spoken, might yet turn out to be a proper, industrious, little fellow.

"Well, my lad! Is there anything I can do for you?" asked Major Graham, when Frank led him kindly into the room. "What is your name?"

"Evan Mackay, at your service. Please, Sir, did you lose a pocket-book last Thursday, with your name on the back, and nine gold sovereigns inside?"

"Yes! that I did, to my cost! Have you heard anything of it?"

The boy silently drew a parcel from his pocket, and without looking up or speaking, he modestly placed it on the table, then colouring very deeply, he turned away, and hurried towards the door. In another minute he would have been off, but Frank sprung forward and took hold of his arm, saying, in the kindest possible manner, "Stop, Evan! Stop a moment! That parcel seems to contain all my uncle's money. Where did you get it? Who sent it here?"

"I brought it, Sir! The direction is on the pocket-book, so there could be no mistake."

"Did you find it yourself, then?"

"Yes! it was lying in the street that night when I ran for a doctor to see my mother, who is dying. She told me now to come back directly, Sir, so I must be going."

"But let us give you something for being so honest," said Frank. "You are a fine fellow, and you deserve to be well rewarded."

"I only did my duty, Sir. Mother always says we should do right for conscience' sake, and not for a reward."

"Yes! but you are justly entitled to this," said Major Graham, taking a sovereign out of the purse. "I shall do more for you yet, but in the mean time here is what you have honestly earned to-day."

"If I thought so, Sir,"—— said the poor boy, looking wistfully at the glittering coin. "If I was quite sure there could be no harm——; but I must speak first to mother about it, Sir! She has seen better days once, and she is sadly afraid of my ever taking charity. Mother mends my clothes, and teaches me herself, and works very hard in other ways, but she is quite bed-ridden, and we have scarcely anything but the trifle I make by working in the fields. It is very difficult to get a job at all sometimes, and if you could put me in the way of earning that money, Sir, it would make mother very happy. She is a little particular, and would not taste a morsel that I could get by asking for it."

"That is being very proud!" said Harry.

"No, Sir! it is not from pride," replied Evan "but mother says a merciful God has provided for her many years, and she will not begin to distrust Him now. Her hands are always busy, and her heart is always cheerful. She rears many little plants by her bedside, which we sell, and she teaches a neighbour's children, besides sewing for any one who will employ her; for mother's maxim always was, that there can be no such thing as an idle Christian."

"Very true!" said Lady Harriet. "Even the apostles were mending their nets and labouring hard, whenever they were not teaching. Either the body or the mind should always be active."

"If you saw mother, that is exactly her way; for she does not eat the bread of idleness. Were a stranger to offer us a blanket or a dinner in charity, she would rather go without any than take it. A very kind lady brought her a gown one day, but mother would only have it if she were allowed to knit as many stockings as would pay for the stuff. I dare not take a penny more for my work than is due; for she says, if once I begin receiving alms, I might get accustomed to it."

"That is the good old Scotch feeling of former days," observed Major Graham. "It was sometimes carried too far then, but there is not enough of it now. Your mother should have lived fifty years ago."

"You may say so indeed, Sir! We never had a drop of broth from the soup-kitchen all winter, and many a day we shivered without a fire, though the society offered her sixpence a-week for coals, but she says, 'The given morsel is soon done;' and now, many of our neighbours who wasted what they got, feel worse off than we, who are accustomed to suffer want, and to live upon our honest labour. Long ago if mother went out to tea with any of our neighbours, she always took her own tea along with us."

"But this is being prouder than anybody else," observed Frank, smiling. "If my grandmama goes out to a tea-party, she allows her friends to provide the fare."

"Very likely, Sir! but that is different when people can give as good as they get Last week a kind neighbour sent us some nice loaf-bread, but mother made me take it back, with her best thanks, and she preferred her own oat-cake. She is mere ready to give than to take, Sir, and divides her last bannock, sometimes, with anybody who is worse off than ourselves."

"Poor fellow!" said Frank, compassionately; "how much you must often have suffered!"

"Suffered," said the boy, with sudden emotion. "Yes! I have suffered! It matters nothing to be clothed in rags,—to be cold and hungry now! There are worse trials than that! My father died last year, crushed to death in a moment by his own cart-wheels,—my brothers and sisters have all gone to the grave, scarcely able to afford the medicines that might have cured them,—and I am left alone with my poor dying mother. It is a comfort that life does not last very long, and we may trust all to God while it lasts."

"Could you take us to see Mrs Mackay?" said Major Graham, kindly. "Laura, get your bonnet."

"Oh Sir! that young lady could not stay half a minute in the place where my poor mother lives now. It is not a pretty cottage, such as we read of in tracts, but a dark, cold room, up a high stair, in the narrowest lane you ever saw, with nothing to sit on but an old chest."

"Never mind that, Evan," replied Major Graham. "You and your mother have a spirit of honour and honesty that might shame many who are lying on sofas of silk and damask. I respect her, and shall assist you if it be possible. Shew us the way."

Many dirty closes and narrow alleys were threaded by the whole party, before they reached a dark, ruinous staircase, where Evan paused and looked round, to see whether Major Graham still approached. He then slowly mounted one flight of ancient crumbling steps after another, lighted by patched and broken windows, till at last they arrived at a narrow wooden flight, perfectly dark. After groping to the summit, they perceived a time-worn door, the latch of which was lifted by Evan, who stole noiselessly into the room, followed by uncle David, and the wondering children.

There, a large, cold room, nearly empty, but exceedingly clean, presented itself to their notice. In one corner stood a massive old chest of carved oak, surrounded with a perfect glow of geraniums and myrtles in full blossom; beside which were arranged a large antique Bible, a jug of cold water, and a pile of coarsely-knitted worsted stockings. Beyond these, on a bed of clean straw, lay a tall, emaciated old woman, apparently in the last stage of life, with a face haggard by suffering; and yet her thin, withered hands were busily occupied with needle-work, while in low, faltering tones, she chanted these words;

> "When from the dust of death I rise,
> To claim my mansion in the skies,
> This, this shall be my only plea,
> Jesus hath liv'd and died for me"

"Mother!" said Evan, wishing to arouse her attention. "Look, mother!"

"Good day, Mrs Mackay," added Major Graham, in a voice of great consideration, while she languidly turned her head towards the door. "I have come to thank you for restoring my purse this morning."

"You are kindly welcome, Sir! What else could we do!" replied she, in a feeble, tremulous voice. "The money was yours, and the sooner it went out of our hands the better."

"It was perfectly safe while it stayed there," added Major Graham, not affecting to speak in a homely accent, nor putting on any airs of condescension at all, but sitting down on the old chest, as if he had never sat on anything but a chest in his life before, and looking at the clean, bare floor with as much respect as if it had been a Turkey carpet. "Your little boy's pocket seems to be as safe as the Bank of Scotland."

"That is very true, Sir! My boy is honest; and it is well to keep a good conscience, as that is all he has in this world to live for. Many have a heavy conscience to carry with a heavy purse; but these he need not envy. If we are poor in this world, we are rich in faith; and I trust the money was not even a temptation to Evan, because he has learned from the best of all Teachers, that it would 'profit him nothing to gain the whole world, and lose his own soul.'"

"True, Mrs Mackay! most true! We have come here this morning to request that you and he will do me the favour to accept of a small recompense."

"We are already rewarded, Sir! This has been an opportunity of testifying to our own hearts that we desire to do right in the eye of God. At the same time, it was Providence who kindly directed my son's steps to the place where that money was lying; and if anything seems justly due to poor Evan, let him have it. My wants are few, and must soon be ended. But, oh! when I look at that boy, and think of the long years he may be struggling with poverty and temptation, my heart melts within me, and my whole spirit is broken. Faith itself seems to fail, and I could be a beggar for him now! It is not money I would ask Sir, because that might soon be spent; but get him some honest employment, and I will thank you on my very knees."

Evan seemed startled at the sudden energy of his mother's manner, and tears sprung into his eyes while she spoke with a degree of agitation so different from what he had ever heard before; but he struggled to conceal his feelings, and she continued, with increasing emotion,

"Bodily suffering, and many a year of care and sorrow, are fast closing their work on me. The moments are passing away like a weaver's shuttle; and if I had less anxiety about Evan, how blessed a prospect it would appear; but that is the bitterness of death to me now. My poor, poor boy! I would rather he was in the way of earning his livelihood, than that he got a hundred a-year. Tell me, Sir!—and, oh! consider you are speaking to a dying creature—can you possibly give him any creditable employment, where he might gain a crust of bread, and be independent!"

"I honour your very proper feeling on the subject, Mrs Mackay, and shall help Evan to the best of my ability," replied Major Graham, in a tone of seriousness and sincerity. "To judge of these fine geraniums, he must be fond of cultivating plants and we want an under gardener in the country; therefore he shall have that situation without loss of time."

"Oh, mother! mother! speak no more of dying! You will surely get better now!" said Evan, looking up, while his thin, pale face assumed a momentary glow of pleasure. "Try now to get better!

I never could work as well, if you were not waiting to see me come home! We shall be so happy now!"

"Yes! I am happy!" said Mrs Mackay, solemnly looking towards heaven, with an expression that could not be mistaken. "The last cord is cut that bound me to the earth! May you, Sir, find hereafter the blessings that are promised to those who **visit the fatherless and widows in their affliction.**"

CHAPTER XII.

THE YOUNG MIDSHIPMAN.

> When hands are link'd that dread to part,
> And heart is met by throbbing heart;
> Ah! bitter, bitter is the smart
> Of them that bid farewell.
>
> HEBER.

NEXT Monday morning, at an early hour, Frank had again found his way with great difficulty to the house of Widow Mackay, where he spent all his pocket-money on two fine scarlet geraniums. If they had been nettles or cabbages, he would have felt the same pleasure in buying them; and his eyes sparkled with animation when he entered uncle David's room, carrying them in his hand, and saying, "I was so glad to have some money! I could spare it quite well. There is no greater pleasure in being rich than to help such people as Evan Mackay and his poor, sick mother!"

"Yes, Frank, I often wonder that any enjoyment of wealth can be considered equal to the exercise of kind feelings, for surely the most delightful sensation in this world is, to deserve and receive the grateful affection of those around us," replied Major Graham. "What a wretched being Robinson Crusoe was on the desert island alone, though he found chests of gold; and yet many people are as unblessed in the midst of society, who selfishly hoard fortunes for themselves, unmindful of the many around who ought to be gratefully receiving their daily benefits."

"I was laughing to read lately of the West India slaves, who collected money all their lives in an old stocking," said Frank, "and who watched with delight as it filled from year to year; but the bank is only a great stocking, where misers in this country lay up treasures for themselves which they are never to enjoy, though, too often, they lay up no treasures for themselves in a better world."

"I frequently think, Frank, if all men were as liberal, kind, and forbearing to each other as the Holy Scriptures enjoin, and if we lived as soberly, temperately, and godly together, what a paradise this world would become; for many of our worst sufferings are brought on by our own folly, or the unkindness of others. And certainly, if we wish to fancy the wretchedness of hell itself, it would only be necessary to imagine what the earth would become if all fear of God and man were removed, and every person lived as his own angry, selfish passions would dictate. Great are the blessings we owe to Christianity, for making the world even what it is now, and yet greater would those blessings be, if we obeyed it better."

"That is exactly what grandmama says, and that we must obey the Gospel from love and gratitude to God, rather than from fear of punishment or hope of reward, which is precisely what we saw in poor Widow Mackay and Evan, who seemed scarcely to expect a recompense for behaving so honestly."

"That was the more remarkable in them, as few Christians now are above receiving a public recompense for doing their duty to God. Men of the world have long rewarded each other with public dinners and pieces of plate, to express their utmost praise and admiration; but of late I never open a newspaper without reading accounts of one clergyman or another, who has been 'honoured with a public breakfast!' when he is presented by an admiring circle with 'a gold watch and appendages!' or a Bible with a complimentary inscription, or a gown, or a pair of bands, worked by the ladies of his congregation! and all this, for labouring among his own people in his own sphere of duty! What would Archbishop Leighton and the old divines have said to any one who attempted to rouse their vanity in this way, with the praise of men!"

"What you say reminds me, uncle David," said Frank, "that we have been asked to present our Universal-Knowledge Master with a silver snuff-box, as a testimonial from the scholars in my class, because he is going soon to Van Diemen's Land, therefore, I hope you will give me half-a-crown to subscribe, or I shall be quite in disgrace with him."

"Not one shilling shall you receive from me, my good friend, for any such purpose! A snuff-box, indeed! your master ought to shew his scholars an example of using none! a filthy waste of health, money, and time. Such testimonials should only be given, as Archbishop Magee says, to persons who have got into some scrape, which makes their respectability doubtful. If my grocer is ever presented with a pair of silver tongs, I shall think he has been accused of adulterating the sugar, and give over employing him directly."

"Laura," said Frank, "you will be having a silver thimble voted to you for hemming six pocket-handkerchiefs in six years."

"I know one clergyman, Dr Seton, who conscientiously refused a piece of plate, which was about to be presented in this way," continued Major Graham. "He accidentally heard that such a subscription was begun among the rich members of his congregation, and instantly stopped it, saying, 'Let your testimonial consist in a regular attendance at church, and let my sole reward be enjoyed hereafter, when you appear as my crown of joy and rejoicing in the presence of our Lord Jesus Christ at his coming.'"

Sir Edward Graham's particular friend, Captain Gordon, at last wrote to say, that the Thunderbolt, 74, having been put in commission for three years, was about to sail for the African station, therefore he wished Frank to join without delay and as a farther mark of his regard, he promised that he would endeavour to keep his young protégé employed until he had served out his time, because a midshipman once paid off, was like a stranded whale, not very easily set afloat again.

Lady Harriet sighed when she read the letter, and looked paler all that day, but she knew that it was right and necessary for Frank to go, therefore she said nothing to distress him on the occasion, only in her prayers and explanations of the Bible that evening, there was a deeper tone of feeling than ever, and a cast of melancholy, which had rarely been the case before, while she spoke much of that meeting in a better world which is the surest hope and consolation of those Christians who separate on earth, and who know not what a day, and still less what many years, may bring forth.

Major Graham tried to put a cheerful face on the matter also, though he evidently felt very sorry in deed about parting with Frank, and took him out a long walk to discuss his future prospects, saying, " Now you are an officer and a gentleman, entitled therefore to be treated with new respect and attention, by all your brother officers, naval or military, in His Majesty's service."

Frank himself, being a boy of great spirit and enterprise, felt glad that the time had really come for his being afloat, and examining all the world over with his own eyes; but he said that his heart seemed as if it had been put in a swing, it fell so low when he thought of leaving his dear, happy home, and then it rose again higher than ever at the very idea of being launched on the wide ocean, and going to the countries he had so often read of, where battles had been fought and victories won.

"Frank!" said Peter Grey, who was going to join the Thunderbolt in about a fortnight afterwards, "you have no idea how beautiful I looked in uniform to-day! I tried mine on, and felt so impatient to use my dirk, I could have eat my dinner with it, instead of employing a common knife."

"You never forget to be hungry, Peter," said Frank, laughing. "But now you are like the old Lord Buchan, who used to say he could cook his porridge in his helmet, and stir it with his broadsword."

"I hope," said Major Graham, "you both intend to become very distinguished officers, and to leave a name at which the world grows pale."

"Certainly," answered Peter. "All the old heroes we read of shall be mere nobodies compared to me! I mean to lose a leg or an arm in every battle,"——

"Till nothing is left of you but your shirt-collar and shoe-strings," interrupted Frank, laughing.

"No! no! What remains of me at last shall die a Peer of the realm," continued Peter. "We must climb to the top of the tree, Frank! What title do you think I should take?"

"Lord Cockpit would suit you best for some time, Peter! It will not be so easy a business to rise as you think. Every one can run a race, but very few can win," observed Major Graham. "The rarest thing on earth is to succeed in being both conspicuous and respectable. Any dunce may easily be either the one or the other, but the chief puzzle with most men is, how to be both. In your profession there are great opportunities, but at the same time let me warn you, that the sea is not a bed of roses."

"No, uncle David! but I hope it will become a field of laurels to us," replied Frank, laughing. "Now tell me in real earnest who you think was the greatest of our naval heroes till now, when Peter is to cut them all out."

"He must wait a few years. It is a long ladder to run up before reaching the top. In France, the king's sons are all born Field-Marshals, but nobody in this country is born an Admiral. The great Lord Duncan served during half a century before gaining his most important victory; but previous to that, he paved the way to success, not by mere animal courage alone, but by being so truly good and religious a man, that his extraordinary firmness and benevolence of character gained the confidence of all those who served with him, and therefore half his success in battle was owing to his admirable conduct during peace."

"So I have heard!" replied Frank; "and when there was mutiny in every other ship, the Admiral's own crew remained faithful to him. How much better it is to be obeyed from respect and attachment than from fear, which is a mean feeling that I hope neither to feel myself, nor to excite in others. I wish to be like Nelson, who asked, 'What is fear? I never saw it!'"

"Yes, Frank! Nelson was said to be 'brave as a lion, and gentle as a lamb.' Certainly both he and Lord Duncan were pre-eminently great; but neither Lord Duncan nor any other enlightened Christian would have said what Lord Nelson did, with his latest breath—'I have not been a great sinner!' No mortal could lift up his eyes at the day of judgment, and repeat those words again; for every man that breathes the breath of life is a great sinner. We are living in God's own world without remembering him continually; and amidst thousands of blessings we disobey him. The chief purpose for which men are created, is to glorify God, and to prepare for entering his presence in a better world; but instead of doing so, we live as if there were no other object to live for, than our own pleasures and amusements on earth. How, then, can we be otherwise than great sinners! I hope, Frank, that you will endeavour to be, like Lord Duncan, not merely a good officer, but also a good Christian; for, besides fighting the battles of your country, you must gain a great victory over yourself, as all men must either conquer their own evil dispositions, or perish for ever."

Lady Harriet was particularly earnest in entreating Frank to write frequently home, observing, that she considered it a religious duty in all children to shew their parents this attention, as the Bible says, that "a wise son maketh a glad father," and that "the father of the righteous shall greatly rejoice;" but, on the contrary, too many young persons leave their parents to mourn in suspense and anxiety as to the health and happiness of those whom they love more than they can ever love any one else.

"Tell us of every thing that interests you, and even all about the spouting whales, flying fish, and dying dolphins, which you will of course see," said Laura. "Be sure to write us also how many albatrosses you shoot, and whether you are duly introduced to Neptune at the Cape."

"Yes, Laura! But Bishop Heber's Journal, or any other book describing a voyage to the Cape, mentions exactly the same thing. It will quite bring me home again when I speak to you all on paper; and I shall be able to fancy what everybody will say when my letter is read. Mrs Darwin sent for me this morning on particular business; and it was to say that she wished me, in all the strange countries where the Thunderbolt touched, to employ my spare moments in catching butterflies, that as many as possible might be added to her museum."

"Capital! How like Mrs Darwin!" exclaimed Major Graham, laughing. "You will of course be running all over Africa, hat in hand, pursuing painted butterflies, till you get a *coup de soleil*, like my friend Watson, who was killed by one. Poor fellow! I was with him then, and it was a frightful scene. He wheeled round several times in a sort of convulsion, till he dropped down dead in my arms."

"I shall gild the legs and bills of some ducks

before leaving home, and send them to her as a present from Sierra Leone," said Peter. "The wings might be dyed scarlet, which would look quite foreign; and if an elephant falls in my way, it shall be stuffed and forwarded by express."

"Uncle David! Do you remember what fun we had, when you sent Mrs Darwin that stuffed bear in a present! I was desired to announce that a foreigner of distinction had arrived to stay at her house. What a bustle she was in on hearing that he brought letters of introduction from you, and intended to remain some time. Then we told her that he could not speak a word of English, and brought 'a Pole' with him; besides which he had once been a great dancer. Oh! how amusing it was, when she at last ventured into the passage to be introduced, and saw her fine stuffed bear."

"Whatever people collect," said Peter, "every good-natured person assists. I mean to begin a collection of crooked sixpences immediately; therefore, pray never spend another, but give me as many as you can spare; and the more crooked the better."

"Sing a song a sixpence!" said Frank, laughing. "Laura should begin to collect diamonds for a necklace, and perhaps it might be all ready before she comes out. I shall return home on purpose to see you then, Laura."

"Pray do, Master Frank," said Mrs Crabtree, with more than usual kindness; "we shall have great rejoicings on the occasion of seeing you back—an ox roasted alive, as they do in England, and all that sort of tomfooleries. I'll dance a jig then myself for joy!—you certainly are a wonderful good boy, considering that I had not the managing of you."

Frank's departure was delayed till after the examination of his school, because Mr Hannay had requested, that, being the best scholar there, he might remain to receive a whole library of prize-books and a whole pocketful of medals; for, as Peter remarked, "Frank Graham deserved any reward, because he learned his lessons so perfectly, that he could not say them wrong even if he wished!"

Harry and Laura were allowed to attend on the great occasion, that they might witness Frank's success; and never, certainly, had they seen anything so grand in their lives before! A hundred and forty boys, all dressed in white trousers and yellow gloves, were seated in rows, opposite to six grave, learned-looking gentlemen, in wigs and spectacles, who seemed as if they would condemn all the scholars to death!

The colour mounted into Harry's cheeks with delight, and the tears rushed into his eyes, when he saw Frank, whose face was radiant with good humour and happiness, take his place as head boy in the school. All his companions had crowded round Frank as he entered, knowing that this was his last appearance in the class; while he spoke a merry or a kind word to each, leaning on the shoulder of one, and grasping the hand of another with cordial kindness; for he liked everybody, and everybody liked him. No one envied Frank being dux, because they knew how hard he worked for that place, and how anxious he had been to help every other boy in learning as cleverly as himself; for all the boobies would have become duxes if Frank could have assisted them to rise, while many an idler had been made busy by his attention and advice. No boy ever received, in one day, more presents than Frank did on this occasion from his young friends, who spent all their pocket-money in pen-knives and pencil-cases, which were to be kept by Frank, in remembrance of them, as long as he lived; and some of his companions had a tear in their eye on bidding him farewell, which pleased him more than all their gifts.

Major Graham took his place, with more gravity than usual, among the judges appointed to distribute the prizes; and now, during more than two hours, the most puzzling questions that could be invented were put to every scholar in succession, while Frank seemed always ready with an answer, and not only spoke for himself, but often good-naturedly prompted his neighbours, in so low a tone that no one else heard him. His eyes brightened, and his face grew red with anxiety, while even his voice shook at first; but before long Frank collected all his wits about him, and could construe Latin or repeat Greek with perfect ease till at length the whole examination was concluded, and the great Dr Clifford, who had lately come all the way from Oxford, was requested to present the prizes. Upon this he rose majestically from his arm-chair, and made a long speech, filled as full as it could hold with Latin and Greek. He praised Homer and Horace for nearly twenty minutes, and brought in several lines of Virgil, after which he turned to Frank, saying, in a tone of great kindness and condescension, though at the same time exceedingly pompous,

"It seems almost a pity that this young gentleman—already so very accomplished a scholar —who is, I may say, a perfect *multum in parvo*, should prematurely pause in his classical career to enter the navy; but in every situation of life his extraordinary activity of mind, good temper, courage, and ability, must render him an honour to his country and his profession."

Dr Clifford now glanced over the list of prizes,

and read aloud—" First prize for Greek—Master Graham!"

Frank walked gracefully forward, coloured, and bowed, while a few words of approbation were said to him, and a splendidly-bound copy of Euripides was put into his hands by Dr Clifford, who then hastily read over the catalogue of prizes to himself, in an audible voice, and in a tone of great surprise,

"First prize for Latin!—Master Graham! First for algebra,—first for geography,—first for mathematics,—all Master Graham!!!—and last, not least, a medal for general good conduct, which the boys are allowed to bestow upon the scholar they think most deserving—and here stands the name of Master Graham again!!"

Dr Clifford paused, while the boys all stood up for a moment and clapped their hands with enthusiam, as a token of rejoicing at the destination of their own medal.

For the first time Frank was now completely overcome,—he coloured more deeply than before, and looked gratefully round, first at his companions, then at his master, and last at Major Graham, who had a tear standing in his eye when he smiled upon Frank, and held out his hand.

Frank's lip quivered for a moment, as if he would burst into tears, but with a strong effort he recovered himself, and affectionately grasping his uncle's hand, hastily resumed his place on the bench, to remain there while his companions received the smaller prizes awarded to them.

Meantime Harry had been watching Frank with a feeling of joy and pride, such as he never experienced before, and could scarcely refrain from saying to every person near him, "That is my brother!" He looked at Frank long and earnestly, wishing to be like him, and resolving to follow his good example at school. He gazed again and again, with new feelings of pleasure and admiration, till gradually his thoughts became melancholy, while remembering how soon they must be separated; and suddenly the terrible idea darted into his mind, "Perhaps we never may meet again!" Harry tried not to think of this; he turned his thoughts to other subjects; he forced himself to look at anything that was going on, but still these words returned with mournful apprehension to his heart, "Perhaps we never may meet again!"

Frank's first action, after the examination had been concluded, was hastily to gather up all his books, and bring a sight of them to Harry and Laura; but what was his astonishment when, instead of looking at the prizes, Harry suddenly threw his arms round his neck, and burst into tears!

"My dear, dear boy! what has happened!" exclaimed Frank, affectionately embracing him, and looking much surprised. "Tell me, dear Harry, has anything distressed you?"

"I don't know very well, Frank! but you are going away,—and—and—I wish I had been a better boy! I would do anything you bid me now!—but I shall never be so happy again—no! never, without you."

"But, dear Harry! you will have Laura and grandmama, and uncle David, all left, and I am coming back some day! Oh! what a happy meeting we shall have then!" said Frank, while the tears stood in his eyes, and drawing Harry's arm within his own, they walked slowly away together.

"I am very, very anxious for you and Laura to be happy," continued Frank, in the kindest manner; "but, dear Harry, will you not take more care to do as you are bid, and not always to prefer doing what you like! Mrs Crabtree would not be half so terrible if you did not provoke her by some new tricks every day. I almost like her myself; for as the old proverb says, 'Her bark is worse than her bite;' and she often reminds me of that funny old fable, where the mice were more afraid of the loud, fierce-looking cock, than of the sleek, smooth-looking cat, for there are people carrying gentler tongues yet quite as difficult to deal with. At the same time, seeing how uncomfortable you and Laura both feel with Mrs Crabtree, I have written a letter to papa, asking, as my last and only request on leaving home, that he will make a change of ministry, and he is always so very kind, that I feel sure he will grant it."

"How good of you, Frank!" said Harry. "I am sure it is our own faults very often when we are in disgrace, for we are seldom punished till we deserve it; but I am so sorry you are going away, that I can think of nothing else."

"So am I, very sorry indeed; but my best comfort, when far from home, would be, to think that you and Laura are happy, which will be the case when you become more watchful to please grandmama."

"That is very true, Frank! and I would rather offend twenty Mrs Crabtrees than one grandmama; but perhaps uncle David may send me to school now, when I shall try to be like you, sitting at the top of the class, and getting prizes for good behaviour."

"Well, Harry! my pleasantest days at school have been those when I was busiest, and you will find the same thing. How delightful it was, going over and over my tasks till they were quite perfect, and then rushing out to the play-ground, where my mind got a rest, while my body was active; you know it is seldom that both mind and body work at once, and the best way of resting the one is, to make the other labour That is probably the reason, Harry, why games are never half so pleasant as after hard study."

"Perhaps," replied Harry, doubtfully; "but I always hate anything that I am obliged to do."

"Then never be a sailor, as I shall be obliged to do fifty things a-day that I would rather not; for instance, to get up in the middle of the night, when very likely dreaming about being at home again; but, as grandmama says, it is pleasant to have some duties, for life would not get well on without them."

"Yes—perhaps—I don't know!—we could find plenty to do ourselves, without anybody telling us. I should like to-morrow, to watch the boys playing at cricket, and to see the races, and the Diorama, and in the evening to shoot our bows and arrows."

"My good Sir! what the better would you, or anybody else, be of such a life as that! Not a thing in this world is made to be useless, Harry; the very weeds that grow in the ground are for some serviceable purpose, and you would not wish to be the only creature on earth living entirely for yourself. It would be better if neither of us had ever been born, than that the time and opportunities which God gives us for improving ourselves and doing good to others, should all be wasted. Let me hope, Harry, when I am away, that you will often consider how dull grandmama may then feel, and how happy you might make her by being very attentive and obedient."

"Yes, Frank! but I could never fill your place! —that is quite impossible! Nobody can do that!"

"Try!—only try, Harry! Grandmama is very easily pleased when people do their best. She would not have felt so well satisfied with me, if that had not been the case."

"Frank!" said Harry, sorrowfully, "I feel as if ten brothers were going away instead of one, for you are so good to me! I shall be sure to mention you in my prayers, because that is all I can do for you now."

"Not all, Harry! though that is a great deal; you must write to me often, and tell me what makes you happy or unhappy, for I shall be more interested than ever, now that we are separated. Tell me everything about my school-fellows, too, and about Laura. There is no corner of the wide world where I shall not think of you both every day, and feel anxious about the very least thing that concerns you."

"My dear boys!" said Major Graham, who had joined them some moments before, "it is fortunate that you have both lived always in the same home; for that will make you love each other affectionately, as long as you live. In England, children of one family are all scattered to different schools, without any person seeming to care whether they are attached or not, therefore their earliest and warmest friendships are formed with strangers of the same age, whom they perhaps never see again, after leaving school. In that case, brothers have no happy days of childhood to talk over in future life, as you both have,—no little scrapes to remember, that they got into together,—no pleasures enjoyed at the same moment to smile at the recollection of, and no friction of their tempers in youth, such as makes everything go on smoothly between brothers when they grow older; therefore, when at last grown up and thrown together, they scarcely feel more mutual friendship and intimacy than any other gentlemen testify towards each other."

"I daresay that is very true," said Frank. "Tom Brownlow tells me when his three brothers come home from Eton, Harrow, and Durham, they quarrel so excessively, that sometimes no two of them are on speaking terms."

"Not at all improbable," observed Major Graham, " In everything we see how much better God's arrangements are than our own. Families were intended to be like a little world in themselves—old people to govern the young ones—young people to make their elders cheerful—grown-up brothers and sisters to shew their juniors a good example—and children to be playthings and companions to their seniors; but that is all at an end in the present system."

"Old Andrew says that large families 'squander' themselves all over the earth now," said Frank, laughing.

"Yes! very young children are thrust into preparatory schools—older boys go to distant academies—youths to College—and young men are shipped off abroad, while who among them all can say his heart is in his own home? Parents, in the mean time, finding no occupation or amusement in educating their children, begin writing books, perhaps theories of education, or novels; and try to fill up the rest of their useless hours with plays, operas, concerts, balls, or clubs. If people could only know what is the best happiness of this life, it certainly depends on being loved by those we belong to; for nothing can be called peace on earth, which does not consist in family affection, built on a strong foundation of religion and morality."

Sir Edward Graham felt very proud of Frank, as all gentlemen are of their eldest sons, and wrote a most affectionate letter on the occasion of his going to sea, promising to meet him at Portsmouth, and lamenting that he still felt so ill and melancholy he could not return home, but meant to try whether the baths in Germany would do him any good. In this letter was enclosed what he called "Frank's first prize-money," the largest sum the young midshipman had ever seen in his life, and before it had been a day in his possession, more than the half was spent on presents to his friends. Not a single person seemed to be forgotten except himself; for Frank was so completely unselfish, that Peter Grey once laughingly said, "Frank scarcely remembers there is such a person as himself in the world, therefore it is astonishing how he contrives to exist at all."

"If that be his worst fault, you show him a very opposite example, Peter," said Major Graham, smiling; "number one is a great favourite with you."

"Frank is also very obliging!" added Lady Harriet; "he would do anything for anybody."

"Ah, poor fellow! he can't help that," said Peter, in a tone of pity. "Some people are born with that sort of desperate activity—flying to assist every one—running up stairs for whatever is wanted—searching for whatever is lost—and picking up whatever has been dropped. I have seen several others like Frank, who were troubled with that sort of turn. He is indulging his own inclination in flying about everywhere for everybody, as much as I do in sitting still!—it is all nature!—you know tastes differ, for some people like apples, and some like onions."

Frank had a black shade of himself, drawn in uniform and put into a gilt frame, all for one shilling, which he presented to his grandmama, who looked sadly at the likeness when he came smiling into her dressing-room, and calling Harry to assist in knocking a nail into the wall, that it might be hung above the chimney-piece. "I need nothing to remind me of you, dear Frank," observed Lady Harriet, "and this is a sad exchange, the shadow for the substance." Frank gave a handsome new red morocco spectacle-case to uncle David, and asked leave to carry away the old one with him as a remembrance. He bought gowns for all the maids, and books for all the men-servants. He presented Mrs Crabtree with an elegant set of tea-cups and saucers, promising to send her a box of tea the first time he went to China; and for Laura and Harry he produced a magnificent magic lantern, representing all the stars and planets, which cost him several guineas. It was exhibited the evening before Frank went away, and caused great entertainment to a large party of his companions, who assembled at tea to take leave of him, on which occasion Peter Grey made a funny speech, proposing Frank's health in a bumper of bohea, when the whole party became very merry, and did not disperse till ten.

Major Graham intended accompanying Frank to Portsmouth, and they were to set off by the mail next evening. That day was a sad one to Harry and Laura, who were allowed a whole holiday; but not a sound of merriment was heard in the house, except when Frank tried to make them cheerful, by planning what was to be done after he came back, or when Major Graham invented droll stories about the adventures Frank would probably meet with at sea. Even Mrs Crabtree looked more grave and cross than usual; and she brought Frank a present of a needle-case made with her own hands, and filled with thread of every kind, saying, that she heard all " midshipmites " learned to mend their things, and keep them decent, which was an excellent custom, and ought to be encouraged; but she hoped he would remember, that " a stitch in time saves nine."

Lady Harriet stayed most of the time in her dressing-room, and tried to conceal the traces of many tears when she did appear; but it was only too evident how sadly her time had been passed alone.

"Grandmama!" said Frank, taking her hand affectionately, and trying to look cheerful; "we shall meet again; perhaps very soon!"

Lady Harriet silently laid her hand upon the Bible, to shew that there she found the certain assurance of another meeting in a better world; but she looked at Frank with melancholy affection, and added, very solemnly and emphatically,

> "'There is no union here of hearts,
> That finds not here an end.'"

"But grandmama! you are not so very old!" exclaimed Laura, earnestly. "Lord Rockville was born ten years sooner; and, besides, young people sometimes die before older people."

"Yes, Laura! young people may die, but old people must. It is not possible that this feeble, aged frame of mine can long remain in the visible world. 'The eye of him that hath seen me shall see me no more.' I have many more friends under the earth now, than on it. The streets of this city would be crowded, if all those I once knew and still remember, could be revived; but my own turn is fast coming, like theirs, and Frank knows, as all of you do, where it is my hope and prayer that we may certainly meet again."

"Grandmama!" said Frank, in a low and broken voice, "it wants but an hour to the time of my departure; I should like much if the servants were to come up for family prayers, and if uncle David would read us the 14th chapter of St John."

Lady Harriet rung the bell, and before long the whole household had assembled, as not one would have been absent on the night of Master Frank's departure from home, which all were deeply grieved at, and even Mrs Crabtree dashed a tear from her cheek as she entered the room.

Frank sat with his hand in Lady Harriet's, while Major Graham read the beautiful and comforting chapter which had been selected, and when the whole family knelt in solemn prayer together, many a deep sob, which could not be conquered, was heard from Frank himself. All being over, he approached the servants, and silently shook hands with each, but could not attempt to speak; after which Lady Harriet led him to her dressing-room, where they remained some time, till, the carriage having arrived, Frank hastened into the drawing-room, clasped Harry and Laura in his arms, and having, in a voice choked with grief, bid them both a long farewell, he hurried out of their presence.

When the door closed, something seemed to fall heavily on the ground, but this scarcely attracted any one's attention, till Major Graham followed Frank, and was shocked to find him lying on the staircase, perfectly insensible. Instead of calling for assistance, however, uncle David carefully lifted

Frank in his own arms, and carried him to the carriage, where, after a few moments, the fresh air and the rapid motion revived his recollection, and he burst into tears.

"Poor grandmama! and Harry and Laura!" cried he, weeping convulsively. "Oh! when shall I see them all again!"

"My dear boy!" said Major Graham, trying to be cheerful; "do you think nobody ever left home before? One would suppose you never expected to come back! Three years seem an age when we look forward, but are nothing after they have fled. The longer we live, the shorter every year appears, and it will seem only the day after to-morrow when you are rushing into the house again, and all of us standing at the door to welcome you back. Think what a joyous moment that will be! There is a wide and wonderful world for you to see first, and then a happy home afterwards to revisit."

"Yes, dear, good, kind uncle David! no one ever had a happier home; and till the east comes to the west, I shall never cease to think of it with gratitude to you and grandmama. We shall surely all meet again. I must live upon that prospect. Hope is the jewel that remains wherever we go, and the hope to which grandmama has directed me, is truly compared to a rainbow, which not only brightens the earth, but stretches to heaven."

CHAPTER XIII.

THE AMUSING DRIVE.

*I would not enter on my list of friends
(Though graced with polish'd manners and fine sense,
Yet wanting sensibility) the man
Who needlessly sets foot upon a worm.*
                                        COWPER.

LADY HARRIET was confined to bed for several days after Frank's departure from home, and during all that week Harry and Laura felt so melancholy, that even Mrs Crabtree became sorry for them, saying, it was quite distressing to see how quiet and good they had become, for Master Harry was as mild as milk now, and she almost wished he would be at some of his old tricks again.

On the following Monday a message arrived from Lady Rockville, to say that she was going a long drive in her phaeton, to visit some boys at Musselburgh school, and would be happy to take Harry and Laura of the party, if their grandmama had no objection. None being made by anybody, they flew up stairs to get ready, while Harry did not take above three steps at a time, and Laura, when she followed, felt quite astonished to find Mrs Crabtree looking almost as pleased as herself, and saying she hoped the expedition would do them both good.

Before five minutes had elapsed Harry was mounted on the dickey, where Lady Rockville desired him to sit, instead of the footman, who was now dismissed, as room could not be made for them both; so after that Harry touched his hat whenever any of the party spoke to him, as if he had really been the servant.

Laura, meanwhile, was placed between Lady Rockville and Miss Perceval, where she could hardly keep quiet a minute for joy, though afraid to turn her head or to stir her little finger, in case of being thought troublesome.

"I am told that the races take place at Musselburgh to-day," said Lady Rockville. "It is a cruel amusement, derived from the sufferings of noble animals; they have as good a right to be happy in the world as ourselves, Laura; but we shall pass that way, so Harry and you will probably see the crowds of carriages."

"Oh, how enchanting! I never saw a race-course in my life!" cried Laura, springing off her seat with delight. "Harry! Harry! we are going to the races!"

"Hurra!" exclaimed Harry, clapping his hands; "what a delightful surprise! Oh! I am so dreadfully happy!"

"After all, my dear Lady Rockville," said Miss Perceval, yawning, "what have horses got legs for, except to run?"

"Yes, but not at such a pace! It always shocked me—formerly at Doncaster, where the jockeys were sometimes paid £1000 for winning—to see how the poor animals were lashed and spurred along the course, foaming with fatigue, and gasping till they nearly expired. Horses, poor creatures, from the hour of their birth till their death, have a sad time of it!"

"Grandmama once read me a beautiful description of a wild horse in his natural state of liberty," said Laura. "Among the South American forests he was seen carrying his head erect, with sparkling eyes, flowing mane, and splendid tail, trotting about among the noble trees, or cropping the grass at his feet, looking quite princely, and doing precisely what he pleased."

"Then look at the contrast," said Lady Rockville, pointing to a long row of cart-horses, with galled sides, shrivelled skins, broken knees, and emaciated bodies, which were all dragging their weary load along. "Animals are all meant for the use of man, but not to be abused, like these poor creatures."

"As for racing," said Miss Perceval, "a thoroughbred horse enters into the spirit of it quite as much as his rider. Did you never hear of Quin's celebrated steed, which became so eager to win, that when his antagonist passed, he seized him violently by the leg, and both jockeys had to dismount, that the furious animal might be torn away. The famous horse Forrester, too, caught hold of his opponent by the jaw, and could scarcely be disengaged."

"Think of all the cruel training these poor creatures went through before they came to that," added Lady Rockville; "of the way in which horses are beaten, spurred, and severely cut with the whip; then, after their strength fails, like the well-known 'high-mettled racer,' the poor animal is probably sold at last to perpetual hard labour and ill-usage."

"Uncle David shewed me one day," said Laura, "that horrid picture which you have probably seen, by Cruickshanks, of the Knackers' Yards in London, where old horses are sent to end their miserable days, after it is impossible to torture them any longer into working. Oh! it was dreadful! and yet grandmama said the whole sketch had been taken from life."

"I know that," answered Lady Rockville. "In these places the wretched animals are literally put to death by starvation, and may be seen gnawing each other's manes in the last agonies of hunger."

"My dear Lady Rockville," exclaimed Miss Perceval, affectedly, "how can you talk of such unpleasant things!—there is an act of Parliament against cruelty to animals, so of course no such thing exists now. Many gentlemen are vastly kind to old horses, turning them out to grass for years, that they may enjoy a life of elegant leisure and rural retirement, to which, no doubt, some are well entitled; for instance, the famous horse Eclipse, which gained his owner £25,000! I wish he had been mine!"

"But think how many are ruined when one is enriched, and indeed both are ruined in morals and good feeling; therefore I am glad that our sex have never taken to the turf. It is bad enough, my dear Miss Perceval, to see that they have taken to the moors; for were I to say all I think of those amazons who lately killed their six brace of grouse on the 12th of August, they would probably challenge me to single combat. Lord Rockville says, 'What with gentlemen doing worsted work, and ladies shouldering double-barrelled guns, he scarcely thinks this can be the same world that he was born in long ago.'"

The carriage at this moment began to proceed along the road with such extraordinary rapidity, that there seemed no danger of their following in the dust of any other equipage, and Miss Perceval became exceedingly alarmed, especially when Lady Rockville mentioned that this was one of the first times she had been driven by her new coachman, who seemed so very unsteady on his seat, she had felt apprehensive, for some time, that he might be drunk.

"A tipsy coachman! Dear Lady Rockville, do let me out! We shall certainly be killed in this crowd of carriages! I can walk home! Pray stop him, Miss Laura! I came to look on at a race, but not to run one myself! This fast driving is like a railroad, only not quite so straight! I do verily believe we are run off with! Stop, coachman!—stop!"

In spite of all Miss Perceval's exclamations and vociferations, the carriage flew on with frightful rapidity, though it reeled from side to side of the road, as if it had become intoxicated like the driver himself, who lashed his horses and galloped along within an inch of hedges and ditches all the way, till at last, having reached the race-course, he pulled up so suddenly and violently, that the horses nearly fell back on their haunches, while he swore at them in the most furious and shocking manner.

Lady Rockville now stood up, and spoke to the coachman very severely on his misconduct, in first driving her so dangerously fast, and then being disrespectful enough to use profane language in her presence, adding, that if he did not conduct himself more properly, she must complain to Lord Rockville as soon as the carriage returned home. Upon hearing this, the man looked exceedingly sulky, and muttered angrily to himself in a tipsy voice, till at last he suddenly threw away the reins, and, rising from the box, he began to scramble his way down, nearly falling to the ground in his haste, and saying, "If your ladyship is not pleased with my driving, you may drive yourself!"

After this the intoxicated man staggered towards a drinking-booth not far off, and disappeared, leaving Miss Perceval perfectly planet-struck with astonishment, and actually dumb during several minutes with wonder at all she heard and saw. There sat Harry, alone on the dickey, behind two spirited blood-horses, foaming at the mouth with the speed at which they had come, and ready to start off again at the slightest hint, while noises on every side were heard enough to frighten a pair of hobby-horses. Piemen ringing their bells—blind fiddlers playing out of tune—boys calling lists of the horses—drums beating at the starting post—ballad-singers squalling at the full pitch of their voices—horses galloping—grooms quarrelling—dogs barking—and children crying.

In the midst of all this uproar, Harry unexpectedly observed Captain Digby on horseback not far off. Without losing a moment, he stood up, waving his handkerchief, and calling to beg he would come to the carriage immediately, as they were in want of assistance; and Lady Rockville told, as soon as he arrived, though hardly able to help laughing while she explained it, the extraordinary predicament they had been placed in. Captain Digby, upon hearing the story, looked ready to go off like a squib with rage at the offending coachman, and instantly seizing the driving-whip, he desired his servant to hold the horses' heads, while he proceeded towards the drinking-booth, flourishing the long lash in his hand, as he went, in a most ominous manner. Several minutes elapsed, during which Harry overheard a prodigious outcry in the tent, and then the drunken coachman was seen reeling away along the road, while Captain Digby, still brandishing the whip, returned, and mounting the dickey himself, he gathered up the reins, and insisted on driving Lady Rockville's phaeton for her. Before long it was ranged close beside a chariot so full of ladies it seemed ready to burst, when Harry was amused to perceive that Peter Grey and another boy, who were seated on the rumble behind, had spread a table-cloth on the roof of the carriage, using it for a dining-table, while they all seemed determined to astonish their appetites by the quantity of oysters and sandwiches they ate, and by drinking at the same time large tumblers of porter. Lady Rockville wished she could have the loan of Harry and Laura's spirits for an hour or two, when she saw how perfectly bewildered with delight they were on beholding the thousands of eager persons assembled on the race-ground,—jockeys riding about in liveries as gay as tulips—officers in scarlet uniform—red flags fluttering in the breeze—caravans exhibiting pictures of the wildest-looking beasts in the world—bands of music—recruiting parties—fire-eaters, who dined on red-hot pokers—portraits representing pigs fatter than the fattest in the world—giants a head and three pairs of shoulders taller than any one else, and little dwarfs, scarcely visible with the naked eye—all of which were shewn to children for half-price!

Lady Rockville very good-naturedly gave Harry half-a-crown, promising that, before leaving the race-ground, he should either buy some oranges to lay the dust in his throat, after so long a drive, or visit as many shows as he pleased for his half-crown; and they were anxiously discussing what five sights would be best worth sixpence each, when a loud hurra was heard, the drums beat, and five horses started off for the first heat. Harry stood up in an ecstacy of delight, and spoke loudly in admiration of the jockey on a grey horse, with a pink jacket, who took the lead, and seemed perfectly to fly, as if he need never touch the ground; but Harry exclaimed angrily against the next rider, in a yellow dress and green cap, who pulled back his own bay horse, as if he really wished to lose. To Laura's astonishment, however, Captain Digby preferred him, and Miss Perceval declared in favour of a light-blue jacket and chestnut horse. Harry now thought everybody stupid not to agree with him, and called out, in the height of his eagerness, "I would bet this half-crown upon the pink jacket!"

"Done!" cried Peter, laughing. "The yellow dress and green cap for my money!"

"Then I shall soon have five shillings!" exclaimed Harry, in great glee; but scarcely had he spoken, before a loud murmuring sound arose among the surrounding crowd, upon hearing which he looked anxiously about, and was astonished to see the green cap and yellow dress already at the winning-post, while his own favourite grey horse cantered slowly along, far behind all the others, carrying the jockey with the pink jacket, who hung his head, and was bent nearly double with shame and fatigue.

Peter Grey gave a loud laugh of triumph when he glanced at Harry's disappointed, angry countenance, and held out his hand for the half-crown, saying, " Pay your debt of honour, Master Harry! It is rather fortunate I won, seeing that not one sixpence had I to pay you with! not a penny to jingle on a milestone. You had more money than wit, and I had more wit than money, so we are well met. Did you not see that the grey horse has fallen fame? Goodbye, youngster! I shall tell all the giants and wild beasts to expect you another day!"

"Harry!" said Lady Rockville, looking gravely at his enraged countenance, " it is a foolish fish that is caught with every bait! I am quite relieved that you lost that money. This is an early lesson against gambling, and no one can ever be rich or happy who becomes fond of it. We were wrong to bring you here at all; and I now see you could easily be led into that dreadful vice, which has caused misery and ruin to thousands of young men. If you had possessed an estate, it would have been thrown away quite as foolishly as the poor half-crown, making you perhaps miserable afterwards for life."

" I thought myself quite sure to win!" exclaimed Harry, still looking with angry astonishment after Peter, who was making odd grimaces, and holding up the half-crown in a most teasing manner.

'I would rather have thrown my money into the sea than given it to Peter."

"Think, too, how many pleasanter and better ways there are, in which you might have spent it!" added Lady Rockville. "Look at that poor blind man, whom you could have relieved, or consider what a nice present you should have given to Laura! But there seem to be no more brains in your head, Harry, than in her thimble!"

"My cousin Peter is quite a young black-leg already," observed Miss Perceval. "I never saw such a boy! So fond of attracting notice, that he would put on a cap and bells if that would make him stared at. Last Saturday he undertook for a bet, to make a ceremonious bow to every lamp-post along Prince's Street, and I wish you could have seen the wondering crowd that gradually collected as he went along, performing his task with the most perfect composure and impudence."

"For cool assurance, I hope there are not many boys equal to him," said Lady Rockville. "He scattered out of the window lately several red-hot halfpence among some beggars, and I am told they perfectly stuck to the poor creatures' fingers when trying to pick them up; and he was sent a message, on his pony, one very cold day lately, to Lady De Vere's, who offered, when he was taking leave, to cut him one of her finest camellias, to which he replied, 'I would much rather you offered me a hot potato!'"

"Peter feels no sympathy in your disappointment, Harry," added Miss Perceval; "but we might as well expect wool on a dog, as friendship from a gambler, who would ruin his own father, and always laughs at those who lose."

"Go and cut your wisdom teeth, Harry!" said Captain Digby, smiling. "Any one must have been born blind not to observe that the grey horse was falling behind; but you have bought half-a-crown's worth of wisdom by experience, and I hope it will last for life. Never venture to bet even that your own head is on your shoulders, or it may turn out a mistake."

"Harry is now the monkey that has seen the world, and I think it will be a whole year of Saturdays before he ever commits such a blunder again," continued Lady Rockville. "We must for this once, not complain of what has occurred to Lady Harriet, because she would be exceedingly displeased; but certainly you are a most ingenious little gentleman for getting into scrapes!"

Harry told upon himself, however, on his return home, because he had always been accustomed to do so, knowing Major Graham and his grandmama never were very angry at any fault that was confessed and repented of, therefore he went straight up stairs and related his whole history to uncle David, who gave him a very serious exhortation against the foolish and sinful vice of gambling. To keep him in mind of his silly adventure that day, Harry was also desired, during the whole evening, to wear his coat turned inside out, a very frequent punishment administered by Major Graham for small offences, and which was generally felt to be a terrible disgrace.

CHAPTER XIV.

THE UNEXPECTED EVENT.

> His shout may ring upon the hill,
> His voice be echoed in the hall,
> His merry laugh like music thrill,
> I scarcely notice such things now.
> WILLIS.

SOME weeks after Frank had left home, while Lady Harriet and Major Graham were absent at Holiday House, Harry and Laura felt surprised to observe that Mrs Crabtree suddenly became very grave and silent,—her voice seemed to have lost half its loudness,—her countenance looked rather pale,—and they both escaped being scolded on several occasions, when Harry himself could not but think he deserved it. Once or twice he ventured to do things that at other times he dared not have attempted, "merely as an experiment," he said, "like that man in the menagerie, who put his head into the lion's mouth without feeling quite sure whether it would be bit off the next moment or not;" but though Mrs Crabtree evidently saw all that passed, she turned away with a look of sadness, and said not a word.

What could be the matter? Harry almost wished she would fly into a good passion, and scold him, it became so extraordinary and unnatural to see Mrs Crabtree sitting all day in a corner of the room, sewing in silence, and scarcely looking up from her work; but still the wonder grew, for she seemed to become worse and worse every day. Harry dressed up the cat in an old cap and frock of Laura's,—he terrified old Jowler, by putting him into the shower-bath,—and let off a few crackers at the nursery window,—but it seemed as if he might have fired a cannon without being scolded by Mrs Crabtree, who merely turned her head round for a minute, and then silently resumed her work. Laura even fancied that Mrs Crabtree was once in tears, but that seemed quite impossible, so she thought no more about it, till one morning, when they had begun to despair of ever hearing more about the business, and were whispering together in a corner of the room, observing that she looked duller than ever, they were surprised to hear Mrs Crabtree calling them both to come near her. She looked very pale, and was beginning to say something, when her voice suddenly became so husky and indistinct, that she seemed unable to proceed; therefore, motioning with her hand for them to go away, she began sewing very rapidly, as she had done before, breaking her threads, and pricking her fingers, at every stitch, while they became sure she was sobbing and crying.

Laura and Harry silently looked at each other with some apprehension, and the nursery now became so perfectly still that a feather falling on the ground would have been heard. This had continued for some time, when at last Laura upon tip-toe stole quietly up to where Mrs Crabtree was sitting, and said to her, in a very kind and anxious voice, " I am afraid you are not well, Mrs Crabtree! Grandmama will send for a doctor when she comes home. Shall I ask her?"

" You are very kind, Miss Laura!—never mind me! Your grandmama knows what is the matter. It will be all one a hundred years hence," answered Mrs Crabtree, in a low, husky voice. " This is a thing you will be very glad to hear!—you must prepare to be told some good news!" added she, forcing a laugh, but such a laugh as Harry and Laura never heard before, for it sounded so much more like sorrow than joy. They waited in great suspense to hear what would follow; but Mrs Crabtree, after struggling to speak again with composure, suddenly started off her seat, and hurried rapidly out of the room. She appeared no more in the nursery that day, but next morning when they were at breakfast, she entered the room with her face very much covered up in her bonnet and evidently tried to speak in her usual loud, bustling voice, though somehow it still sounded perfectly different from common. "Well, children! Lady Harriet was so kind as to promise that my secret should be kept till I pleased, and that no one should mention it to you but myself. I am going away!"

"You!" exclaimed Harry, looking earnestly in Mrs Crabtree's face. "Are you going away?"

"Yes, Master Harry, I leave this house to-day! Now don't pretend to look sorry! I know you are not! I can't bear children to tell stories. Who would ever be sorry for a cross old woman like me?"

"But perhaps I am sorry! Are you in real earnest going away?" asked Harry again, with renewed astonishment. "Oh no! It is only a joke!"

"Do I look as if this were a joke?" asked Mrs Crabtree, turning round her face, which was bathed with tears. "No, no! I am come to bid you both a long farewell! A fine mess you will get into now! All your things going to rack and ruin, with nobody fit to look after them!"

"But Mrs Crabtree! we do not like you to go

away," said Laura, kindly. " Why are you leaving us all on a sudden ? it is very odd ! I never was so surprised in my life !"

" Your papa's orders are come. He wrote me a line some weeks ago, to say that I have been too severe. Perhaps that is all true. I meant it well; and we are poor creatures, who can only act for the best. However, it can't be helped now ! There's no use in lamenting over spilt cream. You'll be the better-behaved afterwards. If ever you think of me again, children, let it be as kindly as possible. Many and many a time shall I remember you both. I never cared for any young people but yourselves, and I shall never take charge of any others. Master Frank was the best boy in the world, and you would both have been as good under my care; but it is no matter now !"

" But it does matter a very great deal," cried Harry, eagerly. " You must stay here, Mrs Crabtree, as long as you live, and a great deal longer ! I shall write a letter to papa all about it. We were very troublesome, and it was our own faults if we were punished. Never mind, Mrs Crabtree, but take off your bonnet and sit down ! I am going to do some dreadful mischief to-night, so you will be wanted to keep me in order."

Mrs Crabtree laid her hand upon Harry's head in silence, and there was something so solemn and serious in her manner, that he saw it would be needless to remonstrate any more. She then held out her hand to Laura, endeavouring to smile as she did so, but it was a vain attempt, for her lip quivered, and she turned away, saying, " Who would believe I should make such a fool of myself! Farewell to you both! and let nobody speak ill of me after I am gone, if you can help it!"

Without looking round, Mrs Crabtree hurried out of the nursery and closed the door, leaving Harry and Laura perfectly bewildered with astonishment at this sudden event, which seemed more like a dream than a reality. They both felt exceedingly melancholy, hardly able to believe that she had ever formerly been at all cross, while they stood at the window, with tears in their eyes, watching the departure of her wellknown blue chest, on a wheelbarrow, and taking a last look of her red gown and scarlet shawl as she hastily followed it.

For several weeks to come, whenever the door opened, Harry and Laura almost expected her to enter, but month after month elapsed, and Mrs Crabtree appeared no more, till one day, at their earnest entreaty, Lady Harriet took them a drive of some miles into the country, to see the neat, little lodging, like a bathing-machine, by the seaside, where she lived, and maintained herself by sewing, and by going out occasionally as a sicknurse. A more delightful surprise certainly never could have been given than when Harry and Laura tapped at the cottage door, which was opened by Mrs Crabtree herself, who started back with an exclamation of joyful amazement, and looked as if she could scarcely believe her eyes on beholding them, while they laughed at the joke till tears were running down their cheeks. "Is Mrs Crabtree at home?" said Harry, trying to look very grave.

"Grandmama says we may stay here for an hour while she drives along the shore," added Laura, stepping into the house with a very merry face. "And how do you do, Mrs Crabtree?"

"Very well, Miss Laura, and very happy to see you. What a tall girl you are become! and Muster Harry, too! looking quite over his own shoulders!"

After sitting some time, Mrs Crabtree insisted on their having some dinner in her cottage; so making Harry and Laura sit down on each side of a large blazing fire, she cooked some most delicious pancakes for them in rapid succession, as fast as they could eat, tossing them high in the air first, and then rolling up each as it was fried, with a large spoonful of jam in the centre, till Harry and Laura at last said, that unless Mrs Crabtree supplied fresh appetites, she need make no more pancakes, for they thought even Peter Grey himself could scarcely have finished all she provided.

Harry had now been several months constantly attending school, where he became a great favourite among the boys, and a great torment to the masters; while, for his own part, he liked it twenty times better than he expected, because the lessons were tolerably easy to a clever boy, as he really was, and the games at cricket and foot-ball in the playground put him perfectly wild with joy. Every boy at school seemed to be his particular friend, and many called him "the holiday maker," because if ever a holiday was wished for, Harry always became leader in the scheme. The last morning of Peter Grey's appearing at school, he got the name of "the copper captain," because Mr Hannay having fined him half-a-crown, for not knowing one of his lessons, he brought the whole sum in halfpence, carrying them in his hat, and gravely counting them all out, with such a painstaking, good-boy look, that any one, to see him, would have supposed he was quite penitent and sorry for his misconduct; but no sooner had he finished the task and ranged all the halfpence neatly in rows along Mr Hannay's desk, than he was desired, in a voice of thunder, to leave the room instantly, and never to return, which accordingly he never did, having started next day on the top of the coach for Portsmouth; and the last peep Harry got of him he was buying a perfect mountain of gingerbread out of an old man's basket, to eat by the way.

Meantime Laura had lessons from a regular day-governess, who came every morning at seven, and never disappeared till four in the afternoon, so, as Mrs Crabtree remarked, "the puir thing was perfectly deaved wi' edication;" but she made such rapid progress that uncle David said it would be difficult to decide whether she was growing fastest in body or in mind. Laura seemed born to be under the tuition of none but ill-tempered people, and Madame Pirouette appeared in a constant state of irritability. During the music-lessons she sat close to the piano, with a pair of sharp-pointed scissors in her hand, and whenever Laura played a wrong note, she stuck their points into the offending finger, saying sometimes, in an angry foreign accent, "Put your toe upon 'dis note! I tell you put your toe upon 'dis note!"

"My finger, I suppose you mean?" asked Laura, trying not to laugh.

"Ah! fingare and toe! dat is all one! Speak not a word! take hold of your tongue."

"Laura!" said Major Graham one day, "I would as soon hear a gong sounding at my ear for half an hour, as most of the fine pieces you perform now. Taste and expression are quite out of date, but the chief object of ambition is, to seem as if you had four hands instead of two, from the torrent of notes produced at once. If ever you wish to please my old-fashioned ears, give me melody, —something that touches the heart and dwells in the memory,—then years afterwards, when we hear it again, the language seems familiar to our feelings, and we listen with deep delight to sounds recalling a thousand recollections of former days, which are brought back by music (real music) with distinctness and interest which nothing else can equal."

During more than two years, while Harry and Laura were rapidly advancing in education, they received many interesting letters from Frank, expressing the most affectionate anxiety to hear of their being well and happy, while his paper was filled with amusing accounts of the various wonderful countries he visited; and at the bottom of the paper, he always very kindly remembered to send them an order on his banker, as he called uncle David, drawn up in proper form, saying, "Please to pay Master Harry and Miss Laura Graham the sum of five shillings on my account. FRANCIS ARTHUR GRAHAM."

In Frank's gay, merry epistles, he kept all his little annoyances or vexations to himself, and in-

variably took up the pen with such a desire to send
cheerfulness into his own beloved home, that his
etters might have been written with a sunbeam,
they were so full of warmth and vivacity. It seemed always a fair wind to Frank, for he looked upon
the best side of every thing, and never teased his
absent friends with complaints of distresses they
could not remedy, except when he frequently mentioned his sorrow at being separated from them,
adding, that he often wished it were possible to
meet them during one day in every year, to tell
all his thoughts, and to hear theirs in return, for
sometimes now, during the night-watches, when all
other resources failed, he entertained himself by
imagining the circle of home all gathered around
him, and by inventing what each individual would
say upon any subjects he liked, while all his adventures acquired a double interest, from considering that the recital would one day amuse his dear
friends when their happy meeting at last took place.
Frank was not so over-anxious about his own comfort, as to feel very much irritated and discom-
posed at any privations that fell in his way; and
once sitting up in the middle of a dark night, with
the rain pouring in torrents, and the wind blowing
a perfect hurricane, he drew his watch-coat round
him, saying good-humouredly to his grumbling companions, "This is by no means so bad! and what-

ever change takes place now, will probably be for the better. Sunshine is as sure to come as Christmas, if you only wait for it, and, in the mean time, we are all more comfortably off than St Patrick, when he had to swim across a stormy sea, with his head under his arm."

Frank often amused his messmates with stories which he had heard from uncle David, and soon became the greatest favourite imaginable with them all, while he frequently endeavoured to lead their minds to the same sure foundation of happiness which he always found the best security of his own. He had long been taught to know that a vessel might as well be steered without rudder or compass, as any individual be brought into a haven of peace, unless directed by the Holy Scriptures; and his delight was frequently to study such passages as these: "When thou passest through the waters, I will be with thee; and through the rivers, they shall not overflow thee: when thou walkest through the fire, thou shalt not be burned; neither shall the flame kindle upon thee. For I am the Lord thy God, the Holy One of Israel, thy Saviour."

CHAPTER XV

AN UNEXPECTED VOYAGE

Full little knowest thou, that hast not tried,
How strange it is in "steam-boat" long to bide,
To fret thy soul with crosses and with cares,
To eat thy heart through comfortless despairs,
To speed to-day—to be put back to-morrow—
To feed on hope—to pine with fear and sorrow.
SPENSER.

As Harry and Laura grew older, they were gradually treated like friends and companions by Lady Harriet and Major Graham, who improved their minds by frequent interesting conversations, in which knowledge and principle were insensibly instilled into their minds, not by formal instruction, but merely by mentioning facts, or expressing opinions and sentiments, such as naturally arose out of the subjects under discussion, and accustoming the young people themselves to feel certain that their own remarks and thoughts were to be heard with the same interest as those of any other person. No surprise was expressed, if they appeared more acute or more amusing than might have been expected,—no angry contempt betrayed itself if they spoke foolishly, unless it were something positively wrong; and thus Major Graham and Lady Harriet succeeded in making that very difficult transition from treating children as toys, to becoming their confidential friends, and most trusted, as well as most respected and beloved associates.

Frank had been upwards of five years cruising on various stations abroad, and many officers who had seen him gave such agreeable reports to Major Graham of his admirable conduct on several occasions, and of his having turned out so extremely handsome and pleasing, that Lady Harriet often wished, with tears in her eyes, it were possible she might live to see him once again, though her own daily-increasing infirmities rendered that hope every hour more improbable. She was told that he spoke of her frequently, and said once when he met an aged person at the Cape, "I would give all I possess on earth, and ten times more, if I had it, to see my dear grandmother as well, and to meet her once more." This deeply affected Lady Harriet, who was speaking one day with unusual earnestness of the comfort it gave, whatever might be the will of Providence in respect to herself, that Frank seemed so happy, and liked his profession so well, when the door flew open, and Andrew hastened into the room, his old face perfectly wrinkled with delight, while he displayed a letter in his hand, saying, in a tone of breathless agitation, as he delivered it to Major Graham, " The post-mark is Portsmouth, Sir!"

Lady Harriet nearly rose from her seat with an exclamation of joy, but, unable for the exertion, she sunk back, covering her face with her hands, and listened in speechless suspense to hear whether Frank had indeed returned. Harry and Laura eagerly looked over Major Graham's shoulder, and Andrew lingered anxiously at the door, till this welcome letter was hurriedly torn open and read. The direction was certainly Frank's writing, though it seemed very different from usual, but the contents filled Major Graham with a degree of consternation and alarm, which he vainly endeavoured to conceal; for it informed him that, during a desperate engagement with some slave-ships off the coast of Africa, Frank had been most severely wounded, from which he scarcely recovered before a violent attack of fever reduced him so extremely, that the doctors declared his only chance of restoration was to be invalided home immediately; " therefore," added he, " you must all unite a prayer for my recovery with a thanksgiving for my return, and I can scarcely regret an illness that restores me to home. My heart is already with you all, but my frail, shattered body must rest some days in London, as the voyage from Sierra Leone has been extremely fatiguing and tedious."

Lady Harriet made not a single remark when this letter was closed, but tears coursed each other rapidly down her aged cheeks, while she slowly removed her hands from her face, and gazed at Major Graham, who seated himself by her side, in evident agitation, and calling back Andrew when he was leaving the room, he said, in accents of unusual emotion, " Desire John to inquire immediately whether any steam-boat sails for London to-day."

" You are right!" said Lady Harriet, feebly. " Oh! that I could accompany you! But bring him to me if possible. I dare not hope to go. Surely we shall meet at last. Now, indeed, I feel my own weakness when I cannot fly to see him. But he will be quite able for the journey. Frank had an excellent constitution,—he—he was—"

Lady Harriet's voice failed, and she burst into a convulsive agony of tears.

A few hours, and uncle David had embarked for London, where, after a short passage, he arrived at his usual lodgings in St James' Place ; but some days elapsed, during which he laboured in vain to discover the smallest trace of Frank, who had omitted, in his hurried letter from Portsmouth, to mention where he intended living in town. One evening, fatigued with his long and unavailing search, Major Graham sat down, at the British Coffeehouse, to take some refreshment before resuming his inquiries, and was afterwards about to leave the room, when he observed a very tall, interesting young man, exceedingly emaciated, who strolled languidly into the room, with so feeble a step that he seemed scarcely able to support himself. The stranger took off his hat, sunk into a seat, and passed his fingers through the dark masses of curls that hung over his pale, white forehead, his large eyes closed heavily with fatigue, his cheek assumed a hectic glow, and his head sunk upon his hand. In a low subdued voice he gave some directions to the waiter, and Major Graham, after gazing for a moment with melancholy interest at this apparently consumptive youth, was about to depart, when a turn of the young man's countenance caused him to start; he looked again more earnestly—every fibre of his frame seemed suddenly to thrill with apprehension, and at last, in a voice of doubt and astonishment, he exclaimed, "Frank!"

The stranger sprung from his seat, gazed eagerly round the room, rushed into the arms of Major Graham, and fainted.

Long and anxiously did uncle David watch for the restoration of Frank, while every means were used to revive him, and when at length he did regain his consciousness, no time was lost in conveying him to St James' Place, where, after being confined to bed and attended by Sir Astley Cooper and Sir Henry Halford during four days, they united in recommending that he should be carried some miles out of town, to the neighbourhood of Hammersmith, for change of air, till the effect of medicine and diet could be fully tried. Frank earnestly entreated that he might be taken immediately to his own home; but this the doctors pronounced quite impossible, privately hinting to Major Graham that it seemed very doubtful indeed whether he could ever be moved there at all, or whether he might survive above a few months.

"Home is anywhere that my own family live with me," said Frank, in a tone of resignation, when he heard a journey to Scotland pronounced impossible. "It is not where I am, but who I see, that signifies; and this meeting with you, uncle David, did me more good than an ocean of physic. Oh! if I could only converse with grandmama for half-an-hour, and speak to dear Harry and Laura, it would be too much happiness. I want to see how much they are both grown, and to hear their merry laugh again. Perhaps I never may! But if I get worse, they must come here. I have many many things to say! Why should they not set off now?—immediately! If I recover, we might be such a happy party to Scotland again. For grandmama, I know it is impossible; but will you write and ask her about Harry and Laura? The sooner the better, uncle David, because I often think it probable——"

Frank coloured and hesitated; he looked earnestly at his uncle for some moments, who saw what was meant, and then added,

"There is one person more, far distant, and little thinking of what is to come, who must be told. You have always been a father to me, uncle David, but he also would wish to be here now. Little as we have been together, I know how much he loves me."

Frank's request became no sooner known than it was complied with by Lady Harriet, who thought it better not to distress Harry and Laura, by mentioning the full extent of his danger, but merely said, that he felt impatient for the meeting, and that they might prepare on the following day, to embark under charge of old Andrew and her own maid Harrison, for a voyage to London, where she hoped they would find the dear invalid already better. Laura was astonished at the agitation with which she spoke, and felt bewildered and amazed by this sudden announcement. She and Harry once or twice in their lives caught cold, and spent a day in bed, confined to a diet of gruel and syrup, which always proved an infallible remedy for the very worst attacks, and they had frequently witnessed the severe sufferings of their grandmama, from which, however, she always recovered, and which seemed to them the natural effects of her extreme old age; but to imagine the possibility of Frank's life being in actual danger never crossed their thoughts for an instant, and, therefore, it was with a feeling of unutterable joy that they stood on the deck of the Royal Pandemonium, knowing that they were now actually going to meet Frank.

Nothing could be a greater novelty to both the young travellers than the scene by which they were now surrounded; trumpets were sounding—bells ringing—sailors, passengers, carriages, dogs, and baggage, all hurrying on board pell-mell, while a jet of steam came bellowing forth from the waste pipe, as if it were struggling to get rid of the huge column of black smoke vomited forth by the chimney. Below stairs they were still more astonished to find a large cabin, covered with gilding, red damask, and mirrors, where crowds of strange-looking people, more than half sick, and very cross, were scolding and bustling about, bawling for their carpet-bags, and trying to be of as much consequence as possible, while they ate and drank trash, to keep off sea-sickness, that might have made any one sick on shore—sipping brandy and water, or eating peppermint drops, according as the case required. Among those in the ladies cabin, Laura and Harry were amused to discover Miss Perceval, who had hastened into bed already, in case of being ill, and was talking unceasingly to any one who would listen, besides ordering and scolding a poor sick maid, scarcely able to stand. Her head was enveloped in a most singular night-cap, ornamented with old ribbons and artificial flowers—she wore a bright-yellow shawl, and had taken into the berth beside her a little Blenheim spaniel, a parrot, and a cage of canary birds, the noisy inhabitants of which sung at the full pitch of their voices till the very latest hour of the night, being kept awake by the lamp which swung from side to side, while nothing could be compared to their volubility except the perpetual clamour occasioned by Miss Perceval herself.

"I declare these little, narrow beds are no better than coffins! I never saw such places! and the smell is like singed blankets and cabbages boiled in melted oil! It is enough to make any body ill! Mary! go and fetch me a cup of tea; and, do you hear? tell those people on deck not to make such a noise—it gives me a headach! Be sure you say that I shall complain to the captain. Reach me some bread and milk for the parrot,— fetch my smelling bottle,—go to the saloon for that book I was reading,—and search again for the pocket-handkerchief I mislaid. It cost ten guineas, and must be found. I hope no one has stolen it! Now, do make haste with the tea! What are you dawdling there for? If you do not stop that noise on deck, Mary, I shall be exceedingly displeased! Some of those horrid people in the steerage were smoking too, but tell the captain that if I come up he must forbid them. It is a trick to make us all sick, and save provisions. I observed a gun-case in the saloon, too, which is a most dangerous thing, for guns always go off when you least expect. If any one fires, I shall fall into hysterics. I shall, indeed! What a creaking noise the vessel makes! I hope there is no danger of its splitting! We ought not to go on sailing after dusk. The captain must positively cast anchor during the night, that we may have no more of this noise or motion but sleep in peace and quietness till morning."

Soon after the Royal Pandemonium had set sail, or rather set fire, the wind freshened, and the pitching of the vessel became so rough, that Harry and Laura, with great difficulty, staggered to seats on the deck, leaving both Lady Harriet's servants so very sick below, that instead of being able to attend on them, they gave nine times the trouble that any other passenger did on board, and were not visible again during the whole voyage. The two young travellers now sat down together, and watched, with great curiosity, several groups of strangers on deck; ladies, half sick, trying to entertain gentlemen in seal-skin travelling-caps and pale cadaverous countenances, smoking cigars; others opening baskets of provisions, and eating with good, sea-faring appetite; while one party had a carriage on the deck so filled with luxuries of every kind, that there seemed no end to the multitude of Perigord pies, German sausages, cold fowls, pastry, and fruit, that were produced during the evening. The owners had a table spread on the deck, and ate voraciously, before a circle of hungry spectators, which had such an appearance of selfishness and gluttony, that both his young friends thought immediately of Peter Grey.

As evening closed in, Harry and Laura began to feel very desolate, thus for the first time in their lives alone, while the wide waste of waters around made the scene yet more forlorn. They had enjoyed unmingled delight in talking over and over about their happy meeting with Frank, and planned a hundred times how joyfully they would rush into the house, and with what pleasure they would relate all that happened to themselves, after hearing from his own mouth the extraordinary adventures which his letters had described. Laura produced from her reticule several of the last she had received, and laughed again over the funny jokes and stories they contained, inventing many new questions to ask him on the subject, and fancying she already heard his voice, and saw his bright and joyous countenance. But now the night had grown so dark and chilly, that both Harry and Laura felt themselves gradually becoming cold, melancholy, and dejected. They made an effort to walk arm-in-arm up and down the deck, in imitation of the few other passengers who had been able to remain out of bed, and they tried still to talk cheerfully; but in spite of every effort, their thoughts became mournful. After clinging together for some time, and staggering up and down, without feeling in spirits to speak, they were still shiveringly cold, yet unwilling to separate for the night, when Harry suddenly stood still, grasping Laura's arm with a look of startled astonishment, which caused her hastily to glance round in the direction where he was eagerly gazing, yet nothing became visible but the dim outline of a woman's figure, rolled up in several enormous shawls, and with her bonnet slouched far over her face.

"I am certain it was she!" whispered Harry, in a tone of breathless amazement; "almost certain!"

"Who!" asked Laura, eagerly.

Without answering, Harry sprung forward, and

seized the unknown person by the arm, who instantly looked round.——It was Mrs Crabtree!

"I am sorry you observed me, Master Harry! I did not intend to trouble you and Miss Laura during the voyage," said she, turning her face slowly towards him, when, to his surprise, he saw that the traces of tears were on her cheek, and her manner appeared so subdued, and altogether so different from former times, that Laura could yet scarcely credit her senses. "I shall not be at all in your way, children, but I —— ——I must see Master Frank again. He was always too good for this world, and he'll not be here long—Andrew told me all about it, and I could not stay behind. I wish we were all as well prepared, and then the sooner we die the better."

Harry and Laura listened in speechless consternation to these words. The very idea of losing Frank had never before crossed their imaginations for a moment, and they could have wished to believe that what Mrs Crabtree said was like the ravings of delirium, yet an irresistible feeling of awe and alarm rushed into their minds.

"Miss Laura! if you want help in undressing, call to me at any time. I was sure that doited body Harrison would be of no service. She never was fit to take care of herself, and far less of such as you. It put me wild to think of your coming all this way with nobody fit to look after you, and then the distress that must follow."

"But surely, Mrs Crabtree, you do not think Frank so very ill?" asked Laura, making an effort to recover her voice, and speaking in a tone of deep anxiety. "He had recovered from the fever, but is only rather too weak for travelling."

"Well, Miss Laura! grief always comes too soon, and I would have held my tongue had I thought you did not know the worst already. If I might order as in former days, it would be to send you both down directly, out of this heavy fog and cold wind."

"But you may order us, Mrs Crabtree," said Harry, taking her kindly by the hand; "we are very glad to see you again! and I shall do whatever you bid me! So you came all this way on purpose for us! How very kind!"

"Master Harry, I would go round the wide world to serve any one of you! Who else have I to care for? But it was chiefly to see Master Frank. Let us hope the best, and pray to be prepared for any event that may come. All things are ordained for good, and we can only make the best of what happens. The world must go round,—it must go round, and we can't prevent it."

Harry and Laura hung their heads in dismay, for

there was something agitated and solemn in Mrs Crabtree's manner, which astonished and shocked them, so they hurried silently to bed; and Laura's pillow was drenched with tears of anxiety and distress that night, though gradually, as she thought of Frank's bright colour and sparkling eyes, his joyous spirit and unbroken health, it seemed impossible that all were so soon to fade away, that the wind should have already passed over them, and they were gone, till by degrees her mind became more calm; her hopes grew into certainties; she told herself twenty times over that Mrs Crabtree must be entirely mistaken, and at last sunk into a restless, agitated slumber

Next day the sun shone, the sky was clear, and every thing appeared so full of life and joy, that Harry and Laura would have fancied the whole scene with Mrs Crabtree a distressing dream, had they not been awakened to recollection before six in the morning, by the sound of her voice, angrily rebuking Miss Perceval and other ladies, who, with too good reason, were grumbling at the hardship of sleeping, or rather vainly attempting to sleep, in such narrow uncomfortable dog-holes. Laura heard Mrs Crabtree conclude an eloquent oration on the subject of contentment, by saying, " Indeed ladies! many a brave man, and noblemen's sons too, have laid their heads on the green grass, fighting for you, so we should put up with a hard bed patiently for one night."

Miss Perceval turned angrily away, and summoned her maid to receive a multitude of new directions. "Mary, tell the Captain that when I looked out last, there was scarcely any smoke coming out of the funnel, so I am sure he is saving fuel, and not keeping good enough fires to carry us on! I never knew such shabbiness! Tell the engineer, that I insist on his throwing on more coals immediately. Bring me some hot water, as fast as possible. These towels are so coarse, I cannot on any account use them. After being accustomed to such pocket-handkerchiefs as mine, at ten guineas each, one does become particular. Can you not find a larger basin? This looks like a soup-plate, and it seems impossible here to get enough of hot water to wash comfortably."

"She should be put into the boiler of the steamboat," muttered Mrs Crabtree. "I wish them animal-magnifying doctors would put the young lady to sleep till we arrive in London."

"Now!" continued Miss Perceval, "get me another cup of tea. The last was too sweet, the one before not strong enough, and the first half cold, but this is worse than any. Do remember to mention, that yesterday-night the steward sent up a tin tea-pot a thing I cannot possibly suffer again.

We must have the urn, too, instead of that black tea-kettle; and desire him to prepare some butter-toast. I am not hungry, so three rounds will be enough. Let me have some green tea this time; and see that the cream is better than last night, when I am certain it was thickened with chalk or snails. The jelly, too, was execrable, for it tasted like sticking-plaster. I shall starve if better can't be had; and the table-cloth looked like a pair of old sheets. Tell the steward all this, and say he must get my breakfast ready on deck in half an hour; but meantime, I shall sit here with a book while you brush my hair."

The sick, persecuted maid seemed anxious to do all she was bid; so, after delivering as many of the messages as possible, she tried to stand up and do Miss Perceval's hair, but the motion of the vessel had greatly increased, and she turned as pale as death, apparently on the point of sinking to the ground, when Laura, now quite dressed, quietly slipped the brush out of her hand, and carefully brushed Miss Perceval's thin locks, while poor Mary silently dropped upon a seat, being perfectly faint with sickness.

Miss Perceval read on, without observing the change of abigails, till Harry, who had watched this whole scene from the cabin-door, made a hissing noise, such as grooms do when they currycomb a horse, which caused the young lady to look hastily round, when great was Miss Perceval's astonishment to discover her new abigail, with a very painstaking look, brushing her hair, while poor Mary lay more dead than alive on the benches. "Well! I declare! was there ever anything so odd!" she exclaimed in a voice of amazement. "How very strange! What can be the matter with Mary! There is no end to the plague of servants!"

"Or rather to the plague of mistresses!" thought Laura, while she glanced from Miss Perceval's round, red, bustling face, to the poor suffering maid, who became worse and worse during the day, for there came on what sailors call "a capful of wind," which gradually rose to a "stiff breeze," or what the passengers considered a hurricane; and, towards night, it attained the dignity of a real undeniable "storm." A scene of indescribable tumult then ensued. The captain attempted to make his voice heard above the roaring tempest, using a torrent of unintelligible nautical phrases, and an incessant volley of very intelligible oaths. The sailors flew about, and every plank in the vessel seemed creaking and straining, but high above all, the shrill tones of Miss Perceval were audibly heard exclaiming,

"Are there enough of 'hands' on board? Is there any danger? Are you sure the boiler will not burst? I wish steam-boats had never been invented! People are sure to be blown up to the clouds, or sunk to the bottom of the ocean, or scalded to death, like so many lobsters. I cannot stand this any longer! Stop the ship, and set me on shore instantly!"

Laura clung closer to Harry, and felt that they were like two mere pigmies, amid the wide waste of waters, rolling and tossing around them, while his spirits, on the contrary, rose to the highest pitch of excitement with all he heard and saw, till at length, wishing to enjoy more of the "fun," he determined to venture above board. By the time Harry's nose was on a level with the deck, he gazed around, and saw that not a person appeared visible except two sailors, both lashed to the helm, while all was silent now, except the deafening noise made by the wild waves, and the stormy blast, which seemed as if it would blow his teeth down his throat. Harry thought the two men looked no larger than mice in such a scene, and stood, clinging to the bannisters, perfectly entranced with astonishment and admiration at the novelty of all he saw, and thinking how often Frank must have been in such scenes, when suddenly a wave washed quite over the deck, and he felt his arm grasped by Mrs Crabtree, who desired him to come down immediately, in a tone of authority which he did not even yet feel bold enough to disobey; therefore, slowly and reluctantly he descended to the cabin, where the only living thing that seemed well enough to move, was Miss Perceval's tongue.

"Steward!" she cried, in sharp, angry accents. "Steward! here is water pouring down the sky-lights like a shower-bath! Look at my band-box swimming on the floor! Mary! tiresome creature! don't you see that? My best bonnet will be destroyed! Send the captain here! He must positively stop that noise on deck; it is quite intolerable! My head aches, as if it would burst like the boiler of a steam-boat! Stupid man! Can't he put into some port, or cast anchor? How can he keep us all uncomfortable in this way! Mary! Mary! I say! are you deaf? Steward! send one of the sailors here to take care of this dog! I declare poor Frisk is going to be sick! Mary! Mary! This is insufferable! I wish the Captain would come and help me to scold my maid! I shall certainly give you warning, Mary."

This awful threat had but little effect on one who thought herself on the brink of being buried beneath the waves, besides being too sick to care whether she died the next minute or not; and even Miss Perceval's voice became drowned at last in the tremendous storm which raged throughout the night, during which the captain rather increased

Laura's panic, if that were possible, by considerately putting his head into the cabin now and then to say, "Don't be afraid, ladies! There is no danger!"

"But I must come up and see what you are about, Captain!" exclaimed Miss Perceval.

"You had better be still, ma'am," replied Mrs Crabtree. "It is as well to be drowned in bed as on deck."

Nothing gives a more fearful idea of the helplessness of man, and the wrath of God, than a tempestuous sea during the gloom of midnight; and every mind on board became awed into silence and solemnity during this war of elements, till at length, towards morning, while the hurricane seemed yet raging with undiminished fury, Laura suddenly gave an exclamation of rapture, on hearing a sailor at the helm begin to sing "Tom Bowling." "Now I feel sure the danger is over," said she, "otherwise that man could not have the heart to sing! If I live a century, I shall always like a sailor's song for the future."

It is seldom that any person's thankfulness after danger bears a fair proportion to the fear they felt while it lasted; but Harry and Laura had been taught to remember where their gratitude was due, and felt it the more deeply next day, when they entered the Yarmouth Roads, and were shewn the masts of several vessels, appearing partly above the water, which had on various occasions been lost in that wilderness of shoals, where so many melancholy catastrophes have occurred.

After sailing up the Thames, and duly staring at Greenwich Hospital, the hulks, and the Tower of London, they landed at last; and having offered Mrs Crabtree a place in the hackney coach, they hurried impatiently into it, eager for the happy moment of meeting with Frank. Harry, in his ardour, thought that no carriage had ever driven so slowly before. He wished there had been a rail road through the town; and, far from wasting a thought upon the novelties of Holborn or Piccadilly, he and Laura gained no idea of the metropolis more distinct than that of the Irishman who complained he could not see London for the quantity of houses. One only idea filled their hearts, and brightened their countenances, while they looked at each other with a smile of delight, saying, " Now, at last, we are going to see Frank!"

CHAPTER XVI.

THE ARRIVAL.

What is life?—— a varied tale,
Deeply moving, quickly told.
                    WILLIS.

"Oh! what a lovely cottage!" exclaimed Laura, in an ecstacy of joy, when they stopped before a beautiful house, with large, airy windows down to the ground; walls that seemed one brilliant mass of roses; rich flowery meadows in front, and a bright, smooth lawn behind, stretching down to the broad bosom of the Thames, which reflected on its glassy surface innumerable boats, filled with gay groups of merry people. "That is such a place as I have often dreamed of, but never saw before! It seems made for perfect happiness!"

"Yes! how delightful to live here with Frank and uncle David!" added Harry. "We shall be sailing on the water all day!"

The cottage-gate was now opened, and Major Graham himself appeared under the porch; but instead of hurrying forward, as he always formerly did, to welcome them after the very shortest separation, he stood gravely and silently at the door, without so much as raising his eyes from the ground; and the paleness of his countenance filled both Harry and Laura with astonishment. They flew to meet him, making an exclamation of joy; but after embracing them affectionately, he did not utter a word, and led the way, with hurried and agitated steps, into a sitting-room.

"Where is Frank?" exclaimed Harry, looking eagerly round. "Why is he not here? Call him down! Tell him we are come!"

A long pause ensued; and Laura trembled when she looked at her uncle, who was some moments before he could speak, and sat down taking each of them by the hand, with such a look of sorrow and commiseration, that they were filled with alarm.

"My dear Harry and Laura!" said he, solemnly, "you have never known grief till now; but if you love me listen with composure. I have sad news to tell, yet it is of the very greatest consequence that you should bear up with fortitude. Frank is extremely ill; and the joy he felt about your coming has agitated him so much, that he is worse than you can possibly conceive. It probably depends upon your conduct now, whether he survives this night or not. Frank knows you are here; he is impatient for you to embrace him; he becomes more and more agitated every moment the meeting is delayed; yet if you give way to childish grief, or even to childish joy, upon seeing him again, the doctors think it may cause his immediate death. You might hear his breathing in any part of this house. He is in the lowest extreme of weakness! It will be a dreadful scene for you both. Tell me, Harry and Laura, can you trust yourselves? Can you, for Frank's own sake, enter his room this moment, as quietly as if you had seen him yesterday, and speak to him with composure?"

Laura felt, on hearing these words, as if the very earth had opened under her feet,—a choking sensation arose in her throat,—her colour fled,—her limbs shook,—her whole countenance became convulsed with anguish,—but making a resolute effort, she looked anxiously at Harry, and then said, in a low, almost inaudible voice,

"Uncle David! we are able,—God will strengthen us. I dare not think a moment. The sooner it is done the better. Let us go now."

Major Graham slowly led the way without speaking, till he reached the bed-room door, where he paused for a moment, while Harry and Laura listened to the gasping sound of Frank struggling for breath.

"Remember you will scarcely know him," whispered he, looking doubtfully at Laura's pallid countenance; "but a single expression of emotion may be fatal. Shew your love for Frank now, my dear children. Spare him all agitation;—forget your own feelings for his sake."

When Harry and Laura entered the room Frank buried his face in his hands, and leaned them on the table, saying, in convulsive accents, "Go away, Laura!—oh go away just now! I cannot bear it yet!—leave me!—leave me!"

If Laura had been turned into marble at the moment, she could not have seemed more perfectly calm, for her mind was wound up to an almost supernatural effort, and advancing to the place where he sat, without attempting to speak, she took Frank by the hand—Harry did the same; and not a sound was heard for some moments, but the convulsive struggles of Frank himself, while he gasped for breath, and vainly tried to speak, till at length he raised his head and fixed his eyes on Laura. Then, for the first time, was she struck with the dreadful conviction that this meeting was but a prelude to their immediate and final separation. The pale, ashy cheek, the hollow eye, the sharp and altered features, all told a tale of anguish such as she had never before conceived, and a cold tremor passed through her frame, as she stood amazed and bewildered with grief, while the past, the present, and the future seemed all one mighty heap of agony. Still she gazed steadily on Frank, and said nothing, conscious that the smallest indulgence of emotion would bring forth a torrent which nothing could control, and determined, unless her heart ceased to beat, that he should see nothing to increase his agitation.

At length, in a low, faint, broken voice, Frank was able to speak, and looking with affectionate sympathy at Laura, he said, " Do not think, dear sister, that I always suffer as you see me now. This joy has been too much for me. I shall soon feel easier."

Major Graham observed a livid paleness come over Laura's countenance, when she attempted to answer, and seeing it was impossible to sustain the trial a moment longer, he made a pretext to hurry her away. Harry instantly followed, and rushing into a vacant room, he threw himself down in an agony of grief, and wept convulsively, till the very bed shook beneath him. Hours passed on, and Major Graham left them to exhaust their grief in weeping together, but every moment seemed only to increase their agitation, as the conviction be came more fearfully certain, that Frank was indeed lost to them for ever. This, then, was the meeting they had so often and so joyously anticipated! Laura sunk upon her knees beside Harry, and prayers were mingled with their tears, while they asked for consolation, and tried to feel resigned "Alas!" thought she, solemnly, "how truly did grandmama say, 'If the sorrows of this world are called "light afflictions," what must be those from which Christ died to save us!' It is merciful that we are not forbid to weep; for, oh! who ever lost such a brother?—the kindest—the best of brothers! —dear, dear Frank!—can nothing be done! Uncle David," added Laura, clinging to Major Graham, when he entered the room, "oh! say something to us about Frank getting better,—do you think he will? May we have a hope?—one single hope to live upon, that Frank may possibly be spared; do not turn away—do not look so very sad—think how young Frank is,—and the doctors are so skilful —and—and—oh, uncle David! he is dying! I see it! I must believe it!" continued she, wringing her hands with grief. "You cannot give us one word of hope, though the whole world would be nothing without him."

"My dear,—my very dear Laura! remember that consoling text in Holy Scripture, 'Be still, and know that I am God;'—we have no idea what He can do in saving us from sorrow, or in comforting us when it comes; therefore let us seek peace from Him, and believe that all shall indeed be ordered well, even though our own hearts were to be broken with affliction. Frank has seen old nurse Crabtree, and is now in a refreshing sleep; therefore I wish you to take the opportunity of sitting in his room, and accustoming yourselves, if possible, to the sight of his altered appearance. He is sometimes very cheerful, and always patient; therefore we must keep up our own spirits, and try to assist him in bearing his sufferings, rather than increase them by shewing what we feel ourselves. I was pleased with you both this morning—that meeting was no common effort; and now we must shew our submission to the Divine will, difficult as that may be, by a deep heartfelt resignation to whatever He ordains."

Harry and Laura still felt stupified with grief, but they mechanically followed Major Graham into Frank's room, and sat down in a distant corner behind his chair, observing with awe and astonishment his pallid countenance, his emaciated hands, and his drooping figure, while scarcely yet able to believe that this was indeed their own beloved Frank. After they had remained immoveably still for some time, though shedding many bitter tears, as they gazed on the wreck of one so very dear, he suddenly started awake, and glanced anxiously round the room, then with a look of deep disappointment, he said to uncle David, in low, feeble accents,

"It was only a dream! I have often dreamed the same thing, when far away at sea—that would have been too much happiness! I fancied Harry and Laura were here!"

"It was no dream, dear Frank! we are here," said Laura, trying to speak in a quiet, subdued voice.

"My dear sister! then all is well; but pray sit always where I can see you. After wishing so long for our meeting, it appears nearly impossible that we are together at last."

Frank became exhausted with speaking so much, but pointed to a seat near himself, where Harry and Laura sat down, after which he gazed at them long and earnestly, with a look of affectionate pleasure; while his smile, which had lost all its former cheerfulness, was now full of tenderness and sensibility. At length his countenance gradually changed, while large tears gathered in his eyes, and coursed each other silently down his cheeks. Thoughts of the deepest sadness seemed passing through his mind during some moments, but checking the heavy sigh that rose in his breast, he rivetted his hands together, and looked towards heaven with an expression of placid submission, saying these words in a scarcely audible tone, though evidently addressed to those around,

"Weeping endureth for a night, but joy cometh in the morning."—"We know that if our earthly house of this tabernacle be dissolved, we have a building of God, an house not made with hands, eternal in the heavens."—"Weep ye not for the dead, neither bemoan him; *but* weep sore for him that goeth away: for he shall return no more, nor see his native country."*

These words fell upon the ear of Harry and Laura like a knell of death, for they now saw that Frank himself believed he was dying, and it appeared as if their last spark of hope expired when they heard this terrible dispensation announced from his own lips. He seemed anxious now that they should understand his full meaning, and receive all the consolation which his mind could afford, for he closed his eyes, and added in solemn accents,

"I must have died at some time, and why not now? If I leave friends who are very dear on earth, I go to my chief best friend in heaven. The whole peace and comfort of my mind rest on thinking of our Saviour's merits. Let us all be ready to say, 'The will of the Lord be done.' Think often,

* Jeremiah xxii. 10

Harry and Laura, of those words we so frequently repeated to grandmama formerly:

> 'Take comfort, Christians, when your friends
> In Jesus fall asleep;
> Their better being never ends;
> Why then dejected weep?
>
> Why inconsolable, as those
> To whom no hope is giv'n?
> Death is the messenger of peace,
> And calls 'my' soul to heav'n.'"

Frank's voice failed, his head fell back upon the pillows, and he remained for a length of time with his eyes closed in solemn meditation and prayer, while Laura and Harry, unable so much as to look at each other, leaned upon the table, and wept in silence.

Laura felt as if she had grown old in a moment,—as if life could give no more joy—and as if she herself stood already on the verge of the grave. It appeared like a dream that she had ever been happy, and a dreadful reality to which she was now awakened. " Behold, God taketh away! who can hinder Him? who will say unto Him, What doest thou!" " Cease ye from man, whose breath is in his nostrils." These were texts which forced themselves on her mind, with mournful emphasis, while she felt how helpless is earthly affection when the dispensations of God are upon us. All her love for Frank could not avert the stroke of death,—all his attachment to her must now be buried in the grave,—and the very tenderness they felt for each other only embittered the sorrow of this dreadful moment.

From that day, Harry and Laura, according to the advice of uncle David, testified their affection for Frank, not by tears and useless lamentations, though these were not always to be controlled in private, but by the incessant, devoted attention with which they watched his looks, anticipated his wishes, and thought every exertion a pleasure which could in the slightest degree contribute to his comfort. Frank, on his part, spared their feelings, by often concealing what he suffered, and by speaking of his own death, as if it had been a journey on which he must prepare with readiness to enter reminding them, that never to die was never to be happy, as all they saw him endure from sickness, became nothing to what he endured from struggling against sin and temptation, which were the great evils of existence,—and that from all these he would be for ever freed by death. "Those who are prepared for the change," added he, solemnly, "can neither live too long, nor die too soon; for when God gives us His blessing, He then sends heaven, as it were, into the soul before the soul ascends to heaven; and I trust to being gifted with faith and submission for all that may be ordained during my few remaining hours upon earth."

Yet, with every desire to feel resigned, Frank himself was sometimes surprised out of his usual fortitude, especially when thinking that he must never more hope to see Lady Harriet, towards whom he cast many a longing and affecting thought, saying once, with deep emotion, " If I could only see grandmama again, I should feel quite well!" One evening, as he sat near an open window, gazing on the rich tints of twilight, and breathing with more than usual ease, a wandering musician paused with her guitar, and sung several airs with great pathos and expression. At length she played the tune of " Home! sweet home!" to which Frank listened for some moments with intense agitation, till, clasping his hands and bursting into tears, he exclaimed, in accents of powerful emotion,

" Home! That happy home! Oh! never—never more,—*my* home is in the grave."

Laura wept convulsively while he added, in broken accents, " I shall still be remembered——still lamented——you must not love me too well, Laura, —not as I love you, or your sorrow would be too great; but long hence, when Harry and you are happy together, surrounded with friends, think sometimes of one who must for ever be absent,— who loved you better than them all,—whose last prayer will be for you both. Oh! who can tell what my feelings are! I can do nothing now but cause distress and anguish to those who love me best!'

"Frank, I would not exchange your affection for the wealth of worlds. As long as I live, it will be my greatest earthly happiness to have had such a brother; and if we are to suffer a sorrow that I cannot name, and dare not think of, you are teaching me how to bear it, and leaving us the only comfort we can have, in knowing that you are happy."

"Many plans and many hopes I had for the future, Laura," added Frank; "but there is no future to me now in this world. Perhaps I may escape a multitude of sorrows, but how gladly would I have shared all yours, and ensured my best happiness, by uniting with Harry and you in living to God. If you both learn more by my death than by my life, then, indeed, I do rejoice. With respect to myself it matters but little, a few years or hours sooner; for I may say, in the words of Job, 'Though He slay me, yet will I trust in Him.'"

Frank's sufferings increased every day, and became so very great at last, that the doctor proposed giving him strong doses of laudanum, to bring on a stupor and allay the pain; but when this was mentioned to him he said, "I know it is my duty to take whatever you prescribe, and I certainly shall; but if we can do without opiates, let me entreat you to refrain from them. Often formerly at sea I used to think it very sad how few of those I attended in sickness, were allowed by the physician to die in possession of their senses on account of being made to take laudanum, which gave them false spirits, and temporary ease. Let me retain my faculties as long as they are mercifully granted to me. I can bear pain,—at least, God grant me strength to do so,—but I cannot willingly enter the presence of my Creator in a state little short of intoxication."

Many days of agony followed this resolution on the part of Frank; but though the medicine, which would have brought some hours of oblivion, lay within reach, he persevered in wishing to preserve his consciousness, whatever suffering it might cost; and though now and then a prayer for bodily relief was wrung from him in his acute agony, the most frequent and fervent supplications that he uttered night and day were, in an accent of intense emotion, " God, have mercy upon my soul."

Harry and Laura were surprised to find the fields and walks near London so very rural and beautiful as they appeared at Hammersmith, and to meet with much more simplicity and kindness among the common people than they had anticipated. The poorer neighbours, who became aware of their affliction, testified a degree of sympathy which frequently astonished them, and was often afterwards remembered with pleasure, one instance of which seemed peculiarly touching to Laura. Frank always suffered most acutely during the night, and seldom closed his eyes in sleep till morning, therefore she invariably remained with him, to beguile those weary hours; while any remonstrance on his part against so fatiguing a duty, became a mere waste of words, as she only grew sadder and paler, saying, there would be time enough to take care of herself, when she could no longer be of use to him. The earliest thing that gave any relief to Frank's cough every day, generally was a tumbler of milk, warm from the cow, which had been ordered for him, and was brought almost as soon as the dawn of light. Once, when Frank had been unusually ill, and sighed in restless agony till morning, Laura watched impatiently for day, and when the milkman was seen at six o'clock, slowly trudging through the fields, and advancing leisurely towards the house, Laura hurried eagerly down to meet him, exclaiming, in accents of joy, while she held out the tumbler, "Oh, I am so glad you are come at last!"

"At last, Miss!! I am as early as usual!" replied he, gruffly. "It's not many poor folks that gets up so soon to their work, and if you had to labour as hard as me all day, you would maybe think the morning came too soon."

"I am seldom in bed all night," answered Laura, sadly. "My poor, sick brother cannot rest till this milk is brought, and I wait with him, hour after hour till day-light, wearying for you to come."

The old dairyman looked with sorrowful surprise at Laura, while she, thinking no more of what had passed, hurried away; but next morning, when sitting up with Frank, she became surprised to observe the milkman a whole hour earlier than usual, plodding along towards his cattle at a peculiarly rapid pace. He stayed not more than five minutes, only milking one cow, though all the others gathered round him, and as soon as he had filled his little pail, he came straight towards Major Graham's cottage, and knocked at the door. Laura instantly ran down to thank him with her whole heart for his kind attention, after which, as long as Frank continued ill, the old dairyman rose long before his usual time, to bring this welcome refreshment.

Frank desired Laura to beg that he would not take so much trouble, or else to insist on his accepting some remuneration, but the old man would neither discontinue the custom, nor receive any recompense.

"Let me see this kind, good dairyman, to thank

him myself," said Frank, one night, when he felt rather easier; and next morning, Laura invited poor Teddy Collins to walk up stairs, who looked exceedingly astonished, though very much pleased at the proposal, saying, "Maybe, Ma'am, the poor, young gentleman would not like to see a stranger like me!"

"No one is a stranger who feels for him as you have done," replied Laura, leading the way, and Frank's countenance lighted up with a smile of pleasure when they entered his room. He held out his thin, emaciated hand to Teddy, who looked earnestly and sorrowfully in his face as he grasped hold of it, saying, "You look very poorly, Sir! I'm afraid indeed you are sadly ill."

"That I am! as ill as any one can be on this side of eternity! My tale is told, my days are numbered; but I would not go out of this world without saying how grateful we both feel for your attention. As a cup of cold water given in Christian kindness shall hereafter be rewarded, I trust also that your attention to me may not be forgotten."

"You are heartily welcome, Sir! It is a great honour for a poor, old man like me to oblige anybody. I shall not long be able for work now, seeing that I am upwards of threescore and ten, and my days are already full of labour and sorrow."

"To both of us, then, the night is far spent, and

the day is at hand," replied Frank. "How strange it seems, that, old as you are, I am still older; my feeble frame will be sooner worn out, and my body laid at rest in the grave! Let me hope that you have already applied your heart to wisdom; for every child of earth must, sooner or later, find how short is every thing but eternity. While I appear before you here as a spectacle of mortality, think how soon and how certainly you must follow. May you then find, as I do, that even in the last extreme of sickness and sorrow, there is comfort in looking forward to such blessings as 'eye hath not seen, nor ear heard.' Farewell, my kind friend! In this world we shall meet no more, but there is another and a better."

The old man, apparently unwilling to withdraw, paused for some moments after Frank had ceased to speak. He muttered a few inaudible words in reply, and then slowly and sorrowfully left the room, while Frank's head sunk languidly on the pillows, and Laura retired to her room, where, as usual, she wept herself to sleep.

When Harry and Laura first arrived at Hammersmith, Frank felt anxious that they should walk out every day for the benefit of their health; but finding that each made frequent excuses for remaining constantly with him at home, he invented a plan which induced them to take exercise regularly.

Being early in June, strawberries were yet so exceedingly rare, that they could scarcely be had for any money; but the doctor had allowed his patient to eat fruit. Frank asked his two young attendants to wander about in quest of gardens where a few strawberries could be got, and to bring him some. Accordingly, they set out one morning; and after a long, unsuccessful search, at last observed a small green-house near the road, with one little basket in the window, scarcely larger than a thimble, containing two or three delicious Kean's seedlings, perfectly ripe. These were to be sold for five shillings; but hardly waiting to ascertain the price, Laura seized this welcome prize with delight, and paid for it on the spot. Every morning afterwards, her regular walk was to hasten with Harry towards this pretty little shop, where they talked to the gardener about poor Frank being so very ill, and told him that this fine fruit was wanted for their sick brother at home.

One day the invalid seemed so much worse than usual, that neither Harry nor Laura could bear to leave him a moment; so they requested Mrs. Crabtree to fetch the strawberries, which she readily agreed to do; but on drawing out her purse in the shop, and saying that she came to buy that little basket of fruit at the window, what was her astonishment when the gardener looked civil and sorry, answering that he would not sell those strawberries if she offered him a guinea a-piece.

"No!" exclaimed Mrs Crabtree, getting into a rage; "then what do you put them up at the window for? There is no use pretending to keep a shop, if you will not sell what is in it! Give me these strawberries this minute, and here's your five shillings!"

"It is quite impossible," replied the gardener, holding back the basket. "You see, Ma'am, every day last week, a little Master and Miss came to this here shop, buying my strawberries for a young gentleman who is very ill; and they look both so sweet and so mournful like, that I would not disappoint them for all the world. They seem later to-day than usual, and are, maybe, not coming at all; but if I lose my day's profits, it can't be helped. They shall not walk here for nothing if they please to come!"

When Mrs Crabtree explained that she belonged to the same family as Harry and Laura, the gardener looked hard at her to see if she were attempting to deceive him; but feeling convinced that she spoke the truth, he begged her to carry off the basket to his young friends, positively refusing to take the price.

CHAPTER XVII.

THE LAST BIRTH-DAY.

Mere human pow'r shall fast decay,
And youthful vigour cease;
But they who wait upon the Lord
In strength shall still increase.

FRANK felt no unnatural apathy or indifference about dying, for he looked upon it with awe, though not with fear; nor did he express any rapturous excitement on the solemn occasion, knowing that death is an appointed penalty for transgression, which, though deprived of its sharpest sting by the triumphs of the Cross, yet awfully testifies to all succeeding generations, that each living man has individually merited the utmost wrath of God, and that the last moment on earth, of even the most devoted Christian, must be darkened by the gloom of our original sin and natural corruption. Yet, "as in Adam all die, so in Christ are all made alive;" and amidst the throng of consolatory and affecting meditations that crowded into his mind on the great subject of our salvation, he kept a little book in which were carefully recorded such texts and reflections as he considered likely to strengthen his own faith, and to comfort those he left behind—saying, one day, to Major Graham,

"Tell grandmama, that though my days have been few upon the earth, they were happy! When you think of me, uncle David, after my sufferings are over, it may well be a pleasing remembrance, that you were always the best, the kindest of friends. Oh! how kind!—but I must not—cannot speak of that——. This is my birth-day! my last birth-day! Many a joyous one we kept together, but those merry days are over, and these sadder ones too shall cease; yet the time is fast approaching, so welcome to us both,

'When death-divided friends at last
Shall meet to part no more.'"

In the evening, Major Graham observed that Frank made Mrs Crabtree bring everything belonging to him, and lay it on the table, when he employed himself busily in tying up a number of little parcels, remarking, with a languid smile,

"My possessions are not valuable, but these are for some old friends and messmates, who will be pleased to receive a trifling memorial of one who loved them. Send my dirk to Peter Grey, who is quite reformed now. He is the bravest officer and the kindest friend in the world! Here are all the letters any of you ever sent me; how very often they have been read! but now, even that intercourse must end; keep them, for they were the dearest treasures I possessed. At Madras, formerly, I remember hearing of a nabob who was bringing his whole fortune home in a chest of gold, but the ropes for hoisting his treasure on board were so insufficient, that the whole gave way, and it fell into the ocean never to be recovered. That seemed a very sudden termination of his hopes and plans, but scarcely more unexpected than my own. ' We are a wind that passeth away, and cometh not again.' Many restless nights are ordained for me now, probably that I may find no resource but prayer and meditation. Others can afford time to slumber, but I so soon shall sleep the sleep of death, that it becomes a blessing to have such hours of solitary thought, for preparing my heart and establishing my faith, during this moment of need."

"Yes, Frank! but your prayers are not solitary, for ours are joined to yours," added Laura. "I read in an old author lately, that Christian friends in this world might be compared to travellers going along the same road in separate carriages—sometimes they are together—often they are apart—sometimes they can exchange assistance, as we do now—and often they jostle against each other, till at last, having reached the journey's end, they are removed out of these earthly vehicles into a better state, where they shall look back upon former circumstances, and know even as they are known."

Laura was often astonished to observe the change which had taken place in her own character and feelings, within the very short period of their distress. Her extreme terror of a thunderstorm formerly had occasioned many a jest to her brothers, when Harry used, occasionally, to roll heavy weights in the room above her own, to imitate the loudest peals, while Frank sometimes endeavoured to argue her out of that excessive apprehension with which she listened to the most distant surmise of a storm. Now, however, at Hammersmith, long after midnight, the moon, on one occasion, became completely obscured by dense heavy clouds, and the air felt so oppressively hot, that Frank, who seemed unusually breathless, drew closer to the window. Laura supported his head, and was deeply occupied in talking to him, when suddenly a broad flash of lightning glared into the room, followed by a crash of thunder, that seemed to crack the very heavens. Again and again, the lightning gleamed in her face with such vividness, that Laura fancied she could distinguish the heat of it, and yet she stirred not, nor did a single exclamation, as in former days, arise on her lips.

"Pray, shut the window, Laura," said Frank. languidly raising his eyes; "and be so kind as to close the shutters!"

"Why, Frank?—you never used to be alarmed by thunder!"

"No! nor am I now, dear Laura. What danger need a dying person fear? Some few hours sooner or later would be of little consequence—

> Come he slow, or come he fast,
> It is but Death that comes at last.

Yet, Laura, do you think I have forgotten old times? Oh! no!—not while I live. You attend to my feelings, and surely it is my duty to remember yours."

"Never mind me, Frank!" whispered Laura. "I have got over all that folly. When real fears and sorrows come, we care no more about those that were imaginary."

"True, my dear sister; and there is no courage or fortitude like that derived from faith in a superintending Providence. Though all creation reel, we may sleep in peace, for, to Christians, 'danger is safe, and tumult calm.'"

When Frank grew worse, he became often delirious. Yet, as in health, he had been habitually cheerful, his mind generally wandered to agreeable subjects. He fancied himself walking on the bright meadows, and picking flowers by the river side,—talking to Peter Grey,—meeting Lady Harriet, and even speaking to his father, as if Sir Edward had been present; while Harry and Laura listened, weeping and trembling, to behold the wreck of such a mind and heart as his. One evening he seemed unusually well, and requested that his arm-chair might be wheeled to the open window, where he gazed with delight at the hills and meadows,—the clouds and glittering water,—the cattle standing in the stream,—the boats reflected on its surface,—and the roses fluttering at every casement.

"Those joyous little birds!—their song makes me cheerful," said he, in a tone of placid enjoyment. "I have been in countries where the birds never sing, and the leaves never fade; but they excited no sympathy or interest. Here we have notes of gladness both in sunshine and storm, teaching us a lesson of grateful contentment,—while those drooping roses preach a sermon to me, for as easily might they recover freshness and bloom as myself. We shall both lie low before long in the dust, yet a spring shall come hereafter to revive even the 'ashes of the urn.' Then, uncle David, we meet again,—not as now, amidst sorrow and suffering, with death and separation before us, but blessed by the consciousness that our sins are forgiven,—our trials all ended,—and that our afflictions, which were but for a moment, have worked out for us a far more exceeding, even an eternal weight of glory."

Some hours afterwards, the doctor entered. After receiving a cordial welcome from Frank, and feeling his pulse, he instantly examined his arms and neck, which were covered entirely over with small red spots, upon observing which, the friendly physician suddenly changed countenance, and stole an alarmed glance at Major Graham.

"I feel easier and better to-day, doctor, than at any time since my illness," said Frank, looking earnestly in his face. "Do you think this eruption will do me good? Life has much that would be dear to me, while I have friends like these to live for. Can it be possible that I may yet recover?"

The doctor turned away, unable to reply, while Frank intensely watched his countenance, and then gazed at the pale, agitated face of Major Graham. Gradually the hope which had brightened in his cheek began to fade,—the lustre of his eye became dim,—his countenance settled into an expression of mournful resignation,—and covering his face with his hands, he said, in a voice of deep emotion,

"I see how it is!—God's will be done!"

The silence of death succeeded, while Frank laid his head on the pillow and closed his eyes. A few natural tears coursed each other slowly down his cheek; but at length, an hour or two afterwards, being completely exhausted, he fell into a gentle sleep, from which the doctor considered it very doubtful if he would ever awaken, as the red spots indicated mortification, which must inevitably terminate his life before next day.

Laura retired to the window, making a strenuous effort to restrain her feelings, that she might be enabled to witness the last awful scene; and fervently did she pray for such strength to sustain it with fortitude, as might still render her of some use to her dying brother. Her pale countenance might almost have been mistaken for that of a corpse, but for the expression of living agony in her eye; and she was sunk in deep, solemn thought, when her attention became suddenly roused by observing a chariot and four drive furiously up to the gate, while the horses were foaming and panting as they stopped. A tall gentleman, of exceedingly striking appearance, sprung hurriedly out, walked rapidly towards the cottage door, and in another minute entered Frank's room, with the animated look of one who expected to be gladly welcomed, and to occasion an agreeable surprise.

Harry and Laura shrunk close to their uncle, when the stranger, now in evident agitation, gazed round the room with an air of painful astonishment, till Major Graham looked round, and instantly started up with an exclamation of amazement, "Edward! is it possible! This is indeed a con‑ ....ation! you are still in time!"

"In time!!" exclaimed Sir Edward, grasping his brother's hand with vehement agitation. "Do you mean to say that Frank is yet in danger!"

Major Graham mournfully shook his head, and undrawing the bed-curtains, he silently pointed to the sleeping countenance of Frank, which was as still as death, and already overspread by a ghastly paleness. Sir Edward then sunk into a chair, and clenched his hands over his forehead with a look of unspeakable anguish, saying, in an under tone, "Worn out as I am, in mind and body, I needed not this to destroy me! Say at once, brother, is there any hope?"

"None, my dear Edward! None! Even now he is insensible, and I fear with little prospect of ever becoming conscious again."

At this moment, Frank opened his eyes, which were dim and glassy, while it became evident that he had relapsed into a state of temporary delirium.

"Get more candles! how very dark it is!" he said. "Who are all those people? Send away everybody but grandmama! I must speak to her alone. Never tell papa of all this, it would only distress him—say nothing about me. Why do Harry and Laura never come? They have been absent more than a week! Who took away uncle David too?"

Laura listened for sometime in an agony of grief, till at last, unable any longer to restrain her feelings, she clasped Frank in her arms, and burst into tears, exclaiming, in accents of piercing distress, "Oh Frank! Frank! have you forgotten poor Laura?"

"Not till I am dead!" whispered he, while a momentary gleam of recollection lighted up his face. "Not even then! Laura' we meet again."

Sir Edward now wished to speak, but Frank had relapsed into a state of feeble unconsciousness, from which nothing could arouse him; once or twice he repeated the name of Laura in a low, melancholy voice, till it became totally inaudible—his breath became shorter—his lips became livid—his whole frame seemed convulsed—and some hours afterwards, all that was mortal of Frank Graham ceased to exist. About four in the morning his body was at rest, and his spirit returned to God who gave it.

The candles had burned low in their sockets, and still the mourners remained, unwilling to move from the awful scene of their bereavement. Mrs Crabtree at length, who laid out the body herself, extinguished the lights, and flung open the window-curtains. Then suddenly a bright blaze of sunshine streamed into the room, and rested on the cold, pale face of the dead. To the stunned and bewildered senses of Harry and Laura, the brilliant dawn of morning seemed like a mockery of their distress. Many persons were already passing by—the busy stir of life had begun, and a boy strolling along the road whistled his merry tune as he went gaily on.

"We are indeed mere atoms in the world!" thought Laura, bitterly, while these sights and sounds fell heavily on her heart. "If Harry and I had been dead also, the sun would have shone as brightly the birds sung as joyfully, and those people been all as gay and happy as ever! Nobody is thinking of Frank—nobody knows our misery—the world is going on as if nothing had happened, and we are breaking our hearts with grief!"

Laura's agony became calm as she gazed on the peaceful and almost happy expression of those beautiful features, which had now lost all appearance of suffering. The eyes, from which nothing but kindness and love had beamed upon her, were now closed for ever; the lips which had spoken only words of generous affection and pious hope, were silent; and the heart which had beat with every warm and brotherly feeling, was for the first time insensible to her sorrows; yet Laura did not give way to the strong excess of her grief, for it sunk upon her spirit with a leaden weight of anguish, which tears and lamentations could not express, and could not even relieve. She rose and kissed, for the last time, that beloved countenance which she was never to look upon again till they met in heaven, and stole away to the silence and solitude of her own room, where she tried in vain to collect her thoughts. All seemed a dreary blank. She did not sigh—she could not weep; but she sat in dark and vacant abstraction, with one only consciousness filling her mind—the bitter remembrance that Frank was dead—that she could be of no further use to him—that she could have no future intercourse with him—that even in her prayers she could no longer have the comfort of naming him; and when at last she turned to his own Bible, which he had given her, to seek for consolation, her eyes refused their office, and the pages became blistered with tears.

After Frank's funeral, Sir Edward became too ill to leave his bed; and Major Graham remained with him in constant conversation; while Harry and Laura did everything to testify their affection and to fill the place now so sadly vacant.

On the following Sunday, several of the congregation at Hammersmith observed two young strangers in the rector's pew, dressed in the deepest mourning, with pale and downcast countenances, who glided early into church, and sat immoveably still, side by side, while Mr Palmer gave out for his text, the affecting and appropriate words which Frank himself had often repeated during his last illness : " In an hour that ye think not, the Son of man cometh."

Not a tear was shed by either Harry or Laura, —their grief was too great for utterance; yet they listened with breathless interest to the sermon, intended not only to console them, but also to instruct other young persons from the afflicting event of Frank's death.

Mr Palmer took this opportunity to describe all the amiable dispositions of youth, and to shew how much of what is pleasing may appear before religion has yet taken entire possession of the mind; but he painted in glowing colours the beautiful consistency and harmony of character which must ensue after that happy change, when the Holy Spirit renews the heart, and influences the life. It almost seemed to Harry and Laura as if Frank were visibly before their eyes, when Mr Palmer spoke in eloquent terms of that humility which no praise could diminish,—that benevolence which attended to the feelings as well as the wants of others,—that affection which was ever ready to make any sacrifice for those he loved,—that docility which obeyed the call of duty on every occasion,—that meekness in the midst of provocation which could not be irritated,—that gentle firmness in maintaining the truths of the Gospel, which no opposition could intimidate,—that cheerful submission to suffering which saw a hand of mercy in the darkest hour, —and that faith which was ever " forgetting those things which are behind, and reaching forth unto those things which are before, pressing toward the mark for the prize of the high calling of God in Christ Jesus."

It seemed as if years had passed over the heads of Harry and Laura during the short period of their absence from home—that home where Frank had so anxiously desired to go! All was changed within and around them,—sorrow had filled their hearts; and, no longer merry, thoughtless, young creatures, believing the world one scene of frolicsome enjoyment and careless ease, they had now witnessed its realities,—they had felt its trials,—they had experienced the importance of religion,—they had learned the frailty of all earthly joy,—and they had received, amidst tears and sorrow, the last injunction of a dying brother, to " call upon the Lord while He is near, and to seek Him while He may yet be found."

" Uncle David," said Laura, one day, several months after their return home, "Mrs Crabtree first endeavoured to lead us aright by severity, —you and grandmama then tried what kindness would do, but nothing was effectual till now, when God Himself has laid His hand upon us. Oh! what a heavy stroke was necessary to bring me to my right mind; but now, while we weep many bitter tears, Harry and I often pray together that good may come out of evil, and that we who mourn so deeply, may find our best, our only comfort from above."

    Unthinking, idle, wild, and young,
    I laugh'd, and talk'd, and danc'd, and sung;
    And, proud of health, and frolic vain,
    Dream'd not of sorrow, care, or pain,
    Concluding, in those hours of glee,
    That all the world was made for me.
    But when the days of trial came,
    When sorrow shook this trembling frame,
    When folly's gay pursuits were o'er,
    And I could dance or sing no more;
    It then occur'd how sad 'twould be
    Were this world only made for me.
        PRINCESS AMELIA.

POSTSCRIPT.

It is now many years since a merry deputation of young people presented themselves before the author to make a united request that she would publish a continuation of HOLIDAY HOUSE. One lively little girl of nine years old then expressed herself exceedingly dissatisfied with the last chapter, which she had re-written, in large text, on a plan of her own, to render it more cheerful; and they all exacted a promise, that the narrative should be one day brought to a happy conclusion. Years have since fled away, bringing sorrow upon sorrow, which prevented the author from fulfilling the expectations of her lively young friends, but she has at length been able to do so. As most of those who were children when Holiday House was published are now grown up, the characters in this volume have all reäppeared in their maturer years, and act their parts with a degree of felicity, to satisfy the benevolent sympathy of her young friends, in a tale entitled

THE MYSTERIOUS MARRIAGE; or,
SIR EDWARD GRAHAM.

LONDON: *Warwick House,*
Dorset Buildings, Salisbury Square.

A LIST OF

WARD, LOCK & CO.'S
ILLUSTRATED GIFT BOOKS
STANDARD WORKS,
AND
Popular Volumes for Children,
Suitable for Rewards and Presents.

BEETON'S GREAT BOOK OF POETRY: From Cædmon and King Alfred's Boethius to Browning and Tennyson; with a separate Selection of American Poems. Containing nearly Two Thousand of the Best Pieces in the English Language. With Sketches of the History of the Poetry of our Country, and Biographical Notices of the Poets. NEW EDITION, Illustrated. In One handsome Volume, royal 8vo, cloth gilt, gilt edges, price 21s.; or in half-calf, 25s.

Four Hundred English Poets are represented in this Volume. A separate collection of American Poems, with Biographies, is added to these. Thus, in one book, a view of the Growth and Changes of the English Language, as seen in its Highest Developments, is possible. Not less than a Thousand Volumes have been examined in order to form a selection worthy to receive respect and regard from all Lovers of the Divine Art of Poesy.

NOBLE THOUGHTS IN NOBLE LANGUAGE: A Collection of Wise and Virtuous Utterances, in Prose and Verse, from the Writings of the Known Great and the Great Unknown. With an Index of Authors. Compiled and Analytically Arranged by HENRY SOUTHGATE, Author of "Many Thoughts of Many Minds," &c. Royal 8vo, cloth gilt, gilt edges, 10s. 6d.; half-calf, or half-morocco, 15s.; elegant morocco, bevelled boards, 21s.

Contains Selections from the Works of 700 Authors, and will especially recommend itself to those who can appreciate and value the Best Thoughts of our Best Writers.

DALZIEL'S ILLUSTRATED GOLDSMITH. Comprising "The Vicar of Wakefield," "The Traveller," "The Deserted Village," "The Haunch of Venison," "The Captivity: an Oratorio," "Retaliation," Miscellaneous Poems, "The Good-Natured Man," "She Stoops to Conquer," and a Sketch of the Life of Oliver Goldsmith by H. W. DULCKEN, Ph.D. With 100 Pictures, drawn by G. J. PINWELL, engraved by the Brothers DALZIEL. Beautifully bound, cloth, full gilt, gilt edges, price 10s. 6d.

BEETON'S BOOK OF ENGLISH POETRY: From Chaucer to Pope. With Biographical Notices of the Poets, and numerous full-page Illustrations. Handsomely bound, cloth gilt, gilt edges, 10s. 6d.

BEETON'S BOOK OF FAVOURITE MODERN POETS OF ENGLAND AND AMERICA. With Biographical Notices and numerous full-page Illustrations. Handsomely bound, cloth gilt, gilt edges, 10s. 6d.

SABBATH BELLS CHIMED BY THE POETS. With Coloured and other Illustrations by BIRKET FOSTER and other Artists. Cloth gilt, gilt edges, price 10s. 6d.

London: WARD, LOCK & CO., Salisbury Square, E.C.

FINE ART BOOKS.

THE DORÉ GIFT BOOK OF ILLUSTRATIONS TO TENNYSON'S IDYLLS OF THE KING. With Descriptive Letterpress and Quotations from Tennyson's Poems, by Permission. In One Magnificent royal 4to Volume, containing 37 Engravings on Steel, from the Original Drawings by GUSTAVE DORÉ. Cloth, richly gilt, gilt edges, price 42s.

GUSTAVE DORÉ'S ILLUSTRATIONS TO THE ARTHURIAN LEGENDS. Royal 4to, handsomely bound, cloth, richly gilt, gilt edges, price 12s. each.

1. The Story of King Arthur and Queen Guinevere. From the Traditions of the Mythical period of British History, Welsh, Breton, Norman, and Italian Chroniclers and Romancists, and later Ballad and Idyllic Poetry. With Nine Engravings on Steel, from Drawings by GUSTAVE DORÉ.

2. The Story of Merlin the Enchanter and Vivien, as related by the old British and Breton Chroniclers and in later Poetry. With Nine Engravings on Steel, from Drawings by GUSTAVE DORÉ.

3. The Story of Enid and Geraint. From the old Welsh, French, German, and Scandinavian Legends. With Nine Engravings on Steel, from Drawings by GUSTAVE DORÉ.

4. The Story of Elaine. From the Arthurian Legends collected by Sir THOMAS MALORY and later Writers. With Nine Engravings on Steel, from Drawings by GUSTAVE DORÉ.

"This edition, although illustrated by the same remarkable drawings of Gustave Doré which originally appeared in the fine, large and costly folio published some years ago, is really a new work, containing much valuable matter referring to the Arthurian legends. . . . As popular gift-books they are precisely what they should be—beautifully printed on the thickest paper, handsomely bound, and moderate in price."—*The Times.*

VIVIEN. By ALFRED TENNYSON, D.C.L. With Nine superb Engravings on Steel from Drawings by GUSTAVE DORÉ. Folio, cloth gilt, gilt edges, 21s.

THOMAS HOOD, Illustrated by Gustave Doré. With Nine Engravings on Steel, from Drawings by GUSTAVE DORÉ, and many Woodcuts. Folio, cloth gilt, gilt edges, 21s.

THOMAS HOOD, Illustrated by Birket Foster. With Twenty-two Drawings by BIRKET FOSTER, engraved on Steel. Large 4to, cloth gilt, gilt edges, 21s.

THOMAS HOOD, again Illustrated by Birket Foster. With Twenty-two Drawings by BIRKET FOSTER, engraved on Steel. Large 4to, cloth gilt, gilt edges, 21s.

THOMAS HOOD, Illustrated by Birket Foster. The Two Series in One Volume, handsomely bound, half-morocco, 42s. Forty-four Drawings by BIRKET FOSTER, exquisitely Engraved on Steel.

KEATS' POETIC ROMANCE, ENDYMION. Illustrated by E. J. POYNTER, A.R.A. With Six Magnificent Proof Engravings by F. JOUBERT, from Paintings by E. J. POYNTER. Folio, cloth gilt, gilt edges, Proofs, 42s.

London: WARD, LOCK & CO., Salisbury Square, E.C.

USEFUL AND ENTERTAINING BOOKS.

DALZIEL'S ILLUSTRATED ARABIAN NIGHTS' ENTERTAINMENTS.
With upwards of 200 Illustrations by J. E. MILLAIS, R.A., J. TENNIEL, J. D. WATSON, A. B. HOUGHTON, G. J. PINWELL, and T. DALZIEL, together with Initial Letters, Ornamental Borders, &c., engraved by the Brothers DALZIEL. In One handsome Volume, cloth, richly gilt back, sides, and edges, price 21s.

TRAVELS IN PORTUGAL.
By JOHN LATOUCHE. Third and Cheaper Edition, with Photograph and Map. Crown 8vo, cloth gilt, price 6s.
"Mr. Latouche's travels are delightfully written... His book is as fair as it is pleasant; as full of information as it is sparkling with humour."—*Spectator.*

BEETON'S HOUSEHOLD AMUSEMENTS & ENJOYMENTS.
Acting Charades, Burlesques, Conundrums, Enigmas, Rebuses, and Puzzles. With Coloured Frontispiece and many other Illustrations. Crown 8vo, cloth gilt, gilt edges, 5s.

THE HANDY BOOK OF GAMES FOR GENTLEMEN.
By Captain CRAWLEY, Author of "The Billiard Book," the articles on Billiards and Bagatelle in "The Encyclopædia Britannica," "The Card-Player's Manual," &c. Billiards, Bagatelle, Whist, Loo, Cribbage, Chess, Draughts, Backgammon, Ecarté, Picquet, All Fours, &c., &c. Illustrated. Crown 8vo, cloth gilt, 5s.

Mrs. BEETON'S Book of HOUSEHOLD MANAGEMENT.
IMPROVED AND ENLARGED EDITION. Comprising every kind of practical information on Domestic Economy and Modern Cookery. Containing 1,350 PAGES, 4,000 RECIPES AND INSTRUCTIONS, and 1,000 ENGRAVINGS and COLOURED PLATES. With accurate descriptions as to Quantities, Time, Costs, and Seasons of the various dishes, directions for Carving, Hints on the Management of Children, the Arrangement and Economy of the Kitchen, Duties of Servants, the Doctor, Legal Memoranda, and 250 Bills of Fare to suit the Seasons from January to December. Strongly bound, half-roan, price 7s. 6d.; cloth gilt, gilt edges, 8s. 6d.; half-calf, 10s. 6d.
* *As a Wedding Gift, Birthday Book, or Presentation Volume at any period of the year, or upon any anniversary whatever, Mrs. Beeton's "Household Management" is entitled to the very first place. In half-calf binding, price half a guinea, the book will last a lifetime, and save money every day.*

WARD AND LOCK'S HOME BOOK. A Domestic Cyclopædia.
Uniform with, and a Companion Volume to "Mrs. Beeton's Book of Household Management." Profusely Illustrated with Coloured and other Plates and about 600 Engravings in the text. Strongly bound, half-roan, price 7s. 6d.; half-calf, 10s. 6d.
Among the subjects treated of in WARD AND LOCK'S HOME BOOK will be found: The Way to Build, Buy, Rent, and Furnish a House—The Management of the Home—The Treatment of Children—Needlework in all its Branches—Home Dressmaking—The Toilet—Modern Etiquette—Employment of Leisure Hours, &c.

BEETON'S BOOK OF NEEDLEWORK. Consisting of 670
Needlework Patterns, with full Descriptions and Instructions as to working them. Every stitch described and engraved with the utmost accuracy, and the quantity of material requisite for each pattern stated. Handsomely bound, cloth gilt, gilt edges, price 7s. 6d.
* *Just as* THE BOOK OF HOUSEHOLD MANAGEMENT *takes due precedence of every other Cookery Book, so this Collection of Needlework Designs has become the book,* par excellence, *for Ladies to consult, both for Instruction in Stitches and all kinds of work, and Patterns of elegant style and irreproachable good taste.*

London: WARD, LOCK & CO., *Salisbury Square, E.C.*

HIGH CLASS BOOKS OF REFERENCE.

THE HAYDN SERIES OF MANUALS.

"The most universal book of reference in a moderate compass that we know of in the English language."—*The Times.*

HAYDN'S DICTIONARY OF DATES. Relating to all Ages and Nations; for Universal Reference. Containing about 10,000 distinct Articles, and 80,000 Dates and Facts. Sixteenth Edition, Enlarged, Corrected and Revised by BENJAMIN VINCENT, Librarian of the Royal Institution of Great Britain. In One thick Vol., medium 8vo, cloth, price 18s.; half-calf, 24s.; full or tree-calf, 31s. 6d.

"It is certainly no longer now a mere Dictionary of Dates, but A COMPREHENSIVE DICTIONARY OR ENCYCLOPÆDIA OF GENERAL INFORMATION."—*The Times.*

"It is BY FAR THE READIEST AND MOST RELIABLE WORK OF THE KIND."—*The Standard.*

VINCENT'S DICTIONARY OF BIOGRAPHY, Past and Present. Containing the Chief Events in the Lives of Eminent Persons of all Ages and Nations. By BENJAMIN VINCENT, Librarian of the Royal Institution of Great Britain, and Editor of "Haydn's Dictionary of Dates." In One thick Vol., medium 8vo, cloth, 7s. 6d.; half-calf, 12s.; full or tree-calf, 18s.

"It has the merit of condensing into the smallest possible compass the leading events in the career of every man and woman of eminence. It is very carefully edited, and must evidently be the result of constant industry, combined with good judgment and taste."—*The Times.*

The CHEAPEST BOOK PUBLISHED on DOMESTIC MEDICINE, &c.

HAYDN'S DOMESTIC MEDICINE. By the late EDWIN LANKESTER, M.D., F.R.S., assisted by Distinguished Physicians and Surgeons. New Edition, including an Appendix on Sick Nursing and Mothers' Management. With 32 full pages of Engravings. In One Vol., medium 8vo, cloth gilt, 7s. 6d.; half-calf, 12s.

"Very exhaustive, and embodies an enormous amount of medical information in an intelligible shape."—*The Scotsman.*

"THE FULLEST AND MOST RELIABLE WORK OF ITS KIND."—*Liverpool Albion.*

HAYDN'S BIBLE DICTIONARY. For the use of all Readers and Students of the Old and New Testaments, and of the Apocrypha. Edited by the late Rev. CHARLES BOUTELL, M.A. New Edition, brought down to the latest date. With 100 pages of Engravings, separately printed on tinted paper. In One Vol., medium 8vo, cloth gilt, 7s. 6d.; half-calf, 12s.

"No better one than this is in the market. . Every local preacher should place this dictionary in his study, and every Sunday-school teacher should have it for reference."—*The Fountain.*

UNIFORM WITH "HAYDN'S BIBLE DICTIONARY."

WHISTON'S JOSEPHUS. An entirely New Library Edition of WILLIAM WHISTON's translation of the Works of FLAVIUS JOSEPHUS. Comprising "The Antiquities of the Jews," and "The Wars of the Jews." With Memoir of the Author. Marginal Notes giving the Essence of the Narrative, and 100 pages of Engravings, separately printed on tinted paper. In One Vol., medium 8vo, cloth gilt, 7s. 6d.; half-calf, 12s.

"The present edition is cheap and good, being clearly printed, and, as already remarked, serviceably embellished with views and object drawings, not one of which is irrelevant to the matter."—*The Daily Telegraph.*

London: WARD, LOCK & CO., Salisbury Square, E.C.

THE PEOPLE'S STANDARD CYCLOPÆDIAS.

EVERYBODY'S LAWYER (Beeton's Law Book). Entirely New Edition, Revised by a BARRISTER. A Practical Compendium of the General Principles of English Jurisprudence; comprising upwards of 14,600 Statements of the Law. With a full Index, 27,000 References, every numbered paragraph in its particular place, and under its general head. Crown 8vo, 1,680 pp., cloth gilt, 7s. 6d.

*** *The sound practical information contained in this voluminous work is equal to that in a whole library of ordinary legal books, costing many guineas. Not only for every non-professional man in a difficulty are its contents valuable, but also for the ordinary reader, to whom a knowledge of the law is more important and interesting than is generally supposed.*

BEETON'S DICTIONARY OF GEOGRAPHY: A Universal Gazetteer. Illustrated by Maps—Ancient, Modern, and Biblical, and several Hundred Engravings in separate Plates on toned paper. Containing upwards of 12,000 distinct and complete Articles. Post 8vo, cloth gilt, 7s. 6d.; half-calf, 10s. 6d.

BEETON'S DICTIONARY OF BIOGRAPHY: Being the Lives of Eminent Persons of All Times. Containing upwards of 10,000 distinct and complete Articles, profusely Illustrated by Portraits. With the Pronunciation of Every Name. Post 8vo, cloth gilt, 7s. 6d.; half-calf, 10s. 6d.

BEETON'S DICTIONARY OF NATURAL HISTORY: A Popular and Scientific Account of Animated Creation. Containing upwards of 2,000 distinct and complete Articles, and more than 400 Engravings. With the Pronunciation of Every Name. Crown 8vo, cloth gilt, 7s. 6d.; half-calf, 10s. 6d.

BEETON'S BOOK OF HOME PETS: How to Rear and Manage in Sickness and in Health. With many Coloured Plates, and upwards of 200 Woodcuts from designs principally by HARRISON WEIR. With a Chapter on Ferns. Post 8vo, half-bound, 7s. 6d.

THE TREASURY OF SCIENCE, Natural and Physical. Comprising Natural Philosophy, Astronomy, Chemistry, Geology, Mineralogy, Botany, Zoology and Physiology. By F. SCHOEDLER, Ph.D. Translated and Edited by HENRY MEDLOCK, Ph.D., &c. With more than 500 Illustrations. Crown 8vo, cloth gilt, 7s. 6d.

A MILLION OF FACTS of Correct Data and Elementary Information concerning the entire Circle of the Sciences, and on all subjects of Speculation and Practice. By Sir RICHARD PHILLIPS. Carefully Revised and Improved. Crown 8vo, cloth gilt, 7s. 6d.

THE TEACHER'S PICTORIAL BIBLE AND BIBLE DICTIONARY. With the most approved Marginal References, and Explanatory Oriental and Scriptural Notes, Original Comments, and Selections from the most esteemed Writers. Illustrated with numerous Engravings and Coloured Maps. Crown 8vo, cloth gilt, red edges, 8s. 6d.; French morocco, 10s. 6d.; half-calf, 10s. 6d.

THE SELF-AID CYCLOPÆDIA, for Self-Taught Students. Comprising General Drawing; Architectural, Mechanical, and Engineering Drawing; Ornamental Drawing and Design; Mechanics and Mechanism; the Steam Engine. By ROBERT SCOTT BURN, F.S.A.E., &c. With upwards of 1,000 Engravings. Demy 8vo, half-leather, price 10s. 6d.

London: WARD, LOCK & CO., Salisbury Square, E.C.

REFERENCE BOOKS FOR THE PEOPLE.

BEETON'S NATIONAL REFERENCE BOOKS,
FOR THE PEOPLE OF GREAT BRITAIN AND IRELAND.

*** In an age of great competition and little leisure the value of Time is tolerably well understood. Men wanting facts like to get at them with as little expenditure as possible of money or minutes. BEETON'S NATIONAL REFERENCE BOOKS *have been conceived and carried out in the belief that a set of Cheap and Handy Volumes in Biography, Geography, History (Sacred and Profane), Science, and Business, would be thoroughly welcome, because they would quickly answer many a question. In every case the type will be found clear and plain.*

STRONGLY BOUND IN CLOTH, PRICE ONE SHILLING EACH.
(Those marked thus * can be had cloth gilt, price 1s. 6d.)

1. *Beeton's British Gazetteer: A Topographical and Historical Guide to the United Kingdom.
2. Beeton's British Biography: From the Earliest Times to the Accession of George III.
3. Beeton's Modern Men and Women: A British Biography, from the Accession of George III. to the Present Time.
4. *Beeton's Bible Dictionary. A Cyclopædia of the Geography, Biography, Narratives, and Truths of Scripture.
5. *Beeton's Classical Dictionary: A Cyclopædia of Greek and Roman Biography, Geography, Mythology, and Antiquities.
6. *Beeton's Medical Dictionary. A Guide for every Family, defining, with perfect plainness, the Symptoms and Treatment of all Ailments, Illnesses, and Diseases.
7. Beeton's Date Book. A British Chronology from the Earliest Records to the Present Day.
8. Beeton's Dictionary of Commerce. Containing Explanations of the principal Terms used in, and modes of transacting Business at Home and Abroad.
9. Beeton's Modern European Celebrities. A Biography of Continental Men and Women of Note who have lived during the last Hundred Years, or are now living.

Beeton's Guide Book to the Stock Exchange and Money Market. With Hints to Investors and the Chances of Speculators. Entirely New Edition, post 8vo, linen boards, 1s.

Beeton's Investing Money with Safety and Profit. New and Revised Edition. Post 8vo, linen covers, 1s.

Beeton's Ready Reckoner. With New Tables, and much Information never before collected. Post 8vo, strong cloth, 1s.

Webster's Sixpenny Ready Reckoner. 256 pp., cloth, 6d.

Beeton's Complete Letter Writer, for Ladies and Gentlemen. Post 8vo, strong cloth, price 1s.

Beeton's Complete Letter Writer for Ladies. In linen covers, 6d.

Beeton's Complete Letter Writer for Gentlemen. Price 6d.

The New Letter Writer for Lovers. In linen covers, price 6d.

Webster's Shilling Book-keeping. A Comprehensive Guide, comprising a Course of Practice in Single and Double Entry. Post 8vo, cloth, 1s.

London: WARD, LOCK & CO., Salisbury Square, E.C.

ILLUSTRATED POETICAL WORKS.

" The power of English Literature is in its Poets."

MOXON'S POPULAR POETS.

NEW AND ENLARGED EDITIONS, with Red Border Lines, Critical Memoirs by WILLIAM MICHAEL ROSSETTI, and Illustrations.

The press and the public, alike in Great Britain and her Colonies, and in the United States, unite in their testimony to the immense superiority of Messrs. Moxon's Popular Poets over any other similar collections published by any other house. Their possession of the Copyright works of Coleridge, Hood, Keats, Shelley, Wordsworth, and other great National Poets, places this series above rivalry.

1. Byron's Poetical Works.
2. Longfellow's Poetical Works.
3. Wordsworth's Poetical Works.
4. Scott's Poetical Works.
5. Shelley's Poetical Works.
6. Moore's Poetical Works.
7. Hood's Poetical Works.
8. Keats' Poetical Works.
9. Coleridge's Poetical Works.
10. Burns' Poetical Works.
11. Tupper's Proverbial Philosophy. The Four Series Complete in One Vol., with Portrait.
12. Milton's Poetical Works.
13. Campbell's Poetical Works.
14. Pope's Poetical Works.
15. Cowper's Poetical Works.
16. Humorous Poems.
17. American Poems.
18. Mrs. Hemans' Poetical Works.
19. Thomson's Poetical Works.
20. Poetic Treasures.
21. Hood's Poetical Works. Second Series.
22. J. G. Whittier's Poetical Works.
23. J. R. Lowell's Poetical Works.
24. Young's Poetical Works.
25. Shakespeare's Complete Works.
26. Keble's Christian Year.
27. Poe's Poetical Works.

With Red Border Lines, Critical Memoir, and Illustrations, handsomely bound, cloth gilt, gilt edges,

PRICE 3s. 6d. PER VOLUME.

Also to be had in the following varieties of binding—Morocco, 7s. 6d.; morocco extra, 8s.; tree calf, 10s. 6d.; relief leather, 12s.

MOXON'S FIVE SHILLING POETS.

Crown 8vo, cloth gilt, bevelled boards, gilt top, 5s.; half-morocco, 6s.

Hood's Serious Poems. With Preface by THOMAS HOOD the Younger, and numerous Illustrations.

Hood's Comic Poems. With Preface by THOMAS HOOD the Younger, and numerous Illustrations.

Shelley's Poetical Works. With Portrait.

Keats' Poetical Works. With a Memoir by Lord HOUGHTON.

Longfellow's Poetical Works. With Memoir by WILLIAM MICHAEL ROSSETTI. Illustrated.

Scott's Poetical Works. With Memoir by WILLIAM MICHAEL ROSSETTI. Illustrated.

Hood's Poetical Works. 1st Series. With Memoir by WILLIAM MICHAEL ROSSETTI. Illustrated.

London: WARD, LOCK & CO., Salisbury Square, E.C.

FOR HOME READING.

THE HOME TREASURE LIBRARY.
Handsomely bound, cloth gilt, gilt edges, price 3s. 6d. each.

It is the intention of the Publishers that a tone of pure morality and lofty aim shall characterise the whole of the volumes in this Library, while at the same time the type, paper, and binding shall be of the best description; this, added to the Illustrations, will render these books, both as to interior and exterior, everything that could be desired, and worthy of a place in the Library of every Home.

1. Shiloh. By Mrs. W. M. L. JAY. With Coloured Illustrations.
2. The Prince of the House of David. Coloured Illustrations.
3. Miss Edgeworth's Moral Tales. With Coloured Illustrations.
4. Miss Edgeworth's Popular Tales. Coloured Illustrations.
5. The Throne of David. By Rev. J. H. INGRAHAM. Illustrated.
6. The Pillar of Fire. By Rev. J. H. INGRAHAM. Illustrated.
7. Anna Lee. By T. S. ARTHUR. Illustrated.
8. The Wide, Wide World. By E. WETHERELL. Coloured Illusts.
9. Queechy. By the same. With Coloured Illustrations.
10. Melbourne House. By the same. Coloured Illustrations.
11. Sceptres and Crowns, and The Flag of Truce. By the same. With Coloured Illustrations.
12. The Fairchild Family. By Mrs. SHERWOOD. Coloured Illusts.
13. Stepping Heavenward, and Aunt Jane's Hero. By Mrs. E. PRENTISS. With Coloured Illustrations.
14. Mabel Vaughan. By Miss CUMMING. Coloured Illustrations.
15. Dunallan. By GRACE KENNEDY. Coloured Illustrations.
16. Father Clement. By the same. With Coloured Illustrations.
17. Holden with the Cords. By Mrs. JAY. Coloured Illustrations.
18. Uncle Tom's Cabin. By Mrs. H. B. STOWE. With a Sketch of the Life of Rev. JOSIAH HENSON. Coloured and other Illustrations.
19. Barriers Burned Away. By E. P. ROE. Coloured Illustrations.
20. Little Women and Good Wives. By Miss ALCOTT. With Coloured Illustrations.
21. From Jest to Earnest. By E. P. ROE. Coloured Illustrations.
22. Near to Nature's Heart. By E. P. ROE. Coloured Illustrations.
23. Opening of a Chestnut Burr. By E. P. ROE. Col. Illust.
24. What Can She Do? By E. P. ROE. Coloured Illustrations.
25. The Old Helmet. By E. WETHERELL. Coloured Illustrations.
26. Daisy. By the same. With Coloured Illustrations.
27. A Knight of the Nineteenth Century. Coloured Illustrations.
28. Woman our Angel. By A. S. ROE. Coloured Illustrations.
29. The Lamplighter. By Miss CUMMING. Coloured Illustrations.
30. A Face Illumined. By E. P. ROE. Coloured Illustrations.
31. The Story of Stories. By Mrs. LEATHLEY. Illustrated.

London: WARD, LOCK & CO., Salisbury Square, E.C.

ILLUSTRATED GIFT BOOKS.

THE GOOD WORTH LIBRARY;

In the GOOD WORTH LIBRARY *no works have been admitted in which the three requisites for good worth in a book,—namely, the promotion of knowledge, the furtherance of wisdom, and the charm of amusement—are not combined, and whose perusal will not satisfy the mind, as with good, wholesome and strengthening food.*

Fully Illustrated and handsomely bound, cloth gilt, 3s. 6d. each.

1. **Bunyan's Pilgrim's Progress**, from this World to that which is to Come. With Memoir of the Author by H. W. DULCKEN, PH.D., and 100 Illustrations by THOMAS DALZIEL, Engraved by DALZIEL Brothers.

2. **The Swiss Family Robinson**; or, The Adventures of a Swiss Pastor and his Family on an Uninhabited Island. Translated by HENRY FRITH. With Coloured Plates and upwards of 200 Engravings.

3. **Andersen's Stories for the Young.** By HANS CHRISTIAN ANDERSEN. With many full-page and other Engravings.

4. **Andersen's Popular Tales for Children.** By HANS CHRISTIAN ANDERSEN. With many full-page and other Engravings.

5. **Anne and Jane Taylor's Poetry for Children.** Containing the Original Poems, Hymns for Infant Minds, and Rhymes for the Nursery. With many Engravings.

7. **Fifty Celebrated Women**: Their Virtues and Failings, and the Lessons of their Lives. With many Engravings.

8. **Fifty Celebrated Men**: Their Lives and Trials, and the Deeds that made them Famous. With many Engravings.

9. **Robinson Crusoe.** By DANIEL DEFOE. With Memoir of the Author and many Engravings.

10. **The Wonders of the World**, in Earth, Sea, and Sky. By UNCLE JOHN. With 123 Engravings.

11. **Evenings at Home**; or, The Juvenile Budget Opened. By Mrs. BARBAULD and Dr. AIKEN. With many Engravings.

12. **The Gentlemen Adventurers**; or, Antony Waymouth. By W. H. G. KINGSTON. With full-page Engravings.

13. **Sandford and Merton** (The History of). By THOMAS DAY. With 100 Engravings by DALZIEL Brothers.

14. **The Boy's Own Sea Stories.** Being the Adventures of a Sailor in the Navy, the Merchant Service, and on a Whaling Cruise. Told by Himself. With full-page Engravings.

16. **Great Inventors**: The Sources of their Usefulness, and the Results of their Efforts. With 109 Engravings.

17. **The Marvels of Nature**; or, Outlines of Creation. With 400 Engravings by DALZIEL Brothers.

18. **The Boy's Own Book of Manufactures and Industries of the World.** With 365 Engravings by DALZIEL Brothers.

London: WARD, LOCK & CO., *Salisbury Square, E.C.*

ILLUSTRATED GIFT BOOKS.

THE GOOD WORTH LIBRARY—*continued.*

19. Famous Boys, and How they Became Famous Men. With many Engravings.
20. Triumphs of Perseverance and Enterprise. By THOMAS COOPER. With many Engravings.
21. The Crusades and Crusaders. The Story of the Struggle for the Holy Sepulchre. By J. G. EDGAR. With full-page Engravings.
22. The Merchant's Clerk; or, Mark Wilton. By Rev. C. B. TAYLER, M.A. With full-page and other Engravings.
23. The Young Marooners; or, The Adventures of Robert and Harold on the Florida Coast. With many Engravings.
24. Holiday House. By CATHERINE SINCLAIR. With full-page Engravings.
25. The Boy's Book of Modern Travel and Adventure. With many Engravings.
26. Mary Bunyan, the Blind Daughter of John Bunyan. By SALLIE ROCHESTER FORD. With full-page Engravings.
27. The Scottish Chiefs. By JANE PORTER. With full-page Engravings.
30. Life Thoughts. Gathered from the Extemporaneous Discourses of HENRY WARD BEECHER. With Red Border Lines.
31. The Christian Life. Bible Helps and Counsels for Every Day throughout the Year. With Red Border Lines.
32. The Perfect Life. By WILLIAM E. CHANNING.
33. Sacred Heroes and Martyrs. By J. T. HEADLEY. Revised and Edited by J. W. KIRTON, LL.D., Author of "Buy your Own Cherries."
34. Religion and Science; or, The Truth Revealed in Nature and Scripture. By JOSEPH LE CONTE.
35. Getting On in the World; or, Hints on Success in Life. By WILLIAM MATHEWS, LL.D.
36. Household Stories. By the Brothers GRIMM, W. HAUFF, &c. With numerous Engravings.

CHILDREN AT JERUSALEM: A Sketch of Modern Life in Syria. By Mrs. HOLMAN HUNT. Elegantly bound, cloth gilt, coloured edges, price 3s. 6d.

LITERARY CURIOSITIES AND ECCENTRICITIES. Collected and Edited by W. A. CLOUSTON. A Book of Anecdotes, Laconic Sayings, and Gems of Thought in Prose and Poetry. Crown 8vo, cloth gilt, 2s. 6d.

THE TRUE HISTORY OF A LITTLE RAGAMUFFIN. By JAMES GREENWOOD, Author of "Journeys through London," "A Night in a Workhouse," "Silas the Conjuror," &c. With full-page Illustrations. Crown 8vo, cloth gilt, price 3s. 6d.

London: WARD, LOCK & CO., *Salisbury Square, E.C.*

ILLUSTRATED BOOKS.

THE FAMILY CIRCLE LIBRARY.

A Series of Popular Books, specially designed for Gifts and Rewards, and for Family Reading and Reference.

Fully Illustrated and handsomely bound, cloth gilt, 3s. 6d. each.

1. **Margaret Catchpole (The History of).** By Rev. R. COBBOLD. With Coloured Plates and other Illustrations.
2. **Beatrice; or, The Unknown Relatives.** By CATHERINE SINCLAIR. With Coloured Plates.
3. **Amy and Hester; or, The Long Holidays.** By H. A. FORD. With Coloured Frontispiece and many Engravings.
4. **Wonders and Beauties of the Year.** Popular and Poetical Descriptions of the Wild Flowers, Birds, and Insects of the Months. By H. G. ADAMS. With Coloured Frontispiece and many Engravings.
5. **Wonders and Curiosities of Animal Life.** By GEORGE KEARLEY. With Coloured Frontispiece and many Engravings.
6. **Nature's Gifts, and How we Use them.** A Familiar Account of our Everyday Wants, Comforts, and Luxuries. By GEORGE DODD. With Coloured Frontispiece and other Illustrations.
7. **Modern Society; or, The March of Intellect.** By CATHERINE SINCLAIR. With Coloured and other Illustrations.
8. **Herbert Lovell; or, Handsome He who Handsome Does.** By Rev. F. W. B. BOUVERIE. With Coloured and other Illustrations.
9. **The Sailor Hero; or, The Frigate and the Lugger.** By Captain ARMSTRONG, Author of "The Cruise of the *Daring*." With full-page Illustrations.
10. **The Cruise of the "Daring."** A Tale of the Sea. By Capt. ARMSTRONG, Author of "The Sailor Hero." With full-page Illustrations.
11. **Life's Contrasts; or, The Four Homes.** By Mrs. GOTHER MANN. With Coloured Frontispiece and other Illustrations.
12. **Popular Preachers of the Ancient Church:** Their Lives and their Works. By Rev. W. WILSON. With Illustrations.
13. **Edwin and Mary; or, The Mother's Cabinet.** With Coloured Frontispiece and other Illustrations.
14. **The Book of Children's Hymns and Rhymes.** With Coloured Frontispiece and many Engravings.
15. **Looking Heavenward:** A Series of Tales and Sketches for the Young. By JANE C. SIMPSON. With Coloured Frontispiece and many Engravings.
16. **Character and Culture.** By the BISHOP of DURHAM, Canon DALE, &c. With Passages selected from the Works of Eminent Divines.
17. **Pilgrims Heavenward.** Essays of Counsel and Encouragement for the Christian Life. With Coloured Frontispiece.

London: WARD, LOCK & CO., Salisbury Square, E.C.

FOR EVERY HOME.

THE FAMILY CIRCLE LIBRARY—*continued.*

18. **Preachers and Preaching, in Ancient and Modern Times.** By the Rev. HENRY CHRISTMAS. With Portraits.
19. **Julamerk; or, The Converted Jewess.** By Mrs. WEBB. With Coloured and other Illustrations.
20. **Fern Leaves from Fanny's Portfolio.** First and Second Series Complete. With numerous Illustrations.
21. **Orange Blossoms:** A Book for All who have Worn, are Wearing, or are likely to Wear Them. Edited by T. S. ARTHUR. With numerous Illustrations.
22. **The Martyrs of Carthage; or, The Christian Converts.** A Tale of the Times of Old. With numerous Illustrations.
23. **Modern Accomplishments; or, The March of Intellect.** By CATHERINE SINCLAIR, Author of "Beatrice," "Modern Society," &c. With Coloured Plates.
26. **Poe's Tales of Mystery, Imagination, and Humour.** By EDGAR ALLAN POE. With numerous Illustrations.
27. **Ballads and Poetical Tales.** Selected from PERCY, RITSON, EVANS, JAMIESON, SCOTT, &c.
28. **Beeton's Book of Birds;** Showing how to Rear and Manage them in Sickness and in Health. With Coloured Plates by HARRISON WEIR, and over 100 Engravings.
29. **Beeton's Book of Poultry and Domestic Animals:** How to Rear and Manage them in Sickness and in Health. With Coloured Plates by HARRISON WEIR, and over 100 Engravings.
31. **Journeys through London; or, Bye-ways of the Modern Babylon.** By JAMES GREENWOOD, Author of "A Night in a Workhouse," &c. With 12 double-page Engravings.
32. **Fanny Fern's New Stories for Children.** By the Author of "Fern Leaves." Illustrated.
33. **Adventures of Captain Hatteras.** Containing "The English at the North Pole," and "The Ice Desert." By JULES VERNE. With Coloured Plates.
34. **Twenty Thousand Leagues Under the Sea.** First and Second Series Complete. By JULES VERNE. With Coloured Plates.
35. **The Wonderful Travels.** Containing "Journey into the Interior of the Earth," and "Five Weeks in a Balloon." By JULES VERNE. With Coloured Plates.
36. **The Moon Voyage.** Containing "From the Earth to the Moon," and "Round the Moon." By JULES VERNE. With Coloured Plates.
37. **The Boy's Handy Book of Games and Sports.** With Hundreds of Illustrations.
38. **The Boy's Handy Book of Natural History.** With about 100 full-page Engravings by W. HARVEY.

London: WARD, LOCK & CO., *Salisbury Square, E.C.*

PURE LITERATURE BY CHOICE AUTHORS.

THE GOOD TONE LIBRARY.

The volumes included under this head are those really High-class Works which are most calculated to elevate the mind and give a high tone to the character. Containing all the interest of a novel without the objectionable features so frequently attaching to that class of literature, these Works, designed for the perusal of the Youth of Both Sexes, will be warmly welcomed. The names of the Authors are in themselves sufficient evidence of careful selection, and will assure the public that good taste and purity of spirit constitute the leading features of the "GOOD TONE LIBRARY."

Post 8vo, elegantly bound, cloth gilt.

1. **The Prince of the House of David.** By Rev. J. H. INGRAHAM. With Coloured Frontispiece.
2. **The Wide, Wide World.** By ELIZABETH WETHERELL. With Coloured Frontispiece.
3. **Queechy.** By ELIZABETH WETHERELL. With Coloured Frontispiece.
4. **Melbourne House.** By ELIZABETH WETHERELL. With Coloured Frontispiece.
5. **Uncle Tom's Cabin.** By Mrs. H. B. STOWE. With Sketch of the Life of Rev. JOSIAH HENSON. Coloured and other Illustrations.
6. **Stepping Heavenward.** By E. PRENTISS. With Coloured Frontispiece.
7. **History of the Fairchild Family.** By Mrs. SHERWOOD. With Coloured Frontispiece.
8. **Anna Lee**: the Maiden, the Wife, and the Mother. By T. S. ARTHUR. With Illustrations.
9. **Flower of the Family.** By E. PRENTISS. With Coloured Frontispiece.
10. **From Jest to Earnest.** By E. P. ROE. With Coloured Frontispiece.
11. **The Throne of David.** By Rev. J. H. INGRAHAM. Illustrated.
12. **The Pillar of Fire.** By Rev. J. H. INGRAHAM. Illustrated.
13. **Shiloh**; or, Without and Within. By Mrs. W. M. L. JAY. With Coloured Frontispiece.
14. **Holiday House.** By CATHERINE SINCLAIR. With Coloured Frontispiece.
15. **Little Women.** By LOUISA M. ALCOTT. With Coloured Frontispiece.
16. **Good Wives.** Sequel to, and by the Author of, "Little Women." With Coloured Frontispiece.
17. **The Lamplighter.** By Miss CUMMING. With Coloured Frontispiece.
18. **The Old Helmet.** By the Author of "Queechy," &c. With Coloured Frontispiece.
19. **Freston Tower.** By Rev. R. COBBOLD, Author of "Margaret Catchpole," &c. Illustrated.

London: WARD, LOCK & CO., Salisbury Square, E.C.

POPULAR BOOKS BY GOOD AUTHORS.

THE FAMILY GIFT SERIES.

A cheap Issue of Popular Books, suitable for Prizes and Rewards.

Crown 8vo, cloth gilt, price 2s. 6d. each.

1. **The Swiss Family Robinson.** Translated by HENRY FRITH. With Coloured Frontispiece and over 200 Engravings.
2. **Bunyan's Pilgrim's Progress.** With a Memoir of the Author by H. W. DULCKEN, Ph.D., and 100 Engravings.
3. **Robinson Crusoe.** By DANIEL DEFOE. With Biographical Sketch of the Author, and many Engravings.
4. **The History of Sandford and Merton.** By THOMAS DAY. With 100 Engravings by DALZIEL Brothers.
5. **Famous Boys, and How they became Great Men.** By the Author of "Clever Boys." With many Illustrations.
6. **Fifty Celebrated Women:** Their Virtues and Failings, and the Lessons of their Lives. With Portraits and other Illustrations.
7. **The Gentlemen Adventurers;** or, Antony Waymouth. By the late W H G. KINGSTON. With full-page Engravings.
8. **Evenings at Home.** By Dr. AIKIN and Mrs. BARBAULD. With many Illustrations.
9. **The Adventures of Captain Hatteras.** By JULES VERNE. Containing "The English at the North Pole," and "The Ice Desert." With Coloured Plates.
10. **Twenty Thousand Leagues Under the Sea.** First and Second Series Complete. By JULES VERNE. With Coloured Plates.
11. **The Wonderful Travels.** Containing "Journey into the Interior of the Earth," and "Five Weeks in a Balloon." By JULES VERNE. With Coloured Plates.
12. **The Moon Voyage.** Containing "From the Earth to the Moon," and "Round the Moon." By JULES VERNE. Coloured Plates.
13. **Getting On in the World;** or, Hints on Success in Life. By W. MATHEWS, LL.D. First and Second Series Complete.
14. **The Boy's Own Book of Manufactures and Industries of the World.** With 365 Engravings.
15. **Great Inventors:** The Sources of their Usefulness, and the Results of their Efforts. With 109 Engravings.
16. **Marvels of Nature;** or, Outlines of Creation. 400 Engravings.
17. **The Boy's Own Sea Stories.** With full-page Engravings.
18. **Household Stories.** By the Brothers GRIMM, W. HAUFF, &c. With many Illustrations.
19. **Fifty Celebrated Men:** Their Lives and Trials, and the Deeds that made them Famous. With Portraits and other Illustrations.
20. **The Wonders of the World,** in Earth, Sea, and Sky. With 123 Engravings.
21. **The Triumphs of Perseverance and Enterprise.** By THOMAS COOPER. With many Engravings.

London: *WARD, LOCK & CO., Salisbury Square, E.C.*

POPULAR BOOKS BY GOOD AUTHORS.

THE FAMILY GIFT SERIES,—*continued.*

22. **Keble's Christian Year**: Thoughts in Verse for the Sundays and Holy Days throughout the Year. With full-page Engravings.
23. **A Face Illumined.** By E. P. ROE, Author of "From Jest to Earnest," &c.
24. **The Scottish Chiefs.** By Miss JANE PORTER.
25. **What Can She Do?** By E. P. ROE, Author of "A Face Illumined," &c.
26. **Barriers Burned Away.** By the Same.
27. **Opening of a Chestnut Burr.** By the Same.
28. **Orange Blossoms.** By T. S. ARTHUR. Illustrated.
29. **Mary Bunyan, the Blind Daughter of John Bunyan.** By SALLIE ROCHESTER FORD. With full-page Engravings.
30. **The History of Margaret Catchpole.** By Rev. RICHARD COBBOLD. With numerous Illustrations.
31. **Julamerk; or, The Converted Jewess.** By the Author of "Naomi." With numerous Illustrations.
32. **Herbert Lovell; or, Handsome He who Handsome Does.** With numerous Illustrations.
33. **Amy and Hester; or, The Long Holidays.** Illustrated.
34. **Edwin and Mary; or, The Mother's Cabinet.** Illustrated.
35. **Wonders and Curiosities of Animal Life.** By GEORGE KEARLEY. With many Engravings.
36. **Wonders and Beauties of the Year.** By H. G. ADAMS. With many Engravings.
37. **Modern Society; or, The March of Intellect.** By CATHERINE SINCLAIR. With numerous Illustrations.
38. **Beatrice; or, The Unknown Relatives.** By CATHERINE SINCLAIR. With numerous Illustrations.
39. **Looking Heavenward**: A Series of Tales and Sketches for the Young. With numerous Illustrations.
40. **Life's Contrasts; or, The Four Homes.** Illustrated.
41. **Nature's Gifts, and How we Use Them.** With numerous Illustrations.
42. **Pilgrims Heavenward**: Essays of Counsel and Encouragement for the Christian Life.
43. **The Book of Children's Hymns and Rhymes.** Illustrated.
44. **Preachers and Preaching, in Ancient and Modern Times.** By Rev. HENRY CHRISTMAS. With Portraits.
45. **Character and Culture.** By the Hon. and Rt. Rev. the BISHOP OF DURHAM, Canon DALE, &c.
46. **Popular Preachers**: Their Lives and their Works. By Rev. W. WILSON. With Illustrations.
47. **The Boy's Handy Book of Games and Sports.** With Hundreds of Illustrations.
48. **The Boy's Handy Book of Natural History.** With about 100 full-page Engravings by W. HARVEY.

London: WARD, LOCK & CO., *Salisbury Square, E.C.*

ERCKMANN-CHATRIAN'S STORIES.

WARD, LOCK AND CO.'S
ERCKMANN - CHATRIAN LIBRARY.

Either to the young who are learning history, to the old who desire to gain lessons from experience, or to the more feminine minds who delight in stories of entrancing interest, the exquisite volumes of MM. ERCKMANN-CHATRIAN *appeal in tones of wholesome and invigorating effect.*

Post 8vo, picture wrapper, price 1s. each; cloth gilt, 2s. 6d.; cloth gilt, those marked thus (*), with page Engravings, 2s. 6d. each; gilt edges, 3s. 6d.

The addition to these volumes of the charming Illustrations of SCHULER, BAYARD, *and others, render them in every way perfect.*

*1. Madame Thérèse.
2. The Conscript.
*3. The Great Invasion.
4. The Blockade.
*5. The States-General.
*6. The Country in Danger.
7. Waterloo.
*8. Illustrious Dr. Matheus.
*9. Stories of the Rhine.
*10. Friend Fritz.
*11. Alsatian Schoolmaster.
*12. The Polish Jew.
13. Master Daniel Rock.
*15. Year One of the Republic.
*16. Citizen Bonaparte.
*17. Confessions of a Clarionet Player.
*18. The Campaign in Kabylia
*19. The Man Wolf.
*20. The Wild Huntsman.

DOUBLE VOLUMES. Crown 8vo, picture boards, 2s. each.

1. Under Fire. ("Madame Thérèse," and "The Blockade.")
2. Two Years a Soldier. ("The Conscript," and "Waterloo.")
3. The Story of a Peasant, 1789-1792. ("The States-General," and "The Country in Danger.")
4. The Story of a Peasant, 1793-1815. ("Year One of the Republic," and "Citizen Bonaparte.")
5. The Mysterious Doctor. ("Dr. Matheus," and "Friend Fritz.")
6. The Buried Treasure. ("Stories of the Rhine," and "Clarionet Player.")
7. The Old Schoolmaster. ("The Alsatian Schoolmaster," and "Campaign in Kabylia.")
8. Weird Tales of the Woods. ("The Man Wolf," and "The Wild Huntsman.")

In new and handsome binding, cloth gilt, gilt top, price 5s. each.

The Story of a Peasant, 1789-1792. Containing "The States-General," and "The Country in Danger." With 57 full-page Engravings.

The Story of a Peasant, 1793-1815. Containing "Year One of the Republic," and "Citizen Bonaparte." With 60 full-page Engravings.

London: *WARD, LOCK & CO., Salisbury Square, E.C.*

PRETTY GIFT BOOKS FOR THE YOUNG.

THE MERCIE SUNSHINE SERIES.

Ornamental boards, price ONE SHILLING per volume; or cloth gilt, price 2s.

1. Mercie Sunshine's Chats about Animals. Illustrated.
2. Mercie Sunshine's Chats about Birds. Profusely Illustrated.
3. The Sunny Home. By MERCIE SUNSHINE. Illustrated.
4. The Shilling Nursery Rhymes for Children. Illustrated.
5. The Shilling Nursery Rhymes and Stories. Illustrated.
6. The Shilling Funny Nursery Rhymes. Illustrated.
7. Old Nursery Tales. With Coloured and other Illustrations.
8. The Cinderella Nursery Story Book. With Illustrations.
9. Nursery Stories and Pictures for the Young. Illustrated.
10. Nursery Songs. With Coloured and other Illustrations.
11. Nursery Ballads. With Coloured and other Illustrations.
12. Nursery Stories. With Coloured and other Illustrations.
13. Sunny Hours. By MERCIE SUNSHINE. Profusely Illustrated.
14. Wonderful Days; or, Stories for the Little Ones. Illustrated.
15. Wonderful Deeds. With Coloured and other Illustrations.
16. Wonderful Lives. With Coloured and other Illustrations.
17. The Wonderful Story; or, The Life of Jesus for the Little Ones. With Coloured and other Illustrations.
18. Wonderful Sayings. With Coloured and other Illustrations.
19. The Children's Picture Annual. Third Series. Illustrated.
20. The Children's Picture Annual. Fourth Series. Illustrated.

THE GOOD GIFT LIBRARY FOR LITTLE PEOPLE.

Elegantly bound, cloth gilt, price 6d. each; ornamental wrapper, 3d.

There are no books more suitable for children than these. Of a high moral tone, they impart a reverence and love for the Creator and His works, while their cheapness brings them within the reach of all.

1. Little Susy's Little Servants. 1st Series. By the Author of "Stepping Heavenward."
2. Little Susy's Little Servants. 2nd Series. By the same.
3. Little Susy's Birthdays. 1st Series. By the same.
4. Little Susy's Birthdays. 2nd Series. By the same.
5. Little Susy's Teachers. 1st Series. By the same.
6. Little Susy's Teachers. 2nd Series. By the same.
7. Original Poems. 1st Series. By ANN and JANE TAYLOR.
8. Original Poems. 2nd Series. By the same.
9. Original Poems. 3rd Series. By the same.
10. Watts's Divine and Moral Songs.

☞ The above can also be had in SHILLING PACKETS; Packet I. containing Nos. 1, 2, 3, and 4, and Packet II. containing Nos. 5, 6, 7, and 8.

London: WARD, LOCK & CO., *Salisbury Square, E.C.*

GIFT BOOKS FOR THE YOUNG.

THE DAISY MAYFIELD SERIES.
In picture boards, 3s. each ; or cloth gilt, 5s.

1. The Children's Story Book of Pictures, Poetry, and Music. With 200 Illustrations.
2. Merry Sunbeams. With 200 Illustrations.
3. The Child's Own Birthday Present Book. 400 Illustrations.
4. The Mayflower Picture Book. Profusely Illustrated.
5. The Pleasant Hour Picture Book. Profusely Illustrated.

THE CHILDREN'S FORGET-ME-NOT. Containing Stories of the Months, Tales about Animals, Seaside Ditties, &c., with upwards of 100 large Engravings. Boards, 2s. 6d ; cloth gilt, 3s. 6d.

ANN and JANE TAYLOR'S POETRY for CHILDREN. Containing the ORIGINAL POEMS, HYMNS FOR INFANT MINDS, and RHYMES FOR THE NURSERY. With full-page and other Engravings. Crown 8vo, handsomely bound, cloth gilt, price 3s. 6d.

BIBLE STEPS FOR LITTLE PILGRIMS; or, Scripture Stories for Little Folks. Beautifully Illustrated with Coloured Pictures and 135 full-page and other Engravings. Imperial 16mo, cloth gilt, price 5s.

The CHILDREN'S SERIES of ILLUSTRATED GIFT BOOKS.
Handsomely bound in cloth gilt, picture on cover, 3s. 6d. each.

1. Moral Nursery Tales for Children. By the Author of "The Golden Harp." With many Engravings.
2. The Children's Picture Gift Book of Music and Song. With many Engravings. (Also in picture boards, 2s. 6d.)
3. Chats about Animals and Birds. By MERCIE SUNSHINE, Author of "The Sunny Holidays," &c. Beautifully Illustrated.
4. The Sunny Holidays ; or, The Adventures of the Allen Family. By MERCIE SUNSHINE. Beautifully Illustrated.
5. The Book of Brave Old Ballads. With Coloured Illustrations by Sir JOHN GILBERT.
6. Harry's Ladder to Learning. Coloured and other Illustrations.

THE SUNBEAM PICTURE BOOK SERIES.
Imperial 16mo, picture boards, 2s.; cloth gilt, 3s. (Those marked thus *, boards, 2s. 6d.; cloth gilt, 3s. 6d.)

1. The Primrose Picture Book. With nearly 200 Pictures.
2. My Little Friend. With nearly 200 Engravings.
3. The Daisy Picture Book. With about 200 Illustrations.
4. The Keepsake Picture Book. With 200 Illustrations.
5. The Golden Story Book. With 200 Illustrations.
6. The Sunbeam Picture Book. With 200 Illustrations.
*7. Golden Childhood, Midsummer, 1880. With 200 Illustrations.
*8. The Fireside Picture Book. With 200 Illustrations.

London . WARD, LOCK & CO., Salisbury Square, E.C.

PRETTY GIFT BOOKS.

THE PLAY-HOUR PICTURE BOOKS.
Large 4to, very handsomely bound, cloth gilt extra, price 5s. each.
1. Nursery Rhymes, A B C Book. With 58 Coloured and 47 Plain Illustrations.
3. Little Tot's Pleasure Book. With 42 Coloured Illustrations (many full-page).
4. Child's Own Picture Book of Animals. With 34 Coloured Illustrations (22 full-page) and 56 Engravings.
5. The Nursery Friend. With 24 full-page Coloured Illustrations.

THE "LITTLE PET" SERIES.
Imperial 16mo, boards, 2s. each; New Binding, cloth and silver, 2s. 6d.
1. Our Little Pet's Own Picture Book. With 160 Illustrations.
2. New Comical Nursery Rhymes and Stories. Illustrated.
3. Pretty Little Lessons for Pretty Little Children. Illustrated.
4. Easy Tales and Pleasant Stories. With 200 Engravings.
5. Bible Sketches from the Old and New Testaments. Illust.
6. Sacred Readings for Young Children. With 60 Engravings.
8. The Child's Own Book of Pictures, Tales, and Poetry.
9. Favourite Nursery Rhymes for Nursery Favourites. Illust.
10. Merry Rhymes and Stories for Merry Little Learners.

THE LOTTIE LIGHTHEART SERIES.
Picture boards, 2s.; cloth gilt, 2s. 6d.
1. Brave Old Ballads. With Coloured Plates.
2. Robin Hood, and other Ballads. With Coloured Plates.
3. Moral Nursery Tales for Children. With many Illustrations.
4. Children's Nursery Tales. With many Illustrations.
5. Charlie and Rosie. With about 100 Illustrations.
6. Lottie Lightheart. With about 100 Pictures.
7. The Happy Home Picture Book. With 100 Illustrations.
8. Sunny Child Life. With about 100 Illustrations.

HANS ANDERSEN'S STORY BOOKS.
Fcap. 8vo, cloth gilt, with Coloured Plates and other Illustrations, price 1s. each.
1. THE CHRISTMAS TREE.
2. THE GARDEN OF PARADISE.
3. THE WILLOW TREE.
4. THE SILENT BOOK.
5. THE LITTLE MERMAID.
6. THE SILVER SHILLING.
7. THE SNOW QUEEN.
8. THE ICE MAIDEN.
9. LITTLE IDA'S FLOWERS.
10. LITTLE TUK.
11. WHAT THE MOON SAW.

BIBLE STEPS FOR LITTLE PILGRIMS; or, Scripture Stories for Children. With Coloured Plates and other Illustrations, price 6d.
1. THE STORY OF THE CREATION AND THE DELUGE.—2. THE STORY OF ABRAHAM, ISAAC, AND JACOB.—3. THE STORY OF JOSEPH AND HIS BROTHERS.—4. THE STORY OF MOSES.—5. THE STORY OF THE JUDGES.—6. THE STORY OF DAVID.—7. THE STORY OF THE PROPHETS.—8. THE LIFE OF JESUS.—9. STORIES OF THE PARABLES.—10. STORIES OF THE MIRACLES.—11. STORIES OF THE APOSTLES.

London: WARD, LOCK & CO., Salisbury Square, E.C.

GOOD BOOKS FOR LITTLE PEOPLE.

WARD, LOCK & CO.'S "GOOD AIM" BOOKS.

The feature of this series of Books is to encourage in childhood a spirit of love, gentleness, and cheerfulness, while affording amusement and interest.

Elegantly bound, cloth gilt, price 1s. each.

1. The Original Poems for Children. By ANN and JANE TAYLOR. Illustrated.
2. The Basket of Flowers. Illustrated.
3. Ellen's Idol. By E. S. PHELPS, Author of "The Gates Ajar." With Frontispiece.
5. Sermons on the Wall. By JOHN TILLOTSON. Illustrated.
6. Goldy and Goldy's Friends. By MARY DENSEL. Illustrated.
7. The One Thing Needful; or, Ethel's Pearls. Illustrated.
12. The Orphan Boy; or, From Peasant to Prince. Illustrated.
13. Tom, Tom, the Printer's Son: A Boy's Story. Illustrated.
14. Only a Dandelion. By the Author of "Stepping Heavenward."
15. Follow Me. By the Same. Illustrated.
16. New Year's Bargain. By SUSAN COOLIDGE. Illustrated.
17. In the Beginning; or, From Eden to Canaan. Illustrated.
18. Conquerors and Captives; or, From David to Daniel. Ditto.
19. The Star of Promise; or, From Bethlehem to Calvary. Ditto.
20. The History of the Robins. Illustrated.
21. Hymns for Infant Minds. By ANN and JANE TAYLOR. Illustrated.
22. Rhymes for the Nursery. By ANN and JANE TAYLOR. Illustrated.
23. Little Susy's Six Birthdays. By the Author of "Stepping Heavenward." With many Engravings.
24. Little Susy's Little Servants. By the Author of "Stepping Heavenward." With Coloured Frontispiece and many Engravings.
25. Little Susy's Six Teachers. By the Author of "Stepping Heavenward." With Coloured Frontispiece and many Engravings.
26. On'y a Penny; or, One of the Least of These. By the Author of "A Trap to Catch a Sunbeam." With many Illustrations.
27. The Contented Home. By the Author of "The Basket of Flowers."
28. Help One Another; or, The Way to be Happy. Illustrated.
29. Buried in the Snow: A Tale of the Mountains. Illustrated.
30. The Lost Child; or, A Mother's Love. Illustrated.
31. Summer House Stories. By Miss M. A. PAULL. Illustrated.
32. The Child's Own Book of Poetry. Profusely Illustrated.

London: WARD, LOCK & CO., Salisbury Square, E.C.

ADDENDA TO CATALOGUE.

WARD, LOCK & CO.'S
RECENT PUBLICATIONS.

The FIRST VOLUME of WARD & LOCK'S
UNIVERSAL INSTRUCTOR; or, Self-Culture for All. A Complete Guide to Learning and Self-Education, meeting the requirements of all classes of Students, and forming a perfect System of Intellectual Culture. With Hundreds of Engravings. Medium 8vo, cloth gilt, price 7s. 6d.; half-calf, 10s. 6d.

"We are quite sure that any person who could really master the contents of this one volume, would be one of the most accomplished men of his generation."—*Illustrated London News.*

"The work is excellent, and it is to be hoped it may meet with the popularity it deserves."—*Athenæum.*

"The comprehensive excellence of the work is combined with cheapness. . . An undoubted boon."—*Daily Chronicle.*

WORTHIES OF THE WORLD. Containing Lives of Great Men of all Countries and all Times. With Portraits. Medium 8vo, cloth gilt, price 7s. 6d.; half-calf, 10s. 6d.

"The book is an excellent one for Free Libraries and Young Men's Institutions."—*The Graphic.*

"We know of nothing in the same class of literature equally readable, impartial, and valuable as these sketches."—*Derby Mercury.*

THE MOST COMPLETE AND USEFUL BOOK HITHERTO PRODUCED FOR AMATEURS IN CARPENTRY AND THE CONSTRUCTIVE ARTS.

EVERY MAN HIS OWN MECHANIC. Being a Complete Guide to all Operations in Building, Making, and Mending that can be done by Amateurs in the House, Garden, Farm, &c., including HOUSEHOLD CARPENTRY AND JOINERY, ORNAMENTAL AND CONSTRUCTIONAL CARPENTRY AND JOINERY, and HOUSEHOLD BUILDING ART AND PRACTICE. With about 750 Illustrations of Tools, Processes, Buildings, &c. Demy 8vo, cloth gilt, price 7s. 6d.; half-calf, 10s. 6d.

"There is a fund of solid information of every kind in the work before us, which entitles it to the proud distinction of being a complete 'vade-mecum' of the subjects upon which it treats."—*The Daily Telegraph.*

"It will make the fortune of many a lad."—*Christian Age.*

"Many a boy would be delighted to get this book for a prize."—*Graphic.*

London: WARD, LOCK & CO., Salisbury Square, E.C.

NEW BOOKS AND NEW EDITIONS.

ENTIRELY NEW EDITION, BROUGHT DOWN TO THE AUTUMN OF 1881.
HAYDN'S DICTIONARY OF DATES, for Universal Reference.
By BENJAMIN VINCENT, Librarian of the Royal Institution of Great Britain. SEVENTEENTH EDITION, Enlarged, Revised, and Corrected to Autumn of 1881. Containing 10,000 distinct Articles, and 90,000 Dates and Facts. Medium 8vo, cloth, 18*s.*; half-calf, 24*s.*; full or tree-calf, 31*s.* 6*d.*

THE TIMES says: "Haydn's Dictionary of Dates is the most universal book of reference in a moderate compass that we know of in the English language."

ENTIRELY NEW AND REVISED EDITION.
BEETON'S DICTIONARY of UNIVERSAL INFORMATION, relating to GEOGRAPHY, HISTORY and BIOGRAPHY.
New and Enlarged Edition, containing Several Thousand Additional Articles. By GEO. R. EMERSON. With Maps. In One Handsome Volume, half-leather, 18*s.*

"In proposing to themselves, as the chief aim of their enterprise, a combination of accuracy, compactness, comprehensiveness and cheapness, the publishers have achieved a success which cannot fail to be appreciated by the public."—*Glasgow Herald.*

NEW, IMPROVED AND ILLUSTRATED EDITION OF
DR. ADAM CLARKE'S COMMENTARY on the HOLY BIBLE.
New and Revised Edition, with Additional Notes, bringing up the work to the present Standard of Biblical Knowledge, and Life of the Author by Rev. THORNLEY SMITH, and 100 pages of Engravings, Maps, &c. In Six Volumes, super-royal, cloth, price 52*s.* 6*d.*

"The present edition of Dr. Adam Clarke's well-known Commentary has been made as complete as it well can be."—*Christian World.*

WARD AND LOCK'S BOOK of FARM MANAGEMENT and COUNTRY LIFE.
A Complete Cyclopædia of Rural Occupations and Amusements. The Management of the Farm—The Crops of the Farm—Cows and the Management of the Dairy—The Horse—The Dog—The Fruit and Flower Garden—Trees and Tree Planting—Field Sports and Rural Recreations. Uniform with "Mrs. Beeton's Book of Household Management." With Coloured Plates and many other Illustrations. Large crown 8vo, half-roan, 7*s.* 6*d.*; half-calf, 10*s.* 6*d.*

"It is an exhaustive and yet a popular work; it is practical, yet not dull; scientific, yet readable. A book that ought to be in the hands of every agriculturist."—*Norwich Argus.*

London: WARD, LOCK & CO., *Salisbury Square, E.C.*

NEW BOOKS AND NEW EDITIONS.

A NEW LIFE OF MR. GLADSTONE.

WILLIAM EWART GLADSTONE: Prime Minister of England. A Political and Literary Biography. By GEORGE R. EMERSON, Author of "Life of Lord Beaconsfield," "Life of Raleigh," "Life of Shakespeare," &c., in "Worthies of the World;" Editor of "Beeton's Illustrated Encyclopædia," &c. Demy 8vo, cloth gilt, 6s.

"Readers will find it an instructive study, and will be satisfied, we think, with the manner in which the materials for judgment are here set before them."—*Illustrated London News.*

WASHINGTON IRVING'S SKETCH BOOK. A New Edition. Illustrated with One Hundred and Twenty Engravings on Wood from Original Designs. Large demy 8vo, cloth gilt, 10s. 6d.

CARLETON'S TRAITS AND STORIES of the IRISH PEASANTRY. With the Author's last Corrections, an Introduction, Explanatory Notes, and numerous full-page Plates and other Illustrations by HARVEY, GILBERT, PHIZ, &c. Demy 8vo, cloth gilt, price 7s. 6d.
Also to be had in Two Volumes, price 4s. each.

THE FAMILY ALTAR: A Manual of Domestic Devotion. Containing Morning and Evening Prayers, and Hymns, Portions of Scripture, and Practical Observations for Every Day in the Year. With Engravings. Large 4to, cloth gilt, price 12s. 6d.

THE LADY'S BAZAAR AND FANCY FAIR BOOK. Containing Suggestions upon the Getting-up of Bazaars, and Instructions for making Articles of Embroidery, Cane Work, Crochet, Knitting, Netting, Tatting, Rustic-work and Cone-work; also Directions for Making Skeleton Leaves, Phantom Bouquets, and for Painting on Ivory, China, White-wood, Tapestry, and Terra-Cotta. With 364 Illustrations. Crown 8vo, elegantly bound, cloth gilt, price 5s.

WARD AND LOCK'S
ROYAL EDITION OF THE POETS.

A New and handsome Edition, excellently printed and bound. Edited, with Critical Memoirs, by W. M. ROSSETTI. With Red Line borders and Illustrations.

1. Longfellow.
2. Wordsworth.
3. Hood. 1st Series.
4. Scott.
5. Cowper.
6. Byron.
7. Burns.
8. Moore.
9. Milton.
10. Poetic Treasures, Selected and Edited by Rev. Dr. GILES

Medium 8vo, cloth gilt, gilt edges, 7s. 6d. each; full morocco, 16s.

London: WARD, LOCK & CO., Salisbury Square, E.C.

CHEAP EDITIONS OF STANDARD WORKS.

THE PEOPLE'S STANDARD LIBRARY.

Seventy-six Vols., 1s. each, strongly and attractively bound, cloth gilt.

1. Longfellow.
2. Scott.
3. Wordsworth.
4. Milton.
5. Cowper.
6. Keats.
7. Hood. First Series.
8. Byron.
9. Burns.
10. Mrs. Hemans.
11. Pope.
12. Campbell.
13. Coleridge.
14. Moore.
15. Shelley.
16. Hood. Second Series.
17. Thomson.
18. Tupper's Proverbial Philosophy.
19. Humorous Poems.
20. American Poems.
21. Lowell.
22. Whittier.
23. Shakespeare. Complete.
24. Poetic Treasures.
25. Keble's Christian Year.
26. Young's Poetical Works.
27. Poe's Poetical Works.
28. Ann and Jane Taylor's Poetry for Children.
40. Uncle Tom's Cabin.
41. Evenings at Home.
42. Grimm's Fairy Tales. Illustrated.
43. Robinson Crusoe. 110 Illustrations.
44. Sandford and Merton. 100 Engravings.
45. Bunyan's Pilgrim's Progress. 100 Engravings.
46. The Swiss Family Robinson. 200 Illustrations.
47. Andersen's Popular Stories. Illustrated.
48. Andersen's Popular Tales. Illustrated.
49. The Marvels of Nature. 400 Illustrations.
50. The Scottish Chiefs.
51. The Lamplighter.
52. The Wide, Wide World.
53. Queechy.
54. Poe's Tales of Mystery.
55. Wonders of the World. 123 Engravings.
56. Prince of the House of David.
57. Edgeworth's Moral Tales.
58. Edgeworth's Popular Tales.
59. The Fairchild Family.
60. Two Years Before the Mast.
61. Stepping Heavenward.
62. Baron Munchausen.
63. Fern Leaves and Shadows and Sunbeams.
64. Josephus: Wars of the Jews.
65. Josephus: Antiquities.
66. The Pillar of Fire.
67. The Throne of David.
68. Little Women.
69. Good Wives. Sequel to "Little Women."
70. Melbourne House.
71. De Quincey. With Memoir.
72. De Quincey. 2nd Series.
73. Lord Bacon. With Memoir.
74. Lord Bacon. 2nd Series.
75. Sydney Smith. With Memoir
76. Sydney Smith. 2nd Series.
77. Macaulay. With Memoir.
78. Macaulay. 2nd Series.
79. Macaulay. 3rd Series.
80. Burke's Choice Pieces.
81. Paley's Evidences of Christianity.
82. Paley's Natural Theology
83. Paley's Horæ Paulinæ.
84. Webster's Dictionary of Quotations.

London: WARD, LOCK & CO., Salisbury Square, E.C.

Studious Readers, Authors, and other Literary Persons who lead sedentary lives, and in other ways exhaust the Brain, will find a good and comfortable Corrective in 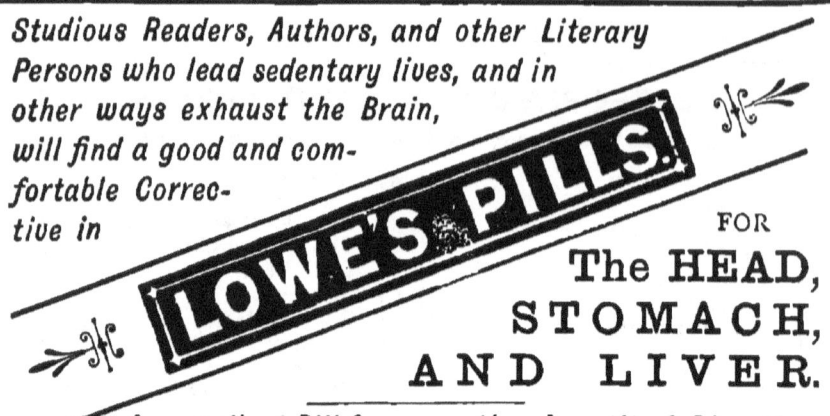 FOR The HEAD, STOMACH, AND LIVER.

An excellent Pill for promoting Appetite & Digestion.

The effect of taking a dose of these Pills at bed-time is exceedingly refreshing, grateful, and soothing, generally giving a quiet sleep and a gentle purge. Their aperient properties are mild and certain, being a medicine equally adapted for Business Men, Working Men, Delicate Females and Children.

They are sold by Chemists and Patent Medicine Vendors in Boxes at 7½d., 1s. 1½d., 2s. 9d., and 11s. each; or post free from the Proprietor on receipt of the price in postage stamps. Freshly made, a great desideratum.

Invented and Prepared by ROBERT HENRY LOWE, 187, Bilston Road, Wolverhampton.

Price 1s., 2s. 6d., and 4s.

The Most Valuable Acquisition to the Toilette

Which has been discovered for many years is

POND'S
AMERICAN WHITE ARECA-NUT
TOOTH PASTE;

Unprecedented as a cleanser for the TEETH, and a sweetener to the breath; its antiseptic properties in arresting decay, and its peculiar preservative qualities in averting TOOTH-ACHE, are indisputable.

PREPARED ONLY BY

POND BROS., 68, Fleet Street, London;
Broadway, New York; Vineland, New Jersey; and Hamilton (City), Canada; Madras; Bombay; Calcutta.

Goodall's Household Specialities.

A Single Trial solicited from those who have not yet tried these splendid Preparations.

YORKSHIRE RELISH.
The Most Delicious Sauce in the World.

This cheap and excellent Sauce makes the plainest viands palatable, and the daintiest dishes more delicious. To Chops, Steaks, Fish, &c., it is incomparable. In Bottles, 6*d*., 1*s*., and 2*s*. each.

GOODALL'S BAKING POWDER.
The Best in the World.

Makes delicious Puddings without Eggs, Pastry without Butter, and beautiful light Bread without Yeast. In 1*d*. Packets; 6*d*., 1*s*., 2*s*., and 5*s*. Tins.

GOODALL'S QUININE WINE.
The Best and most Agreeable Tonic yet introduced.

The best remedy known for Indigestion, Loss of Appetite, General Debility, &c. Restores delicate individuals to health. At 1*s*. 1½*d*. and 2*s*. 3*d*. each Bottle.

GOODALL'S CUSTARD POWDER.
For making Delicious Custards without Eggs, in less time and at Half the Price.

The Proprietors can recommend it to Housekeepers generally as a useful agent in the Preparation of a good Custard. *Give it a Trial.* Sold in Boxes, 6*d*. and 1*s*. each.

GOODALL'S BRUNSWICK BLACK.

For Painting Stoves, Grates, Iron, Tin, &c. 6*d*. and 1*s*. Bottles.

GOODALL'S EGG POWDER.

Its action in Cakes, Puddings, &c., &c., resembles that of the egg in every particular. One Penny Packet will go as far as Four Eggs, and One Sixpenny Tin as far as Twenty-eight. Sold everywhere, in 1*d*. Packets; 6*d*. and 1*s*. Tins.

GOODALL'S BLANC-MANGE POWDER.

Makes Delicious Blanc-Manges in a few minutes. In Boxes, 6*d*. and 1*s*. each.

All the above-named Preparations may be had of all Grocers, Chemists, Patent Medicine Dealers, and Oilmen.

MANUFACTURERS:

GOODALL, BACKHOUSE & CO., White Horse St., Leeds.

RICHARD SMITH & CO.
Nurserymen and Seed Merchants,
WORCESTER.

The undermentioned Descriptive Lists Free on application:
Roses, Fruit and Orchard House Trees, Evergreen and Deciduous Trees and Shrubs, Conifers, Forest Trees, Creepers, Stove and Greenhouse Plants, Herbaceous and Alpine Plants, Bedding Plants, Bulbs, Vegetable, Flower, and Farm Seeds.

These Catalogues contain an immense amount of information, and the prices will be found exceptionally low for the best quality.

BEETHAM'S GLYCERINE and CUCUMBER.
SOFT, WHITE SKIN.
A MOST REFRESHING AND SWEETLY PERFUMED WASH FOR THE SKIN.

By a few applications of this delightful preparation the Skin is rendered *Soft, Smooth,* and *White,* however *Rough, Red* or *Chapped* it may be, and all other blemishes caused by summer's heat or winter's cold removed. It is perfectly Harmless, and may be applied to the Skin of the youngest Child. It allays all irritation caused by the bites of Insects, and for Tourists it is invaluable. Bottles, 1s., 1s. 9d., 2s. 6d., of all Chemists and Perfumers. 1s. size free for 15 stamps by the

Sole Makers—M. BEETHAM & SON, Chemists, Cheltenham.

DR. ROBERTS' CELEBRATED OINTMENT,
CALLED
THE POOR MAN'S FRIEND,

Is confidently recommended to the public as an unfailing Remedy for Wounds of every description, for Ulcerated Sore Legs, even if of twenty years' standing, Cuts, Burns, Scalds, Bruises, Chilblains, Scorbutic Eruptions, and Pimples in the Face, Sore and Inflamed Eyes, Sore Heads, Sore Breasts, Piles, Fistula, &c. Sold in Pots, at 1s. 1½d., 2s. 9d., 11s., and 22s. each. Also his

PILULÆ ANTISCROPHULÆ,

Confirmed by sixty years' experience to be one of the best alterative medicines ever compounded for purifying the blood and assisting nature in all her operations. They form a mild and superior Family Aperient, that may be taken at all times without confinement or change of diet. Sold in Boxes, at 1s. 1½d., 2s. 9d., 4s. 6d., 11s., and 22s. each.

Sold by the Proprietors, BEACH & BARNICOTT, at their Dispensary, Bridport, and by all respectable Medicine Vendors.

SWEET BREATH
SECURED BY USING
HOOPER'S CACHOUS
After Smoking, or Eating Seasoned Food.

They are sold in BOXES ONLY, by every respectable Chemist and Tobacconist. Avoid the many attempted (and possibly injurious) imitations. These are certified by one of the highest analytical authorities to contain no trace of anything injurious to health.

First sold in the year 1844.

www.ingramcontent.com/pod-product-compliance
Lightning Source LLC
Chambersburg PA
CBHW032032220426
43664CB00006B/445